Leonard Kip

Ænone

A Tale of Slave Life in Rome. Second Edition

Leonard Kip

Ænone
A Tale of Slave Life in Rome. Second Edition

ISBN/EAN: 9783337137816

Printed in Europe, USA, Canada, Australia, Japan

Cover: Foto ©ninafisch / pixelio.de

More available books at **www.hansebooks.com**

ÆNONE.

ÆNONE:

A TALE

OF

SLAVE LIFE IN ROME.

BY LEONARD KIP.

SECOND EDITION.

NEW YORK:
PUBLISHED BY JOHN BRADBURN,
107 Nassau Street.
1867.

AFFECTIONATELY INSCRIBED

TO

MY BROTHER.

ÆNONE:

A TALE OF SLAVE-LIFE IN ROME.

CHAPTER I.

WHEN, in the second year of Titus Vespasian, the Roman general Sergius Vanno returned from his armed expedition in the East, and asked for public honors, there were some in the Senate who made objection. It was not fitting—they argued—that formal tokens of national commendation should be too readily bestowed. It had not been so in the time of their fathers. Long years of noble, self-sacrificing zeal and arduous service, crowned with conquests of supreme importance, had then been the only acknowledged title to the prize. It was scarcely proper that the same distinctions which had hitherto been awarded for the acquisition of the most valuable provinces should be granted for the annexation of a mere strip of worthless territory upon the extreme borders of the Empire—wild, rugged, and inhospitable, and inhabited by nomadic tribes, who could only be brought under a nominal authority, and who would never prove otherwise than turbulent and unprofitable subjects. Nor was it a matter to be mentioned with especial laudation that Sergius Vanno had succeeded in repressing, with overwhelming force, a revolt in a few of the Ægean islands. If exploits such as these were to be so liberally recompensed, what honors could there be left to bestow upon deeds of acknowledged brilliancy and importance?

So, with cautious discrimination, spoke some of the senators; and so, in the secrecy of their hearts, most of them thought. But against all this were brought to bear, not only the influence which Sergius naturally commanded as a patrician of the highest rank, but also the far more powerful pressure of popular clamor. Sergius was a favorite with the people. His noble birth and lineage entitled him to their respect. He was of a rare type of manly beauty—was wealthy, and used his gold with liberality—gave abundant largesses to the poorer classes—was lavish in his expenditure upon the arts—did not disdain, at times, to descend from his natural station and associate with his inferiors, thereby pleasing the fancy of the masses for social equality—patronized poets and actors, who, in return, sang or spouted his praise, and thus still further added to his fame—and was noted for a bold, frank, outspoken demeanor, which tended to conciliate all classes with him. These were virtues not always to be found combined in one person. Moreover, he was impulsively brave; and, though still young, was gifted with more than ordinary military genius, and had carried on his campaign with that rashly daring energy which, when rewarded with success, never fails to commend its possessor to popular adulation. In addition to all this, other considerations of a less personal character exerted their influence. Many months had elapsed since Rome had enjoyed any great civic festivity, and the people had begun to long for a new stimulant. The completion of the colossal Flavian amphitheatre had been delayed beyond public expectation; and though its speedy inauguration had been announced, there was serious doubt whether the lower and more turbulent orders of the populace, so long restrained, would possess themselves with sufficient patience to await the occasion with proper calmness. In fact, some outlet must be given to their excited appetite for novelty; and, therefore, after much solemn consideration, the Senate yielded to the public clamor, and voted an ovation.

As a token of national appreciation, therefore, the honor thus bestowed upon Sergius Vanno was not one of the first order; nor were such pageants a novelty to the Roman people. Several times before, within the memory of that generation, victorious generals had entered the city with myrtle wreaths upon their brows, and had exhibited to applauding throngs the gathered wealth of conquered provinces. Nor had many years elapsed since the present emperor—then prince—crowned with the richer and more lavish glories of a triumph, had ridden through the Via Sacra, greeted with welcoming acclamations as the destroyer of the Jewish capital—displaying before him the spoils of the sacred temple, and bringing in his train such thousands upon thousands of captives, that it had seemed as though all Palestine were being emptied into Rome. Compared with such exploits, those of Sergius were of trifling importance. But it now entered little into the minds of the people to make these comparisons. Whatever had been done in past time by other commanders, was not worth considering at present. Whoever might have been renowned before, Sergius Vanno was the hero of to-day. To him should be all the honor which tens of thousands of ringing voices and applauding hands could lavish. And, therefore, once more, as in the days of the past, the balconies of the palaces and villas lining the broad Sacra Via were gorgeous with rich gold and purple tapestries—the Forum glowed bright and resplendent with statues and decorated arches—altars smoked with sacrifice in front of columned temples—and the walls and slopes of the Palatine Hill were joyous with triumphal tokens, while, upon the summit, the house of the Cæsars glittered with banners and brave devices, and such costly adornments as were best fitted to grace the festivity and do honor to the exploits of a much-esteemed subject.

We know the scene. At first—in the full blaze of the noonday sun—the streets standing silent and nearly deserted, except where a few workmen and artisans here and there lingered to complete the festive preparations, or scattered parties of the prætorian guard, in holiday armor, moved slowly to and fro, to watch that order was maintained. Later—when the shadows deepened, and the air grew cooler—the avenues and prominent positions along the established route of the ovation beginning to fill with that great concourse of varied nationalities and conditions which only the imperial city could display. In the open streets a disorderly rabble of slaves and bondmen—pouring in steady streams from their kennels behind the palaces and from the unhealthy purlieus of such quarters as had been spared from the architectural encroachments of the wealthy, and allowed to fester in their own neglected corruption. Gathered together in close fraternity, the Briton, the Goth, the African, and the Jew,—each bearing his badge of life-long servitude, some even wearing marks of recent chastisement, but almost all awaiting the approaching spectacle with pleased and animated countenances, and in seeming forgetfulness that so many of their own number had graced former displays, and, by their degradation, had afforded amusement to other equally unsympathetic concourses. Among them, the lesser Romans—citizens in name, indeed, but, from their poverty and the overbearing exactions of the patricians, almost as much in slavery as those around them—disdainfully asserting their free birth, and in turn contemned by the slaves themselves, as men to whom liberty was but another title for slow starvation, and who would not dare to resent the vilest insults heaped upon them by noble-owned and protected menials—and now equally with the common herd obliged to submit to the strong argument of sword and lance, as, every little while, the soldiers along the line drove the whole writhing crowd, without distinction, into smaller and more confined compass. Here and there, knights and soldiers of high rank—riding up on horseback, and pushing through the struggling mass of slaves to the front, or more leisurely, but to equal purpose, waiting until their own menials had gone before, and, with mingled threats and blows, had cleared out vacant spaces for them. Other crowds, standing in favorable positions upon housetops and upon hastily constructed stagings ; and more especially upon the great amphitheatre, whose arches were blackened with clusters of spectators, and whose summit, in place of the last few layers of stone, so soon to be adjusted, had its deep human fringe. Upon palace balconies, groups of patricians and noble ladies, displaying a dazzling array of gold and purple and rare jewelry, and attended by Ethiopian slaves, who, in glittering armlets, stood behind, holding feathered canopies to shield their mistresses from the sun. All this confusing concourse of wealth and poverty each moment increasing in breadth and density, as every avenue emptied new swarms into the packed arena, until it seemed as though not only all Rome, but half the empire had gathered there.

Later yet, the music of flutes and hautboys—which, for a time, had been only indistinctly heard—breaking upon the ear with a clearer sound, and the van of the procession suddenly emerging into full view from behind the Circus Maximus, and, accompanied by the ringing shout of thousands spreading abroad new and louder welcomes, beginning to file past with rapid steps. First in order, the magistrates in full official robes—the spoils of war—the white sheep dressed for the sacrifice, and the priests bearing the holy vessels of the altar—gay trappings, flaunting standards, and all that could most readily inspire the heart with elation and enthusiasm. After these, and guarded on either side by detached parties of troops, the captives;—of barbaric and Grecian origin mostly, but here and there interspersed with men of other races—Jews, Syrians, and Huns—who, through contiguity of place or love of arms or self-interest, or a kindred hatred of the Roman rule, had been drawn into the battle—and who, having bravely stood their ground, striving for success, and with hearts well prepared for the consequences of failure, had been overtaken by the usual defeat, and dragged into utter and hopeless slavery. Among them, men of the Ethiopian race, also—who, having been slaves in Greece, had fought, not for principle or for freedom, but simply at their owner's bidding, and had thereby, upon being overcome, merely changed one class of masters for another—owners and slaves now knowing no difference in position, but standing involved in the same common fate. Some appearing defiant, others downcast and sullen, a few excited and curious—most of them walking with unfettered limbs, but here and there one heavily chained, betokening a fierce and unsubdued nature, upon which it was still necessary to put restraint. All marching or being dragged along at an equal pace; sometimes with an approximation to military exactness—at other points breaking into a confused mass, as women and children clung despairingly together and prevented the maintenance of any regular order. Around them, the spectators closely pressing, with morbid curiosity, discussing with loud approval the value of whatever of strength or beauty met their eyes, and occasionally greeting some undersized and misshapen victim with jeers of derision. And closing up the straggling line, more soldiers, marching in well-formed ranks, poising aloft myrtle-decked lances, and while interchanging salutations with the eddying crowd, singing in measured cadence their songs of victory.

And at last, as the sun sank yet lower towards the horizon, a yet brighter brilliancy investing the scene, as far down the line new shouts arose, and the struggling throng caught up the loud acclaim and carried it onwards like a great wave, betokening the speedy approach of the most distinguished feature of the procession—the conqueror himself—hailed imperator by his troops—with his most noble friends clustered about him, the myrtle wreath encircling his brow, and his earnest gaze fixed upon the Capitol, the honorable termination of his route.

In every respect, indeed—except in the display of those few distinctive formalities required to mark, as with a legal stamp, the actual and comparative value of the honor—the same old familiar story, so often hitherto rehearsed upon that line of Sacra Via and of Forum. Fresh incense burning upon the altars, which had blazed for other heroes; newly gathered garlands hanging from the arches which had graced past festivities; and surging crowds, heedful only of the present glory, and, with the customary popular fickleness, ready to forget it all as soon as the fleeting pageant should be over, now with indiscriminating zeal cheering the march of Sergius Vanno as frantically as in past days other crowds had greeted the triumphal cars of Cæsar and of Vespasian.

CHAPTER II.

GRADUALLY the sun approached and dipped below the blue line of extended plain which lay between the city and the sea ; the long shadows of afternoon began to blend into the one deeper shade of evening ; the groups of distant buildings became more and more indistinct ; the arches of the Colosseum softly faded away, leaving but a broad mass of unbroken wall ; upon the Palatine Hill the great house of the Cæsars shone less and less gloriously as the sky darkened behind the pile of decorated roofs ; here and there a light gleamed from some distant quarter ; here and there stars began to glisten in the sky.

Then the concourse of people, who had waited so long and patiently, began to break apart. The pageant was not yet entirely over, for fresh battalions of soldiers still marched past at rapid pace, tuning their steady tramp to the cadence of their songs of triumph. But the great feature of the occasion—the conqueror himself—had ridden by ; and what yet remained was but a faint recapitulation of the glories which had gone before. Therefore the patricians retired from their balconies, the horsemen abandoned their stations and plunged down the many streets which led out from the Forum, and the crowd of slaves and menial citizens, already rendered so indistinct in the fading light as to resemble one writhing, struggling monster rather than separate beings, began to stretch out its long arms into the narrow lanes and by-ways, and so gradually to melt away.

Withdrawing from the front balcony of the Vanno palace, where, shielded from the sun, she had sat and watched the procession pass by, Ænone, the young and fair wife of the conqueror, now sought rest and retirement in an inner apartment. Thither one of her women had preceded her, and had drawn forward a cushioned lounge, had beaten up the silken pillows, had placed a table near at hand, with a light repast spread upon it, had trimmed and filled with fresh olive-oil the large bronze lamp which swung from the ceiling, and now stood by awaiting further orders.

Throwing herself upon the lounge, Ænone covered her face with her hands. What unbidden thought was it that came creeping into her heart to trouble her? Why was it that something of the bright joyousness of spirit with which she had looked forward to that day had vanished? Surely nothing had occurred which of itself could bring to her either sorrow or repining. All things had happened as she had anticipated. She had seen her honored lord pass by with the myrtle wreath upon his brow, his most worthy officers at his side, and his bravest guards around him. She had seen that he was strong and without wound, as he had departed from her. She had heard the shouts of applause which had welcomed his approach as though he were a god; and, with her heart generously and unselfishly alive only to his honor, and unable to realize that all this frantic joy and adulation were not the passion of the nation's life, but were merely one single, careless throb of its fevered pulse, she had rejoiced with him, believing that he had indeed done what had made him the greatest of all living men. And, better than all, amid this scene of triumph, he had not seemed unmindful of her, for he had looked up and waved to her a salute, which the responsive crowd had joined in and carried along with redoubled acclamations, and he had sent to her his most trusty slave with a loving message. What, then, could she ask more?

Nothing that she could name, or that if she named to others, would have seemed a reasonable desire. And yet at her heart there was a certain dim, indistinct foreboding of evil, which she could not entirely repress. Was it that, in his glance, as he rode by and beheld her awaiting him, there was less of longing love than of gratified pride? Or did that flush upon his bronzed face indicate too surely his enjoyment of this pageant for its own sake rather than for the pleasure which he might have supposed that she would derive from it? Was it from forgetfulness of her that, after he had ridden past, he did not again look back to wave one more recognition, but rather seemed to gaze eagerly forward to where the assembled senators stood ready to greet him? Or, on the contrary, were all these only vague and empty imaginings, arising from the exhaustion and wearisomeness of long, impatient, waiting?

At length, raising her head, she saw her attendant bondwoman standing at the distance of a few paces, with her hands crossed upon her breast. The steady tramp of marching troops outside had ceased, for the last battalion had passed; and now the only sound was the silver bubbling and plashing of a little fountain that adorned the courtyard upon which the window of the apartment looked out.

"The pageant is over now," said Ænone, "and he will speedily be here. Let me know as soon as my lord returns."

The woman bowed her head in silence; and then, feeling that nothing more was wanted of her, slowly turned to depart. As she did so, a new-comer entered the room— a male slave of Gallic birth, who, by reason of his lofty stature as well as wonderful strength, had been promoted from the lowest order of servitude to become Sergius Vanno's armor-bearer and chief attendant. In that capacity he had fought through the late campaign, and had now returned, bearing among his fellows his own share of honor for successful and daring exploits. He had been released from personal attendance only a few moments before, and was now carrying back his master's sword and buckler, to hang them up in their accustomed place, and himself subside into well-earned idleness. Being the first time, for many months, that he had seen his mistress, he muttered some rough ejaculations expressive of servile devotion, and then stood in lazy attitude awaiting her permission to speak further.

"Your master, Drumo?"

"Will not return to-night," the man responded. "The emperor demands his presence."

"And that will detain him—"

"He knows not how long. But immediately after that, there is to be a brave feast at the house of the poet

Emilius, and it will doubtless be morning before they separate."

"He bade you tell me this?"

The giant nodded.

"It is well. That is all; you can go. You may both go, for I would be alone."

The armor-bearer turned upon his heel and strode away, the sword and buckler, together with his own rougher trappings, rattling at his back as he passed down the hall; and behind him slowly crept away the bondwoman. And Ænone, once more leaning back upon the lounge, gave herself up to sombre reflection.

It was, of course, no more than proper—she mused—that her lord should obey the behests of the emperor and wait upon him. Perhaps new honors would then be showered down; and, at the least, it was no light privilege to stand in the presence of the ruler of the world, and there give personal narration of his exploits. But when that interview was over, what need to join the revels of another household, instead of hurrying back to place his newly won garlands at her feet?

She pondered upon the dubious reputation which attached to the house of the poet Emilius, and recalled the terrible stories which, from time to time, she had heard regarding it. What might be the realities of the scenes there enacted, none could truly tell, except the few most intimate frequenters of that place; but report gave no flattering description of them. Even among the Roman ladies with whom she was associated, and whose information was confined to such stray bits of gossip as they had

"Ten sestertia. I acknowledge it."

"Nay, twenty sestertia, was it not?"

"Twenty sestertia be it, then. What matters the amount, when I paid you upon the moment, and you now have the sum, whatever it may be, in your own purse?"

"True, true," rejoined the other, nodding his head with an air of sage gravity; "whatever it was, of a certainty I now have it. And then, Sergius, you offered against the ten—no, the twenty sestertia—to play the choice of all your new slaves."

"Of my new male slaves, certainly."

"No, of the slaves both male and female. I will tell you how it is that I so especially recollect. It was because I had heard from our lawgiver here, about the beautiful Samian girl you have borne home among your share of the spoils. You did not think, perhaps, that I knew of her; but when I offered to throw the dice, I held her in my mind. And then, when I had won, and told you that I would select her, you said—"

"Exactly what I had said to you before, that you could take your choice from the male slaves," interrupted the other impatiently. "And I have brought you directly hither to make your selection, for fear that when you became sober you would forget the matter altogether, and thereby cheat yourself out of a fairly won prize. Am I not right, comrades? Was not the play as I have stated it?"

"Neither more nor less," the poet answered; and the prætorian captain spoke to the same effect. The comedian still looked unconvinced, and, for the moment, gazed in-

picked up from slaves and menials, and who, standing in unconscious awe of her simple purity of heart, often forebore to speak with her as freely and unguardedly as with each other, she had occasionally heard such startling tales of the wild dissipations there enacted, as surpassed conception, and left her horrified senses no calm refuge except in unbelief. The gorgeous feasts, the night-long libations, the social intimacy with dancing girls and gladiators, the mockery of all that was pure and holy, the derisive insults to the gods themselves—these were practices which the public voice connected with the house of Emilius, not as occasional outbreaks of wild frivolity, but as the fixed habits of his daily life. And if these things were true, what claim of pride or policy could such a place advance to distract her lord from the allegiance due to his own home alone?

But possibly these things might not be true. She reflected that the poet was wealthy; and as long as the world continues to be envious, riches will seldom fail to bring false report upon their possessor. He was a man of genius, also; and all such can scarcely fail to find rivals who will turn satirists and attack them in their homes and daily life. Certainly, it is not difficult for slander to magnify the genial gatherings of kindred spirits into scenes of wild debauchery. And it was also true, that if mere outside appearance is of any value as an index of what is hidden, the slight figure, the pale and almost girlish face, and the winning and courteous demeanor of the poet were far from indicating a man of low and debasing inclinations. Moreover, his writings as surely spoke the contrary; and as she thus reasoned, Ænone lifted from its case a vellum roll with which Emilius himself had presented her, containing many of his poems, exquisitely engrossed. These poems treated not upon the pleasures of wine and love—those fruitful and ever-varying subjects of the Horatian school. Instead of this, they pursued, in deep-sounding and majestically rolling dactyls, the less favorite and trodden track of Socrates and Plato, and discoursed upon temperance and honor—upon the satisfaction derived from a well-spent life, and the delights attending a peaceful death—upon the immateriality of the soul, and the reward bestowed by the gods upon those who have honored them by leading a virtuous career. As Ænone slowly unwound fold after fold of the parchment roll, she felt her heart perplexed within her. She could scarcely believe that none of those tales of reckless dissipation were true, for she remembered that some of them had reached her ear attended by evidence so circumstantial that it was impossible to reject them; but, if true, how account for these grand maxims of lofty morality? What object could their author have in thus uselessly playing the hypocrite, when amatory and bachanalian choruses would not only have been more consonant with his own feelings, but doubtless more acceptable to the world? She had not yet learned what it often takes the wisest man a lifetime to discover—that every inconsistency of conduct is not hypocrisy, but that it is one of the most common idiosyncrasies of the mind to write and believe one thing, and as self-approvingly to feel and act the reverse.

With a sigh she closed the volume, and restored it to its

place within the case. Why ponder upon such things as these ? The real character of the poet Emilius was, after all, a matter of but little consequence to her. Whether the meeting at his house was a wild, reckless orgie, or a mere intellectual gathering of literary genius, it was none the less certain that her lord was tarrying there, away from her side. But perhaps, indeed, even this was a duty which he owed to his fame and station ; and her face brightened up with new hope as the suggestion flashed upon her. It might be that at this feast there would be present some poet of lofty epic powers, or historian of wondrous descriptive talent, ranking as the brightest star of Roman literature ; and either of these, if properly conciliated, would doubtless celebrate her lord's exploits so grandly that in future ages his campaign would shine with far greater lustre than if simply committed to parchment in the dry detail of unadorned fact, and so filed away in the national archives. It was most fitting, therefore, that he should not permit his impatient love for her to allow him to neglect the opportunity of cultivating, by a wise and condescending courtesy, the world-renowned talents of these men, and thereby redoubling the resplendency of his own bright fame.

Easily satisfying her mind with this pleasing reasoning, she retired for the night into the innermost apartment—a retreat adorned with every luxury which could gratify pride and administer to a cultivated taste. The floor was covered with tesselated marbles of different shades and arranged in ingenious and novel patterns. The ceiling was resplendent with allegorical frescoes by the most celebrated masters of the day. There were glowing paintings upon the walls, rich tapestries in the windows, embroidered hangings upon the bed. Beside the tables stood bronze figures holding forth lamps ready trimmed and lighted; fresh flowers had been placed in their allotted vases, and weighed down the air with perfume; and in a deep recess stood the bath ready filled, and scented with carefully plucked rose-leaves floating upon the water. But all this display of magnificent luxury and elaborate taste, if regarded by her at all, now seemed to affect her with weariness rather than with pleasure.

Why, as she lay down upon her couch, and prepared to yield herself up to pleasant slumber, did her thoughts wander back to the time when poverty instead of luxury had been her lot? Why did those olden memories of the past so strongly haunt her? They were, perhaps, never entirely absent from her heart; but now they thronged about her with a force that would not bear repression. Perhaps it was that the very magnificence and pomp of power of which she was now the centre, recalled the memory of the distant past, by virtue of strong contrast alone; perhaps that the unsatisfied longing and vague foreboding of her soul necessarily impressed upon her the consciousness that wealth and honor alone cannot give perfect happiness, and thereby naturally led her thoughts back to the time when she had found true contentment in poverty and loneliness. However that might be, now, as she closed her eyes and shut out the view of the costly adornments around her, more vividly than ever before were pictured to her mind the scenes of her childhood: her father's cottage on the outskirts of Ostia—the olive-grove upon the slope behind—the road-side well, where the villagers would sometimes gather about some invalided soldier from the German army, and listen to his tales of the last campaign—and in front, the bay, sparkling in the bright glare of the sun, and burdened with the corn-freighted ships of Alexandria.

And there, too, was the old wave-worn rock—the scene of her life's only romance—where, stealing out from her father's cabin at the evening hour, and seating herself so close to the water-line that the spray of the tideless sea would dash up and bathe her naked feet, she would wait in all innocence for the coming of the young sailor from Samos. How rapidly those hours used to pass! How pleadingly, on the last evening, he had knelt beside her, with his arm resting upon her knee, and there gazing up into her face, had asked her for one long tress of hair! How foolish she had been to give it to him; and how earnestly he had vowed that he would come back some day, no longer poor and forlorn, but in his own two-masted vessel, with full banks of oars, manned by the slaves whom he would capture, and would then bear her away unto his own home! And how, like a silly girl, she had believed him, as though wandering sailor-boys ever did come back to seek the loving hearts which had trusted them! And so the year had passed away, and, as she might well have known from the first, he had not returned. Nor was it to her regret; for but a little afterwards the youthful patrician, already flushed with budding honors, had chanced to meet her; had loved her with a generous passion, lifting him above all sordid calculation about wealth or social differences, and had taught her in turn to bestow upon him an affection more true and absorbing than she had yet believed her heart was able to contain. And so her first romantic dream had ended, as all such childish dreams are apt to end. Let it go. Her heart had found its true refuge; she could well look back upon the past without regret, and smile at the youthful fancies connected with it.

One prayer to the gods—a further special invocation to her favorite goddess, who at the foot of the couch stretched forth marble arms lovingly towards her—and then the silver tinkling of the little courtyard fountain lulled her softly to sleep.

CHAPTER III.

THE thoughts of Ænone followed her into sleep, and colored her dreams with pleasant memories of the past; and when the morning sun, pouring its beams through the window, awakened her, there was a momentary struggle before she could throw off the fancies of the night and realize that she was no longer in her cottage home. But distinct perception soon returned as she glanced around her and recognized the paintings which adorned her chamber, and the marble goddess still holding forth a welcoming hand, as though in greeting for the return of another day.

Throwing open the window, she sat down for a moment to enjoy the soft breeze, which, laden with perfume, came gambolling fresh from the Alban Hills. The window at which she had placed herself looked out upon a central courtyard, formed by the intersection of the main body of the palace at right angles with the two wings. This court was paved from one side to the other with marble flags of different shades, excepting in the middle, where played the fountain—a circular basin of water upon a rock, in the centre of which two bronze satyrs struggled for a stork, from whose uplifted bill the supplying stream spouted forth. From the end of each wing of the palace the line of the sides was continued by a straight stone wall of considerable height, leading across the whole breath of the Cælian Hill to the slope of its further side, and inclosing an area thickly planted with such flowers, shrubbery, and trees, as the taste of the period considered most essential to a well-appointed garden.

For the moment, the central court was almost deserted, the only appearance of life being a little Nubian slave, who sat upon the coping of the fountain, and lazily played with a tame stork. But all at once Ænone heard mingled voices, and distinguished among them the tones of her husband—deeper than the others, and marked with that quicker and more decided accent acquired by a long course of undisputed authority. At first the sounds seemed stationary, as though the speakers were tarrying in one place for discussion; but in a moment they approached nearer, and the disputants stood in full sight upon a balcony which ran around the interior wall of the palace and overhung the sides of the court.

Foremost and tallest of the group stood Sergius Vanno, recognizable at once by his athletic and graceful figure, reflective face, commanding eye, bright with intelligence, and his agreeable, refined, and attractive presence, as the leading spirit of the group. At his side leaned the poet Emilius, whose weak and slender figure, and mild, girlish expression would hardly appear to sustain the reputation he enjoyed of devoting half his time to the invention and elaboration of new forms of profligacy, and thereby carrying his exploits into realms of vice hitherto undiscovered, even in that age of unbridled indulgence. Behind these stood three others—a captain of the prætorian guard, a tribune of the law, and a comedian of the school of Plautus —each probably carrying the palm of excellence in his especial calling, and all of them doubtless endowed with superior capacities as boon companions in a night-long revel. They had evidently but just left the banqueting hall, and bore indications of having passed a somewhat unquiet night, though in different degrees; for while the captain and comedian still staggered confusedly, and displayed haggard faces and disordered dresses, the superior tact, constitutional strength, or recuperative powers of the others enabled them to maintain such a demeanor of proper sobriety, that but for a slight flush and the companionship in which they were placed, their late excesses might have passed unnoticed.

"It was the choice of all the slaves, both male and female, I tell you," said the comedian, evidently resuming an unfinished dispute. "The choice of all the slaves, Sergius."

"Hear you now this man!" exclaimed Sergius, turning towards his friend Emilius with a quiet smile. "Thrice already have I told him the truth of the matter, and still he persists; well knowing that, if now he can scarcely sustain himself from falling over into the area below, he certainly could not, three hours ago, have been able to tell what play he made, or whether he made any play at all. Nay, Bassus, it was only of the male slaves that I spoke."

"Yet listen to me," insisted the comedian, placing his hand upon the other's shoulder, and leaning heavily upon him. "You do not deny that we gamed?"

"Of a surety I do not."

"Nor that I won money of you?"

quiringly from one to the other, in the hope that some newer recollection would come to the mind of either of them and lead to a recantation. But in that desire he was disappointed, and at last he reluctantly gave up the contest, not daring to protract it longer for fear of provoking a quarrel, and thereby being thrust out of the society to which he was aware his social talents, counteracting his low birth and calling, were his sole passport. And after all, though he had too carelessly made his wager, he had won twenty sestertia and a male slave, and that was something.

"Well, be it so," he assented, with a sigh. "A male slave, since you say it. I had supposed I had spoken more particularly, but it seems that my poor brain was careless and at fault. Only bring the slaves hither quickly, that I may choose and go home, for I must play Castorex this morning, and this head of mine seems likely to split."

"Let it split, then," retorted Sergius with a laugh. "It may save our cracking it some day with a goblet. Ho, there, Drumo!"

He was not obliged to call a second time, for, at the first ring of his voice, the obedient armor-bearer emerged from one of the lower entrances into the court. He also, as well as his master, had been convivially celebrating his return, and now bore the evidences of his frolic in a sad combination of inflamed features, tangled hair, and disordered clothing.

"What ho, master?" he cried, stretching his huge limbs in a yawn and looking up. "Am I wanted?"

"You have been drinking," said Sergius; "go to the

fountain basin there and cleanse yourself. If there were fish in it, I would feel half inclined to cast you in to feed them. After that, come back to me."

The giant grinned, knowing that his master placed too high a value upon him ever to make a dinner of him for the carp, though he might now and then inflict a stripe or two in anger upon his broad shoulders. Then kneeling down at the fountain, he quickly splashed the water into his face and eyes, ran one finger from his forehead to the crown of his head in order to part his disordered locks, pulled away a loose straw from behind his neck, gave his tumbled tunic one jerk to straighten it, and, with the air of a person who had made an elaborate toilet, and could afford to be well satisfied with the result, presented himself for inspection.

"So! Were my new slaves sent in last night?"

The armor-bearer nodded.

"The whole allotment?"

"I suppose so, master. Fifty there should have been, the lictor said, when he brought them, but one had died, and they had thrown him into the Tiber to the fishes. Ho, ho, master, we shall all go one day to feed the fishes or the dogs, or the worms, both you and I alike."

"Silence, you hound!" said Sergius, more by way of habit than because he really minded a familiarity to which he had gradually grown accustomed.

"The others came a little before midnight, and I locked them up below," the Gaul added, pointing to a low range of buildings at the foot of the garden. "They are a well-looking lot, master, but among them all you will not find one to take my place; so, for this time I am safe, and can yet say and do what I please. Ho, ho! And here is the list of them which the messenger brought."

"Never mind the list. It is doubtless all correct," said Sergius, waving the papyrus aside. "Go, now, and bring the slaves hither."

The man nodded, and taking a large key from a nail over his head, disappeared down the garden walk, and in a few moments returned, driving before him the whole body of captives which had fallen to the share of his master. As he had reported, they were of good quality, the best of the prisoners of war having naturally been reserved for the commander of the expedition. The men were mostly stout and athletic, while the women were of healthy and properly agreeable appearance. Of the whole number there were none who seemed to be at all sickly or ill-favored; while the only one who exhibited any signs of deformity was a dwarf, whose withered and twisted figure imparted to him that peculiar grotesque and ape-like appearance which, at that period, was certain to commend him to the taste of wealthy purchasers, and render him of more value than a man of correct proportions. Moreover, as a general thing, the captives seemed more cheerful than they had been the day before, having had the advantage of several hours' rest and of better food than had fallen to their lot at any time during the journey. There were a few who manifested sorrow at having been separated from relatives or friends with whom they had succeeded in travelling to the very gates of the city; and some others, as yet unbroken to misfortune, maintained a rebellious and intractable demeanor. But the majority had already made up their minds that slavery was henceforth their inevitable fate, and that their highest future happiness must be looked for in its alleviation rather than in its abolition ; and they now appeared to take pleasure in the thought that their fortune had led them to a wealthy household, where they would probably experience kind treatment and have easy tasks allotted to them.

Now, having reached the paved court, the captives rested and awaited the inspection of their owner—some sitting upon the marble border of the fountain, some standing by in groups, and through a sort of sympathy holding each others' hands, as though that would give protection. A few gazed moodily upon the ground ; and one or two, overwhelmed with sorrow or nervous apprehension, quietly wept. But the greater portion, impressed with a dim consciousness that their future lot might depend upon their present conduct and appearance, endeavored to assume an air of pleased satisfaction, and thereby possibly win the favorable notice of the group which stood surveying them from the balcony, or at the least the friendly compassion of the older slaves of the household, who began to pour forth from the different doors upon the ground-floor of the palace, and join unbidden in the inspection. Most of these, in the early days of their captivity, had stood up in the centre of similar gaping and gazing crowds, and now in their turn they sated their curiosity upon the new-comers. A few, remembering their own sorrows of those former times, seemed compassionate ; many manifested careless indifference; some wondered whether enough of the present re-enforcement would be retained to materially lighten their own labors ; and others, who had been known to fail in attention to their peculiar departments of industry, trembled lest their places might now be supplied by the new-comers, and themselves be again driven off to market. Whatever their thoughts and feelings, however, no one ventured to approach too near, or speak aloud, excepting the armor-bearer, who, as the privileged slave of the household as well as the marshal of the occasion, moved hither and thither among the captives, encouraging some with rude jokes, shoving others back or forward into suitable positions, and generally endeavoring to set forth the merits of the whole mass in as favorable a light as possible.

"Now stand forward where the noble imperator and his friends can see you," was his command to a well-featured, strong-limbed Rhodian. "Do you think to better your lot by slinking out of sight among the women, and so perhaps be sent off unnoticed to the market, and there be purchased for hard labor in the quarry-pits? Who knows but that if my master sees you, he may make a gladiator of you; and then you can fight before emperors and consuls."

"What care I for your master?" retorted the man. "Let him give me back my wife and my child, whom I yesterday had, and who now are gone."

The armor-bearer shrugged his shoulders.

"Is that all?" he said. "Wives are plenty in this city of Rome. When I first came from Gaul, I, too, had a wife, and, like you, lost her. What then? I suppose that she is happy, wherever she may be; and I—I have not allowed myself to be lonely since. But neither did I let myself fall behind, when I stood in the market; but I pressed forward and struck upon my chest, and called to the highborn and the rich to look upon me, and see how a man could be made, and what he could be good for. And here am I now, a slave, indeed—that cannot be helped—but for all that, a ruler over the other slaves, and my master's favorite and companion. By the immortal gods! there is more manliness in yonder dwarf, with his open face, than in you, with your whimpering and your tears. I will call him forward to teach you a lesson how to act."

At the first beck the dwarf pressed forward with a smile, alternately stretching up to make the most of his diminutive proportions, and then bowing low to crave the good will of the spectators. His appearance brought him instant commendation; and more particularly did the prætorian captain break forth into expressions of appreciation.

"A proper dwarf! a most excellent dwarf! Smaller and more ugly by a quarter than one which I have known to be sold for forty sestertia! And see, Bassus, how he bows and rubs his hands, and shows his teeth at yourself. He has, perhaps, been the buffoon in a Grecian theatre, and in you now recognizes a brother in the art. Take him, therefore, for your choice. At the very least, he will be of value to carry your bag of plays before you, and he may even help you act."

The comedian forced a sickly smile upon his features, not daring to quarrel with his companion, yet not insensible to the sneering tone with which he was addressed. He had, at the first, been struck with the dwarf, and half inclined to choose him. But now the mocking speech deterred him.

"You are disposed to be merry," he said; "nor do you reason well. It is not an ape that an actor wants to carry his plays. There are enough such to listen to them. I will leave the dwarf, therefore, for you to purchase. Perhaps, after all, there may be a place found for him somewhere in your own household. I will make another selection for myself."

And descending from the piazza, he moved in among the captives for the purpose of entering upon a more careful inspection. Eager as he was at all times to make the best of a bargain, he was the more especially anxious now ; for the contemptuous tones of his companions rankled in his heart, and he felt that the more he evinced a capacity to benefit himself, the more he would be likely to disappoint them. Passing deliberately about the slaves, therefore, he scrutinized each face and form before him with the most exact attention ; carefully lifting the eyelid of one, and examining the teeth of another—now pressing his knuckles into an expanded chest, then twisting a muscular arm—causing some to stoop, and others to bend back—and generally practising all those arts and expedients which a professional slave-dealer would employ to guard himself against imposition. Nor was it until the lapse of many minutes that he settled upon his prize.

"I will take this man," he said, dragging the Rhodian forth by the shoulder. "He shall be my slave."

"It is well ; take him," responded Sergius, in his most courtly tone. And for the moment or two, during which his companions yet tarried, he maintained a demeanor so studied and controlled, that it would have required a keen glance to detect in his face his bitter sense of disappointment at the selection which the comedian had made.

CHAPTER IV.

As Sergius turned and entered the house, those who had seen him saluted as the favorite of the emperor, and the idol of the crowd, and thence had believed unbounded happiness must be his never-varying lot, would have been astonished to know how many things there were which rankled painfully in his heart, and, for the moment, made him discontented and fretful.

Thoroughly jealous respecting his military fame, he was not unsuspicious that the cheers of the crowd upon his ovation had been elicited more by the perfection of the pageantry than by a proper appreciation of his own merits; while it was certain that the Senate, though meeting him with the customary congratulations, had delivered them with more form than enthusiasm. And though the emperor had given audience, he had bestowed no new honors upon him. To these disappointments was added the unhappy, self-accusing consciousness of having failed in duty to his own dignity, by passing the night in wild revelry, and among companions, many of whom were beneath him in every quality except their talent for ribald jesting and buffoonery. Moreover, though reputed wealthy, he was at present pressed for money, and had added to his embarrassments by losing at the gaming-table during the past night more than he could well afford to part with; while, to sum up other vexations, the comedian, Bassus, had not only increased the loss by selecting the most valuable slave, but had performed the action in a cool and calculating manner, which was particularly exasperating.

"The low buffoon!" Sergius muttered to himself. "Who would have thought that, half drunken as he was, he would have had the wit to select a slave worth double the sum which had been staked against him, and one whom I had obtained with such trouble, and for my own purposes? Can it be that he pretended his intoxication the more easily to outwit me? I had no fear, but believed that he would be sure to select some slim youth who could be taught to play the flute before him, or act as cup-bearer. What demon put it into his head so suddenly to look for bone and muscle rather than for girlish graces?"

This last suspicion, of having been made the victim of artful dissimulation, added fuel to his vexation, more especially as, turning his head, and glancing into the courtyard, he saw the comedian slipping through a side passage, and the Rhodian obediently following at his heels. This filled up the measure of Sergius' wrath. To his excited fancy the actor bore upon his face an insultingly satisfied smirk of triumph, while the Rhodian appeared larger and stronger than ever. With an exclamation of unavailing anger, Sergius pushed open the door, and stood in the presence of his wife.

It was into the dining-hall that he had plunged. Upon a small table were placed the wine and bread and fruits which formed the customary morning meal among the richer Romans; and beside the table stood Ænone, in an attitude in which hope, and fear, and surprise, and disappointment were equally blended.

Clad in the manner which she knew had always best pleased his fancy, wearing the adornments which, as his gifts, he would most naturally prefer to see upon her, with her curling locks parted as in former days he had liked her to dress them, even striving to impart to her features the peculiar radiant expression which, in other times, had most won his heart—she had impatiently awaited his approach, with a vague fear whispering poisonous surmises to her soul, but yet with a joyful and hopeful assurance of good predominating over all. As soon as these friends of his had departed—she had said to herself—he would no longer delay coming to her. He would meet her with extended arms and the same joyous welcome as of old. He would utter kind and pleasant words expressive of his happiness, and would fold her to his heart. There would she nestle and forget her foolish fears and suspicions of the past night, and would only remember that she was loved. As, however, she now saw the frown upon his face, her heart and courage failed; and in proportion as she had previously fortified her mind with hopeful confidence, a terrible reaction of apprehension overcame her. Could it be that the angry look was for her, and that it could be justified by any word that she had ever spoken, or any duty that she had neglected? With one hand lightly resting upon the table, her right foot thrown forward in impulsive readiness to spring into his extended arms, but her whole form drooping and shrinking with dismay, her face pale, and the smile which she had called upon it now faintly and painfully flickering in a deathlike manner about her whitened lips, as it glided from her control and began to give place to an utter and undisguised fear, she stood awaiting his first word or action.

"Ha, Ænone!"

"My lord—"

Then remembering what was due to her upon their first meeting, he smoothed the frown from off his face, held out his arms, and tenderly embraced her, uttering kind and loving words. It was the same gesture with which he had parted from her when, six months before, the State had called upon him to arouse from the ease and tranquillity of his wedded life and do new service upon the field. Those were the same gentle and affectionate words which he had been wont to utter. And yet to her quickened apprehension, urged on by some secret instinct, it seemed as though the soul of the tender greeting was gone, leaving but the mere form behind. Could it be that during those few months of absence he had learned to think less dearly of her? At the thought, the last faint gleams of the flickering smile died away from her face; while he, unobservant of her distress, and still goaded by the remembrance of his losses, released her from his embrace and threw himself heavily down upon the nearest lounge.

"I am thirsty," he said. "Give me some drink."

She poured some wine into a goblet, and timidly presented it to his lips. The liquid, cooled with snow from the mountains, was refreshing to his palate, and he drank it to the last drop. As he parted with the goblet—rather tossing it away than setting it down—he noticed how she stood before him with whitened face and frightened features, and with the attitude of a shrinking slave rather than of a wife joyous to be of service. His heart smote him for his negligent greeting, and he rose up from the lounge and placed his arm about her.

"Not with you, Ænone, am I vexed," he said, partly comprehending the cause of her emotion. And drawing her nearer, he commenced toying with her waving locks, telling her how for months he had been longing to meet her, and how her looks more than ever delighted him, and otherwise uttering such pleasant and reassuring words as soonest came into his mind. As she began to perceive that it was not for any fault of hers that he had displayed anger, her face gradually lost its expression of dread. But still she could not fail to notice that the words which he spoke were not such as are commonly prompted by a true and unpremeditated affection; but were rather the labored and soulless result of a mere good-natured desire to make atonement for a neglect, and were uttered in all the careless spirit with which one tries to soothe an improperly aggrieved child; and the old smile but feebly played upon her features, struggle with it as earnestly as she could.

"Nay, not at your sweet face is my anger excited, Ænone," he said; "but at that scurvy dog, Bassus. He should himself be a slave and the companion of slaves, were his true station meted out to him."

"He with whom you passed the night?" suggested Ænone.

"Ay, he was one of us," Sergius answered, taking a position nearer the table, and commencing to pick off a crumb of bread as the incentive to a more extended repast. "He was with us, as there always will be some rude and unmannerly intruder in every company; but there were also others, the associates of Emilius. There was Sotus, the Egyptian, a learned astronomer; and Cyope the renowned Greek dramatist; and Spoletius, who is now writing a history of the empire, and, if what he says is true, has already brought his work down to the time of the Emperor Nero—"

"And will carry it on until he reaches the present day? And will then, in their proper place, tell about your achievements, my lord?" exclaimed Ænone, a flush of expectation glowing upon her face, as she thought that here were her conjectures of the preceding evening about to be realized.

"Ay!" responded Sergius; "I presume that he will speak of me and of what you dignify as my achievements, foolishly fond child; and therefore it was meet that I should not neglect the opportunity of being in his presence, in order that he might speak well of me rather than the reverse. Otherwise, you well know that I would have preferred to let revelling have the go-by, and to have come at once to gather you to my heart. But we men, whom the world calls celebrated, must be watchful, and learn to resign pleasure to duty, and guard our fame, or else it may go out like a wasted lamp, and leave us in the darkness of oblivion. We cannot spare our time to give free scope to our love, as though we were poor and unknown."

Ænone reproached herself for her suspicions. Surely she had done wrong in distrusting him for the coldness of his greeting. He may have meant nothing but love and kindness, and have been weighed down by cares and anxieties which she could not comprehend. Had he not said that something had made him angry? He, the great imperator to have been ruffled by the conduct of a low comedian, whose company his interest obliged him to tolerate! She would yet be patient and wait.

"And not only Spoletius, the historian, but also others, poets and philosophers, whose good-will it is proper to secure, and whose conversation would be improving to the gods themselves," continued Sergius, almost blushing as he remembered how little philosophy had been spoken during the past night, excepting that shallow doctrine which inculcates full enjoyment of the passing pleasures of the world, lest death might come and too suddenly end them; and how little poetry had been recited, except as roared forth in the form of bacchanalian choruses. "And even this Bassus it were worth my while to condescend to, lest the notion might seize him to satirize me upon the public stage. And it was to conciliate him that I lost to him twenty sestertia and a well-favored slave. May it not be that I paid too high a price for his friendship, and hence have a right to be angry?"

"But let my lord reflect that he has many slaves—more than he well can find use for; and that, therefore, one less may not be of great consequence to him."

"Nay, but such a slave!" responded Sergius; "tall, almost, as my armor-bearer, and strong as an elephant! A man who was worth to me all those others, thrice over, for the use to which I could have put him. The rest will doubtless be of good account in their way. Some of them will go and dig in my quarries, and a few will be exposed in the market, and will bring their proper price. But this Rhodian—listen! You know that in a few weeks the new

amphitheatre of our emperor will be opened with grand
spectacles lasting many days. At my audience with him
last evening, he spoke thereupon, and of the wild beasts he
had sent for to give dignity to the occasion ; but of this
anon. You know that for months all Rome has been pre-
paring for that event ?"

Ænone nodded assent. Even had she desired, she could
not have remained ignorant that the great colossus of all
amphitheatres was approaching completion, since, from her
window, she could look down the Appian Way and watch
every stone being laid, while, in all societies, the magni-
tude and magnificence of the approaching games were
the theme of universal conversation.

"Well," continued Sergius, "months ago—I hardly
remember how many—I wagered with the proconsul Sardesus that I would furnish for the games the superior
gladiator of the two. Fifteen purses of a hundred sestertia each ; a large sum, but the larger the better, since
I had my armor-bearer in my mind, and felt certain to
win. But since then, I have become attached to this
Drumo. The dog has twice saved my life, and hence has
become too precious to be risked ; for though he would
most likely win the day, yet a chance thrust might
destroy him at the end. I therefore looked around for a
substitute, and found him—this Rhodian slave. Day after
day I marked him in the opposite ranks, fighting against
us, and I gave orders to capture him alive. Twice we
thought we had secured him, and as often did he break
away, killing many of our men. But at last the commander of one of my cohorts obtained possession of his

wife and five children, and sent him word that each day, until he delivered himself up, one of them should be put to death."

"Surely that thing was not done?" exclaimed· Ænone, horror-struck.

"As I live, it was not ordered by me, nor did I learn of the scheme until it was too late to arrest it," responded Sergius ; "else would I have forbidden it. But what would you expect? War has its practices, and mercy is not exactly one of them. And cruelties will happen, do what we may. Whatever transpired, therefore, was the work of the commander of my first cohort, to whom I had given directions to take the man alive, and who knew that it must be done, and without troubling me about the process. Perhaps you do not care to hear the rest?"

"Go on," said Ænone, shuddering with a sickening apprehension of what was to come.

"Well, the first day his oldest child was slain, and the body sent to him ; and the next day the second one slain, and in like manner sent to him ; and so on until but his wife and one child were left. Then he came in and gave himself up."

"And this brave man—fighting for his country—you have made a slave of!" exclaimed Ænone, impetuously. "He has been stripped of his family one by one, and now you would place him in the arena, to be the victim of wild beasts, or at the best, of other slaves !"

"What else would you wish ? The man is of a warlike nature ; and it were better for him to bravely contend for his life in the presence of the emperor himself, than ignominiously to wear it out in the base labor of the quarries. And I will tell you what I meant to have done. I know where are his wife and remaining child, with whom he yesterday entered Rome ; and if in the amphitheatre he had won the victory for me, I would have restored them to him and given him his freedom besides. But all that is passed now. In the heat of the moment I forgot him, and suffered this drunken dog, Bassus, to take his choice ; and he has had too good an eye for what is valuable not to select the Rhodian. Strange, indeed, that I should have been so careless. But throughout all, I never dreamed that his taste would lead him to do more than choose some slight-built boy, who could assist him in his trade. Once, indeed, I feared for the moment that he would select amiss, and take a rarely precious dwarf, whom, both for his appearance and for his knowledge of armor, I had reserved as a gift for your father ; and when that danger was past, I breathed freer, not calculating upon any further mischance."

Ænone remained silent. Ready as she was at all times to give her utmost sympathy to her husband for the slightest annoyance which he might experience, it seemed to her now that his complaining was puerile and unjust, so utterly had the sense of his disappointment been swallowed up, in her thoughts, by the real and tragic woe of the Rhodian captive. Finding day after day his dead children laid at his very door—then separated rudely from all who were left—and in the end brought chained into the arena, and obliged to fight to the death for the pleasure of his conquerors, and perhaps against his own countrymen ;—why should such things be? Ænone was no nerveless creature to faint at the sight of blood. The education of all Romans of that day was adapted to a far different result, and she could look with enjoyment upon the contests of wild beasts, or even view without disapprobation the struggles of gladiators trained to their work as to a profession, and, of their own free will and with full knowledge, taking its risks upon themselves. And yet, for all that, she could not but feel that every hour there were being enacted around her, and as a part of the daily workings of the social system, abuses of power, which, like the present, nothing could justify; and she wondered whether it would last forever, or whether, on the contrary, the outraged gods would not some day arise and pour down upon this imperial Rome the vengeance due to the oppressed.

Sergius partially read her thoughts, and set himself at work to reverse their current and turn it into a more cheerful channel. Drawing his seat closer to her, he began to speak of more pleasant topics, telling of the enlivening incidents of his campaign, rehearsing the exploits of those about him, and dwelling upon the few occasions in which, by some unusual departure from martial customs, mercy had been shown to the weak and helpless, and captives who were not fit for slaves had not been crucified. The gift of fascination was one of his distinguishing traits; and when he chose, he could charm with his winning speech the most obdurate and unloving. Therefore, as he now softly whispered these narrations into Ænone's ears, mingling gentle words of endearment with them, it was not long before she began to yield to the pleasant influence, and was almost ready to believe that she had judged rashly, and that every thing upon earth was not so very wrong. Why, after all, should she presume to criticise matters which did not arouse the discontent of the wisest of men? And if the gods felt really outraged, why did they let their thunders sleep so long?, At the least, it was not the duty of herself, a weak girl, to strive to right the world. Her only domain must be her lord's heart—her only rule of life, his will.

Leaning upon his shoulder, and looking up into his face as she listened, she thought upon the old times, when she had first met him, and how he had then, as now, so successfully exerted his powers of charming, that it had seemed as though no mere earthly love could be good enough reward for him. Could it be that in her distrust she had been the victim of a momentary delusion, and that he would always exert himself hereafter, as now, to please her? Might it not be, after all, that this great happiness, with its tender whisperings and caresses, would ever continue unbroken, as in past times?

"But stay!" he suddenly exclaimed, in the tone of one newly awakened to the existence of a fact whose comparative unimportance had led to its forgetfulness by him. "Let not my own losses make me indifferent to your pleasure, love, for I have not been so. For you, and you alone, I have reserved a gift fit for the palace of the Cæsars."

"A gift, my lord. And for me?"

"Yes; but ask me no questions now. You shall see it to-morrow. A few hours only of mystery and waiting must yet elapse before I will bring it to you. Until then you can enjoy a woman's pleasure and nurse your greedy curiosity—hopeless of solving the enigma until I myself choose to give the clew."

CHAPTER V.

The day wore quietly on, like any other day; for the confusion and turmoil of the ovation were already a half-forgotten thing of the past, and Rome had again subsided into its usual course. In the earlier hours, a city of well-filled streets, astir and vocal with active and vigorous trade and labor; then—as the noontide sun shed from the brazen sky a molten glow, that fell like fire upon the lava pavement, and glanced from polished walls until the whole atmosphere seemed like a furnace—a city seemingly deserted, except by a few slaves, engaged in removing the triumphal arches hung with faded and lifeless flowers, and by a soldier here and there in glistening armor, keeping a lonely watch; and again—as the sun sank towards the west, and, with the lengthening shadows, the intensity of the heat diminished—a city flooded with wealth and fashion, pouring in confused streams hither and thither, through its broadest avenues and forums. Groups of idlers sauntering along to watch the inoccupation of others, and with the prospective bath as the pretence for the stroll—matrons and maidens of high degree, with attendants following them—a rattle of gayly caparisoned chariots, with footmen trotting beside the wheels—guards on horseback—detachments of prætorian soldiers passing up and down—here the car of a senator of the broad purple—there the mounted escort of a Syrian governor—all that could speak of magnificence, wealth, and authority, at that hour thronged the pavement.

Leaving the Vanno palace, Ænone joined herself to this moving concourse. At her side walked one of her bondwomen, and, at a pace or two behind, properly attired, and armed only with a short sword, strode the armor-bearer. Thus attended, she pressed forward along the Appian Way towards the outskirts of the city—past broad palaces and villas, with encircling gardens and open paved courts—past shrubberies, fish-ponds, and statue-crowned terraces—past public baths, through whose broad doorways the people swarmed by hundreds, and whose steps were thronged with waiting slaves; now stopping until the armor-bearer, running to the front, could make a passage for her through some crowd denser than ordinary—then gliding onward with more rapid pace, as the way became clearer—and again arresting herself for a moment, as the stream of people also tarried to watch the approach of the gorgeous chariot and richly uniformed guards of the Emperor Titus Vespasian. At length, turning the corner of a pillar-porticoed temple, which stood back from the street, and up the gentle ascent of whose steps a concourse of priests and attendants were forcing a garland-decked bullock, unconscious of the sacrificial rites which awaited him within, she stood beyond the surging of the crowd and in a quiet little street.

It was a narrow avenue, in whose humble architecture brick took the place of stone; but in no respect mean or filthy, like so many of the streets of similar width in the central portion of the city. Stretching out towards the open country, and not given up to merchandise or slave quarters, its little houses had their gardens and clustering vines about them, supplying with the picturesque whatever was wanting in magnificence, and evidencing a pleasant medium between wealth and poverty. The paved roadway was clean and unbroken; and far down as the eye could reach no life was to be seen, except a single slave with a fruit-basket balanced upon his head, and near him a group of children at play.

Passing down this street, Ænone came to a spot where one of the great aqueducts which supplied the city crossed the roadway diagonally with a single span. At the right hand stood a small brick house, built into the nearest arch so snugly that it seemed as though its occupants could almost hear the gurgling of the water flowing overhead from the hills of Albanus. Like the other houses in its neighborhood, it had a small courtyard in front, planted with a shrub or two. This was the home of her father, the centurion Porthenus. Stopping here, she was about to enter without warning, according to her usual custom; but as she advanced, a dwarf whom she recognized as the same which that morning had so eagerly presented himself for notice in the front of her husband's captives, sprang forward, grinned his recognition of the armor-bearer, made another grimace expressive of mingled respect and admiration for herself, threw open the door, and ushered her in with an outburst of ceremonious pride befitting an imperial reception.

At a back window of the house, from whence the line of aqueduct could be seen for some distance leaping houses and streets in its undeviating course to the centre of the city, sat the centurion. He was a man of medium height, short-necked, and thick-set, with blunted features, and grizzled hair and beard. Two of the fingers of his left hand were wanting, and a broad scar, the trophy of a severe skirmish among the Alemanni, crossed his right cheek and one side of his nose, giving him an expression more curious than pleasing. His general appearance was after the common type of an old war-worn soldier, rough and unscrupulous by nature, hardened by camp life and dissipation, grown cruel by excess of petty authority, overbearing with his inferiors, jovial and complaisant with his equals, cringing to his superiors, and with an air of discontent overlaying every other expression, as though he were continually tortured with the belief that his success in life had not equalled his merits. As Ænone entered, he was bending over a shield, and earnestly engaged in burnishing its brazen mouldings. At his side leaned a short sword, awaiting similar attention, and in a rack beside him were a number of weapons of different varieties and sizes, which had already submitted to his restorative skill, and now shone like glass.

Hearing her light step, he looked up, arose, flung the shield into a corner, and with a roar, as though ordering a battalion, called out to the grinning dwarf, who had followed her in:

"Ho there, ape! A seat for my daughter, the wife of the imperator Sergius Vanno!"

The dwarf sprang forward and dragged out a low bench for her; having done which, he seemed about to yield to his curiosity and remain. But the centurion, disapproving of such freedom, made a lunge at him with the small sword, before which the dwarf retired with a precipitate leap, and joined the bond-woman and armor-bearer outside. Then the father, being left alone with his daughter, embraced her, and uttered such words of welcome as his rough nature suggested.

As regarded his intercourse with her, perhaps the most noticeable traits were the mingled reverence and familiarity with which he treated her. It seemed as though he were actuated by an ever-pervading consciousness that her exalted position demanded the observance of the deepest respect towards her; but that this feeling was connected in his mind with an unceasing struggle to remember that, after all, she was his own child, and as such was not entitled to any undue consideration from him. Upon the present occasion, he first timidly touched her cheek with his lips and uttered a gentle and almost courtly salutation; but immediately recollecting himself, and appearing to become impressed with the belief that his unwitting deference was unworthy of the character of a father, he proceeded to atone for the mistake by a rough and discomposing embrace, and such a familiar and frolicksome greeting as none but a camp-follower would have felt flattered with. Then seating himself before her, he commenced his conversation in a rude and uncouth tone, and with rather a forced affectation of military bluntness; from which, however, as his eye dwelt upon the richness of her apparel and his mind began to succumb to the charm of her native refinement, he gradually and unconsciously subsided, in turn, into his former soft and deferential manner.

"And so the imperator Sergius Vanno, has returned," he said, rolling upon his tongue, with evident satisfaction, that high-sounding title—once the acknowledged appellation of a conqueror, but now claimed as a right by the imperial line alone, and no longer elsewhere bestowed except as an informal and transitory compliment. "It was a splendid ovation, and well earned by a glorious campaign. There is no one in all the Roman armies who could have managed it better."

Nevertheless, with unconscious inconsistency, he immediately began to show wherein the campaign could have been improved, and how many gross mistakes were visible in every portion of it—how the force of Mutius should have been diverged more in advancing inland—how, in the battle along the shore, the three-oared galleys of Agricola should have been drawn up to support the attack—the consequence of this omission, if the leading cohort had met with a repulse—and the like. All this he marked out upon the floor with a piece of coal, taking but little heed that Ænone could not follow him; and step by step, in the ardor of criticism, he advanced so far that he was soon ready to prove that the campaign had been most wofully misconducted, and was only indebted to accident for success.

"But it is of little use for me to talk, if I cannot act as well," he at length concluded, rising from the floor. "And how could I act any part, placed as I am? The father of the wife of the imperator Sergius Vanno should be the leader of a cohort rather than of a mere century; and be otherwise lodged than in this poor place. Then would they listen to him."

He spoke bitterly and enviously, exhibiting in his whole tone as well as in his words his besetting weakness. For awhile Ænone did not answer. It was as far from her duty as from her taste and pleasure to remind him, even if she could have done so to his comprehension, that her husband had already advanced him as far as was possible or fitting, and had otherwise provided for him in various ways as well as could reasonably be expected. The views of the centurion were of a far different nature. In giving his daughter to the patrician he had meanly intended thereby to rise high in life—had anticipated ready promotion beyond what his ignorance would have justified—had supposed that he would be admitted upon an equal social footing among the friends of Sergius, not realizing that his own native roughness and brutishness must have forbidden such a connection—had dazzled his eyes too wilfully with pictures of the wealth and influence and glory that would fall to his lot. As long, therefore, as so many of those gilded imaginings had failed in their promise, it seemed as nothing to him that Sergius, in the first flush of admiration for the daughter, had removed the father from rough provincial to more pleasing and relaxing urban duties, had purchased him a house befitting his station, and had lightened his condition in various ways.

"But we are gradually doing better," Ænone said at length, striving to cheer him by identifying her fortunes more nearly with his own. "This is a finer place than we had to live in at Ostia. Think how narrow and crowded we were then. And now I see that we have a new slave to open for us, while at Ostia we had only old Mitus. Indeed, we are very comfortable."

"Ay, ay," growled the centurion; "a new slave—a dwarf or idiot, or what not—just such a creature as would not bring five sestertia in the market; and therefore the imperator has cast him to me, like a bare bone to a dog. Tell him I thank him for the gift. And in this matter it has been with me as always heretofore—either no luck at all, or too much. How often have I not passed a campaign without taking a prisoner, while they fell in crowds to all around me! And if at last I gained my share, when was it ever of any value to me, being hundreds of miles from a market? And here it is the same again. For months, no slave at all; and then all at once there are two, and I shall be eaten out of my house."

"Two, father?"

"Listen to me. No sooner did your honored lord send me this dwarf, than arrives Tisiphon of the twelfth cohort. He had long owed me a slave; and now that a captive, poor and feeble, and likely to die, had fallen into his hands, he thought it a fair opportunity to acquit himself towards me. But for once Tisiphon has cheated himself. The slave he brought was weak and sick, but it was only from want of food and rest. The fellow will recover, and I will ere long make much of him. Would you see him? Look out of the back window there. He will turn out a fine slave yet, and if this dwarf had not come, would be right pleasing to me. But two of them! How shall I find bread for both?"

Ænone walked to the window, and leaned out. The courtyard behind was but limited in size, containing a few squares of burnt brick arranged for pavement around a small plat of grass at the foot of a single plane-tree. The slave of whom the centurion spoke was seated upon this plat, with his back against the tree, and his head bent over, while, with vacant mind, he watched the play of a small green lizard. As she appeared at the window, he raised his eyes towards her, then dropped them again upon the ground. It was hardly, in fact, as much as could be called a look—a mere glance, rather, a single tremor of the drooping lids, a mute appeal for sympathy, as though there had been an inner instinct which, at that instant, had directed him to her, as one who could feel pity for his trouble and desolation. But at that glance, joined to something strangely peculiar in the captive's figure and attitude, a nervous thrill shot through Ænone's heart, causing her to hold her breath in unreasoning apprehension; a fear of something which she could not explain, a dim consciousness of some forgotten association of the past arising to confront her, but which she could not for the moment identify. And still she looked out, resisting the impulse of dread which bade her move away, fixing a strained gaze upon the captive, in a vain struggle to allay, by one moment of calm scrutiny, that phantom of her memory which, act as she might, would not be repressed, but which each instant seemed to expand into clearer certainty before her.

"Do you see him? Does he appear to you a worthy slave?" cried the centurion.

"A worthy slave indeed," she answered, in a low tone, feeling compelled to make some response.

At her voice the captive again raised his head, and

looked into her face ; not now with a hasty, timid glance, but with the full gaze of one who believes he has been spoken to, and waits for a renewal of the question. And as she met the inquiring look, Ænone turned away and sank back in terror and dismay. She knew it all, now, nor could she longer deceive herself by vain pretences or assurances. The instinct which at the first had filled her soul with that unexplained dread, had not been false to her. For that glance, as it now rested upon her with longer duration and deeper intensity, too surely completed the suggestion which at the first it had faintly whispered to her, flashing into her heart the long-stifled memories of the past, recalling the time when, a few years before, she had sat upon the rock at Ostia, and had gazed down upon eyes lifted to meet her own with just so beseeching an appeal, and telling her too truly that she stood again in the presence of him to whom she had then promised her girlish faith, and whom she had so long since looked upon as dead to her.

"I will call him in," said the centurion, "and you can see him closer."

"Nay, nay, father ; let him remain where he is," she exclaimed, in uncontrollable dread of recognition.

"Ha ! art not afraid, girl ?" demanded the old man. "He can do thee no harm, even were he stronger ; and now that he is weak, a child could lead him with a string. Come hither, sirrah !"

The captive arose, smoothed down his tunic, and, obediently entering the house, awaited commands ; while Ænone, with as quiet movement as possible, shrunk into the most distant corner of the room. What if he should recognize her, and should call upon her by name, not knowing her changed position, or recollecting his own debasement into slavery? What explanation other than the true one could she give to account for his audacity, and save him from the chastisement which the offended centurion would prepare to bestow upon him? This was but a momentary fear, however, since she felt that the increasing gloom of evening, added to her own alteration by dress, and the certainty that he would not expect to meet her thus, furnished a sure protection against recognition, as long as she took care not to risk betrayal by her voice or manner. And, perhaps, after all—and her heart lightened somewhat at the thought—it might be that her reason had too freely yielded to an insane fancy, and allowed her to be deceived by a chance resemblance.

"How is he called?" she inquired, disguising her voice as thoroughly as she could. The instant she had spoken she would have retracted her words, if possible, from the mere fear lest her father, in his response, might mention her name. But it luckily chanced that the centurion did not do so.

"How is he called? Nay, that thing I had not thought to ask as yet. Your name, slave?"

"Cleotos."

At the word, the blood again flew back to her heart. There could now no longer be a doubt. How often had she repeated that name endearingly, in those early days of her first romantic life!

"Cleotos," said the centurion. "It is a brave name. There was once a leader of a full legion with that name, and he did well to the empire. It is, therefore, scarcely a name for a slave to bear. But we will talk some other time about that. It is of thine appearance now, that we will speak. Is he not, after all, a pleasing youth? Did Tisiphon so surely deceive me as he intended, when he gave the man to me? See! there is but little brawn and muscle to him, I grant; and therefore he will not make a good gladiator or even spearman; but he has a comely shape, which will fit him well for a page or palace usher. And, therefore, I will sell him for such. He should bring a good price, indeed, when the marks of his toil and sickness have gone off from him, and he has been fattened into better condition. But two of them!" continued the centurion, suddenly recurring to his former source of grief. "How can I fatten him when there are two of them? How find bread for both? And yet he is not so very thin, now. I will light a lamp, daughter, for it has grown dark, and you shall come nearer and examine him."

"Nay! nay!" exclaimed Ænone, in hurried resistance of this new danger. "Not now. I am no judge of the merits of captives, and it is getting late. I know that my lord will be expecting me, and perchance will be vexed if I delay."

"Be it so, then," responded the other. "And as it is dark, it is not befitting that you should go without escort. Take, therefore—"

"I have the armor-bearer for my escort, father."

"It is something, but not enough," said the centurion "Enough for safety, but not for dignity. Remember that, while on the one hand you are the wife of the imperator

Sergius Vanno, you are also a daughter of the house of Porthenus—a family which was powerful in the far-off days of the republic, long before the house of Vanno had begun to take root," he continued, in a tone of pride. For then, as now, poverty consoled itself for its privations by dreams —whether well or ill founded, it mattered but little—of grandeurs which had once existed ; and it was one of the weaknesses of the centurion to affect superiority of blood, and try to believe that therein he enjoyed compensations beyond any thing that wealth could bestow.

"Of the house of Porthenus," he repeated, "and should therefore be suitably attended. So let this new slave follow behind. And take, also, the dwarf. He is not of soldierly appearance, but for all that he will count as one more."

Fearful of offending her father by a refusal, or of encountering additional risks of recognition by a more prolonged conversation at the doorway, now brightened by the light of the newly risen moon, Ænone hastily assented, and started upon her homeward route. Clinging closely to the side of her bond-woman, not daring to look back for a parting adieu to her father, who stood at the door leaning upon his sword, and grimly smiling with delight at fancying his child at last attended as became a scion of the house of Porthenus—not regarding the half-smothered oaths and exclamations of contempt with which the armor-bearer behind her surveyed his two new companions upon guard—she pressed rapidly on, with the sole desire of reaching her house and securing herself from further danger of recognition.

The moon rose higher, silvering the city with charms of

new beauty, gleaming upon the surface of the swift-rolling Tiber, giving fresh radiance to the marble palaces and temples, adding effect to whatever was already beautiful, diminishing the deformity of whatever was unlovely, even imparting a pleasant aspect of cheerfulness to the lower quarters of the city, where lay congregated poverty and dishonor and crime. The Appian Way no longer swarmed with the crowd that had trodden it an hour ago. The priests had completed the sacrifice and left the temple, the bathers had departed, the slaves no longer lingered upon the porticoes, and the riders in gay chariots no more were to be seen. A calmer and more quiet occupancy of the street had ensued. Here and there a soldier paced to and fro, looking up at the moon and down again at the glistening river, and thought, perhaps, upon other night-watches in Gallia, when just such a moon had gleamed upon the silver Rhone. Here and there two lovers, loth to abandon such a pleasant light and warmth, strolled slowly along, and, as lovers have ever done, bade the moon witness their vows. But not the river or the moonlight did Ænone now linger to look upon, nor lovers' vows did she think about, as she glided hastily towards her own home. The peacefulness and quiet of nature found no response in her heart. Her only emotion was one of dread lest each ray of light might shine too brightly upon her—lest even her walk might betray her—lest every sound might be an unguarded recognition from the poor unconscious captive behind her.

At length she reached her home, passed up the broad flight of steps in front, and stood panting within the doorway. A momentary pause ere she entered; and then, unable to continue the control which she had so far maintained over herself, she turned and cast one hasty, curious glance below. The two new slaves of the centurion stood side by side in the street, gazing up at the palace walls—the dwarf with a grin of almost idiotic glee, the other with a grave air of quiet contemplation. But what was that sudden look of startled recognition that suddenly flashed across the features of the latter? Why did his face turn so ghastly pale in the moonlight, and his limbs seem to fail him, so that he grasped his companion's arm for support? Ænone shrank terrified into the obscurity of the doorway.

But in an instant she recovered her self-possession. It must be that he had been faint or giddy, nothing more. It could not have been recognition that had startled him from his earnest contemplation, for he had not been looking towards her, but, with his body half turned away, had been gazing up at the highest story of the palace.

CHAPTER VI.

And now, having avoided the immediate peril of recognition, Ænone turned into the palace. Even there, however, her disordered fancy pictured dangers still encompassing her. How, after all, could she feel sure that she had not been known? During that clear moonlight passage along the Appian Way, what revelations might not have been made by a chance look or gesture! At the very first she had almost stumbled upon the truth, merely through the magic of one upward glance of the eye of the wearied slave; why, then, might she not have unconsciously revealed herself to him by even a wave of the hand or a turn of the instep, or by some other apparently trivial and unimportant motion? And if so, at what instant might he not forget his fallen condition, and disregard not only his safety but her reputation, by pressing into the palace and claiming the right of speech with her? Rasher deeds were not seldom done under the promptings of desperation. Trembling beneath the sway of such imaginings, each footfall that resounded in the hall seemed like the light and buoyant step of him who had trodden with her the sands of Ostia—each figure that passed by bore, for the instant, the outline of his form—even at the open window the well-known face seemed to peer in at every corner and watch her.

This paroxysm of terror gradually passed away, but was succeeded by other fancies equally productive of inquietude. What if the captive, having recognized her, had whispered his story to the companions with whom he had walked! He would surely not do so if he still loved her ; but what if his love had ceased, and he should be meanly desirous of increasing his own importance by telling how he, a slave, had been the chosen lover of the proudly allied lady before him? Nay, he would never act thus, for it would be a baseness foreign to his nature ; and yet, have not men of the most lofty sense of honor often fallen from their original nobility, and revelled in self-degradation? And it somehow seemed as though, at the last, the dwarf had looked up at her with a strangely knowing leer. And was it merely her imagination that made her think there was a certain sly approach to undue familiarity in the usually deferential deportment of the armor-bearer?

With the next morning, however, came more composed reflections. Though the forebodings of the evening had naturally tinged her dreams with similar vague imaginings of coming trouble, yet, upon the whole, her sleep had brought rest, and the bright sunlight streaming in at the window drove away the phantoms which, during the previous gloom, had so confusedly disported themselves in her bewildered brain. She could now indulge in a more cheering view of her situation ; and she felt that there was nothing in what had transpired of sufficient importance, when coolly weighed and passed upon, to make her anxious or afraid.

In a sick and travel-worn slave she had recognized one

to whom, in her younger days, she had plighted her faith, and who had, in return, given his faith to her. He was now a captive, and she had become one of the nobles of the empire. But his evil lot had not been of her procuring, being merely one of those ill fortunes which are cast broadly over the earth, and whose descent upon any one person more than upon another can be attributed to destiny alone. Nor, in accepting her high position, had she been guilty of breach of faith, for she had long awaited the return of her lover, and he had not come. And through all those years, as she had grown into more mature womanhood, she had vaguely felt that those stolen interviews had been but the unreasoning suggestions of girlish romance, too carelessly indifferent to the exigencies of poverty and diverse nationality; and that, if he had ever returned to claim her, mutual explanation and forgetfulness could have been their only proper course. There was, therefore, nothing for which she could reproach herself, or for which he could justly blame her, were he to recognize her as the wife of another man.

But there was little danger, indeed, that such a recognition could take place. Certainly, now that, apart from her troubled and excited fears of the previous day, she more deliberately weighed the chances, she felt assured that in her rapid passage through the evening gloom, nothing could have betrayed her. And it was not probable that even in open daylight and in face-to-face encounter with him he would be likely to know her. She had recognized him almost at a glance, for not only was his dress composed of the same poor and scant material which had served him years before, but even in form and feature he seemed unchanged, his slight frame having gained no expansion as his manhood had progressed, while his face retained in every line the same soft and almost girlish expression. But with herself all things had altered. It was not merely that the poorly clad maiden who, with naked feet, well-tanned hands, and tangled and loosely hanging curls, had been wont to wander carelessly by the shore of a distant bay, had since become a richly adorned matron of the imperial centre. Beyond all that, there was a greater change, which, though in its gradual progress almost inappreciable to one who had watched her day by day, could not but be remarked after a lapse of many years. The darker hair, the softer complexion, the suave smile into which the merry laugh of girlhood had little by little subsided, the more composed mien, replete with matronly dignity, the refinement of air and attitude insensibly resulting from long-continued instinctive imitation, the superior development of figure—all these, as they were improvements on her former self, were also just so many effective disguises upon which she could safely rely, unless she were to provoke inordinate scrutiny by some unguarded action or expression. But this she would earnestly guard against. She would even put no trust in the natural immunity of which her reason assured her, but would make every thing doubly safe by totally refraining from any encounter with one whose recognition of her would be so painful.

This she could do, and yet not fail in any friendly duty which the remembrance of their former love might enjoin upon her. Unseen in her retirement, she could watch over and protect him, now that in his sorrow and degradation he so greatly needed a friend. She could ameliorate his lot by numberless kindnesses, which he would enjoy none the less for being unable to detect their source. She would cunningly influence her father to treat him with tenderness and consideration. And when the proper time arrived, and she could take her measures without suspicion, she would herself purchase his freedom, and send him back rejoicing to his native land. And when all this was done, and he should again have reached his home, perhaps she might then write to him one line to tell him who it was that had befriended him, and that she had done so in memory of olden times, and that now, when she was so far removed from him, he should give her one kind thought, utter a prayer to the gods in her behalf, and then forget her forever.

So much for her security and her friendly duty. As for the feelings of her heart, she was at rest. Strong in self-confidence, she had no fear that her mind could be influenced to stray from its proper path. It is true that during the previous evening, in the first tumult of troubled thought, she had felt a vague presentiment that a day of temptation might be before her, not as the result of any deliberate choice upon her part, but rather as a cruel destiny to be forced upon her. But now the current of her mind moved more clearly and unobstructedly; and she felt that however chance might control the worldly prosperity of each one, the will and strength to shape his own destiny, for good or evil, are still left to him unimpaired. Away, then, with all thoughts of the past. In her heart there could be but one affection, and to her life there could be but the one course of duty, and in that she would steadfastly walk.

Strengthened, therefore, with the well-assured belief that the impulsive affection of her youth had become gradually tempered by lapse of years into a chaste and sisterly friendship, and that the pleasant memories which clustered about her heart and made her look back half regretfully upon those former days would be cherished only as the mere innocent relics of a girlish romance, she felt no fear that her faith could be led to depart from its lawful allegiance. But aside from all this, there lurked within her breast an uneasy sense of being the holder of a great secret which, in the end, would surely crush her, unless she could share its burden with another. In this desire for confidence, at least, there could be no harm; and her mind rapidly ran over the array of her few friends. For the first time in her life, perhaps, her isolation from close and unfettered companionship with others was forced upon her attention, and her soul grew faint as she thought of her dependence upon herself alone for comfort or advice. To whom, indeed, could she venture to pour out her heart? Not to her father, who, with unreasoning ignorance and little charity, would coarsely form base conclusions about her, and would most likely endeavor to solve the problem by cruelty to the unfortunate slave who had so unwittingly originated it. Not to any of those matrons of whom her rank made her the associate; and who, after gaining her confidence, would either betray it to others, or else, wrongly misconstruing her, and fancying her to be influenced by scruples which they might not have felt, would scarcely fail to ridicule and cast disdain upon all the most tender emotions of her heart. And above all others, not to her husband, to whom, if she dared, she would have wished to reveal every thing, but who had, she feared, at the bottom of his soul, a jealous and suspicious nature, which would be sure to take alarm, and cause him to look upon her story, not as a generous confidence bestowed in the hope of comfort and assistance, but rather as a cunningly devised cover for some unconfessed scheme of wrong against him.

Burdened with these reflections, Ænone slowly passed from her room into the antechamber. Lifting her eyes, she there saw her husband standing at the window, and, at the distance of a pace or two from him, a female figure. It was that of a girl of about eighteen years, small, lithe, and graceful. Her costume, though not in form such as belonged to the freeborn women of Rome, was yet far superior in richness of material to that usually worn by persons of low degree, and was fashioned with a taste which could not fail to assist the display of her graceful perfection of form, indicated in part by the rounded lines of the uncovered neck and arms. As Ænone entered the room, Sergius advanced, and, taking her by the hand, said:

"Yonder is a new slave for you—the present about which I yesterday spoke. I trust it will prove that during my absence I was not unmindful of you. It was at Samos that I obtained her. There, you may remember, we tarried, after taking the town and burning part of the fleet."

Samos! Where had Ænone heard that place mentioned? Searching into the recesses of her memory, it at last flashed upon her. Was it not from Samos that he—Cleotos—had come? And was it fate that forced the recollection of him ever upon her? She turned pale, but by a violent effort succeeded in maintaining her self-possession and looking up with a smile of apparent interest upon her husband as he spoke.

"She had nearly fallen the prey of one of the common soldiers," he continued; "but I, with a few pieces of gold, rescued her from him, picturing to myself the gratification you would feel at being so fitly attended. And that you might the better appreciate the gift, I have retained her till to-day before showing her to you, in order that you might first see her recovered from the toil of travel and in all her renewed beauty. A rare beauty, indeed, but of a kind so different from thine that your own will be heightened by the contrast rather than diminished. How many sestertia I have been offered for her, how many high officers of my forces have desired to obtain her for service upon their own wives, I cannot now remember. But I have refused and resisted all, for I would that you should be known throughout Rome by the beauty of those in waiting about you, even as you are now known by your own beauty. Pray, accept of her, therefore, as your attendant and companion, for it would sorely disappoint me were you to reject such a pleasing gift."

"Let it be as my lord says," responded Ænone. "And if I fail in due utterance of my thanks, impute it not to want of appreciation of the gift, but rather to inability of proper expression."

It was with real gratitude that Ænone spoke; for at the

instant, a thought of cheering import flashed upon her, swelling her heart with joy, and causing her to welcome the captive girl as a gift from the gods. Here, perhaps, as though in direct answer to her prayer for sympathy, might be the one for whom her heart had been longing; coming to her, not laden with any of that haughty pride and ill-befitting knowledge with which the Roman world about her recked, but rather as she herself had once come— with all her unstained provincial innocence of thought yet nestling in her shrinking soul—one, like herself, an exile from a lowly state, and with a heart filled with those simple memories which must not be too carelessly exposed, so seldom do they gather from without any thing but cruel ridicule or cold lack of comprehension—one whom she could educate into an easy intimacy with her own impulses and yearnings, and thus, forgetting all social differences, draw closer and nearer to her as a friend and confidant.

As she thus reflected, she felt the soft pressure of lips upon her left hand, which hung idly at her side, and, looking down, she saw that the captive girl had knelt before her, and, while lightly grasping her fingers, was gazing up into her face with a pleading glance. Ænone's first impulse was to respond with eager warmth to that humble appeal for protection and friendship; and had it not been for the morbid fear she felt lest her husband, who stood looking on, might chide such familiarity, or at the least might cast ridicule upon the feeling which prompted it, she would have raised the captive girl and folded her in her arms. As it was, the impulse was too spontaneous and sudden to be entirely resisted, and she held forth her other hand to lift the kneeling figure, when a strange, intuitive perception of something which she could scarcely explain, caused her to withhold further action.

Something, she knew not what, in the attitude and expression of the captive before her, which sent her warm blood flowing back with a chilled current—something which told her that her hopes of the moment had been smitten with decay as suddenly as they had been raised, and that, instead of a friend, she had perhaps found an enemy. The full dark eye yet gazed up at her with the same apparent moistened appeal for friendly sympathy; but to Ænone's alarmed instinct it now seemed as though behind that glance there was an inner depth of cold, calculating scrutiny. Still, almost unheeding the gentle gesture of the hand extended to raise her, the Greek knelt upon the floor, and, with an appearance of mingled timorousness and humility, laid her lips upon the gathered fingers; but now there appeared to be no natural warmth or glow in the pressure or real savor of lowliness in the attitude, but rather a forced and studied obsequiousness. For the instant Ænone paused, as though uncertain how to act. Then, fearing to betray her doubts, and hoping that her startled instinct might have deceived her, she bent forward once more and raised the captive to her feet.

It had all been the work of an instant; passing so quickly that the pause between the impulse and its completion could hardly have been noticed. But in that instant a change had swept over the expressions of both; and as they now stood opposite and gazed more intently upon each other, the change still progressed. The face of the young Roman matron, but a moment before so glowing with sympathy and radiant with a newly discovered hope of future happiness, now seemed to shrink behind a veil of despairing dread—the fear chasing away the joy as the shadow flits along the wall and banishes the sunlight; while, though every feature of the Greek still seemed clothed with trembling humility, yet, from some latent depths of her nature, a gleam of something strangely wild and forbidding began to play upon the surface, and invest the moistened eye and quivering lip with an undefinable repulsive harshness.

"Your name," said Ænone, rousing herself with exertion, as though from a painful dream.

"They call me Leta," was the reply, uttered in a tone of despairing sadness, and with eyes again cast upon the floor.

"Leta," repeated Ænone, touched in spite of her forebodings by that guise of an unhappiness which might, after all, be real. "It is a fair sounding name, and I shall call you always by it. Poor girl! you are an exile from your native land, and I—I cannot call myself a Roman. We must be friends—must we not?"

She spoke rather in the tone of one hoping against evil auguries than as one indulging in any confident anticipations of the future. The Greek did not answer, but again slowly raised her eyes. At first, as before, with the same studied expression of pleading humility; but, as she glanced forward, and saw Sergius standing behind, and gazing at her with an admiration which he did not attempt to dissemble, a strange glow of triumph and ambitious hope seemed to light up her features. And when, after a hasty glance of almost responsive meaning towards Sergius, she again looked into the face of the other, it was no longer with an assumption of humble entreaty, but rather with an expression of wild, searching intensity. Before it the milder gaze of Ænone faltered, until it seemed as though the two had suffered a relative interchange of position: the patrician mistress standing with troubled features, and with vague apprehension and trembling in her heart, and as though timorously asking for the friendship which she had meant to bestow; and the captive, calmly, and with a look of ill-suppressed triumph, reading the other's soul as though to learn how she could most readily wield supremacy over her.

CHAPTER VII.

For an instant only. When from Ænone's troubled gaze, the half-blinding film which the agitation of her apprehensive mind had gathered, passed away, she no longer saw before her a proudly erect figure, flashing out from dark, wild eyes its defiant mastery, but a form again bent low in timorous supplication, and features once more overspread with a mingled imprint of sorrowful resignation, trusting devotion, and pleading humility.

That gleam of malicious triumph which had so brightened up the face of the slave, had come and gone like the lightning flash ; and, for the moment, Ænone was almost inclined to believe that it was some bewildering waking dream. But her instinct told her that it was no mere imagination or fancy which could thus, at one instant, fill the heart with dread, and change her bright anticipations of coming joy into a dull, aching foreboding of misery. It was rather her inner nature warning her not to be too easily ensnared, but to wait for coming evil with unfaltering watchfulness, and, for the purpose of baffling enmity, to perform the hardest task that can be imposed upon a guileless nature—that of repressing all outward sign of distrust, hiding the torture of the heart within, and meeting smile with smile.

But day after day passed on, and even to her watchful and strained attention there appeared no further indication of any thing that should excite alarm. From morning until night there rested upon the face of the young Greek slave no expression other than that of tender, faithful, and pleased obedience. At the morning toilet, at the forenoon task of embroidery, or at the afternoon promenade, there was ever the same serene gaze of earnest devotion, and the same delighted alacrity to anticipate the slightest wish. Until at last Ænone began again to think that perhaps her perception of that one fleeting look might, after all, be but a flickering dream. And when, at times, she sat and heard the young girl speak, not with apparent method, but rather as one who is unwittingly drawn into discursive prattle, about her cottage home in Samos, and the lowly lover from whom the invading armies had torn her, and watched the moistened eye and the trembling lip with which these memories were dwelt upon, an inward pity and sympathy tempted her to forget her own distrust; until one day she was impelled to act as she had once desired, and began to pour out her whole heart to the young slave as to a friend. The words seemed of themselves to flow to her lips, as bidding the girl be comforted, she told, in one short sentence, how she too had once lived in a tranquil cottage home, away from the bustle and fever of that imperial Rome, and had had her lover of low degree, and that both were still innocently dear to her.

All the while that the story had been welling forth from her lips, that inner instinct which so seldom deceives, told her that she was doing wrong; and when she had ended she would have given worlds not to have spoken. But the words were beyond recall, and she could only gaze stealthily at the listener, and, with a dull feeling of apprehension nestling at the bottom of her heart, endeavor to mark their effect, and to imagine the possible consequences of her indiscretion. But Leta sat bending over her embroidery, and apparently still thinking, with tearful eye, upon her own exile from home. Perhaps she had not even heard all that had been said to her; though if the words had really caught her ear, where, after all, could be the harm? It was no secret in Rome that Sergius Vanno had brought his spouse from a lowly home; and it was surely no crime, that, during those years of poverty which Ænone had passed through before being called to fill her present station, she had once suffered her girlhood fancy to rest for a little while upon one of her own class. And fortunately she had not gone further in her story, but at that point had left it to rest; making no mention of how that long-forgotten lover had so lately reappeared and confronted her.

Still there remained in her heart the irrepressible instinct that it would have been better if she had not spoken. And now, as she silently pondered upon her imprudence, it seemed as though her anxiety had suddenly endowed her brain with new and keener faculties of perception, so many startling ideas began to crowd in upon her. More particularly, full shape and tone seemed for the first time given to one terrible suspicion, which she had hitherto known only in a misty, intangible, and seldom recurring form—the suspicion that, if the passive girl before her were really an enemy, it was not owing to any mere ordinary impulse of fear, or envy, or inexplicable womanish dislike, but rather to secret rivalry.

That, within the past few days, Sergius had more and more exhibited towards herself an indifference, which even his studied attempts to maintain a semblance of his former interest and affection did not fully hide, Ænone could not but feel. That within her breast lurked the terrible thought that perhaps the time had forever passed for her to come to him as to a loving friend, and there fearlessly pour out her tribulations, her secret tears confessed. But throughout all this change, though it became each day more strongly marked, she had tried to cheat herself into the belief that the romantic warmth of a first attachment could not in any case be expected to last for many years—that in meeting indifference she was merely experiencing a common lot—that beneath his coolness there still lurked the old affection, as the lava will flow beneath the hardened crust—and that, if she were indeed losing the appearance of his love, it was merely because the claims of the court, the exigencies of the social world, or the demands of ambition had too, much usurped his attention.

But now a thousand hitherto unregarded circumstances began to creep into her mind as so many evidences that his affection seemed passing from her; not simply because the claims of duty or ambition were stifling in his heart all power to love, but because he had become secretly attached elsewhere. The interested gaze with which he followed the motions of the Greek girl—the solicitude which he seemed to feel that in all things she should be treated, not only tenderly, but more luxuriously than ever fell to the lot of even the highest class of slaves—his newly acquired habit of strolling into the room and throwing himself down where he could lazily watch her—all these, and other circumstances, though individually trivial, could not fail, when united, to give cogency to the one terrible conviction of secret wrong. Whether Leta herself had any perception of all this, who could yet tell? It might be that she was clothed in innocent unconsciousness of her master's admiration, or that, by the force of native purity, she had resisted his advances. And, on the other hand, it might be that not merely now, but long before she had been brought into the house, there had been a secret understanding between the two; and that, with undeviating and unrelenting cunning, she was ever drawing him still closer within the folds of her fascinations. Looking upon her, and noting the humble and almost timorous air with which she moved about, as though seeking kindness and protection, and the eloquence of mute appeal for sympathy which lay half hidden in her dark eyes beneath the scarcely raised lids, and rested in her trembling lips, who could doubt her? But marking the haughtiness of pride with which at times she drew up her slight figure to its utmost height, the ray of scorn and malice which flashed from those eyes, and the lines of firm, unpitying determination which gathered about the compressed corners of those lips, who could help fearing and distrusting her?

Time or chance alone could resolve the question, and meanwhile, what course could Ænone take? She could not send the object of her suspicion to another place; for even if she had the power to do so, she might not be able to accomplish it without such open disturbance that the whole social world of Rome would learn the degrading fact that she had been jealous of her own slave. She could not think—as she was sometimes almost tempted—of forgetting her pride, and humbling herself before her enemy, to beg that she would not rob her of all that affection which had once been lavished upon herself: for, if the Greek girl were innocent, useless and feeble pity would be the only result; while, if she were guilty, it would but lead to further secret wiles and malicious triumph. Nor could she venture to accuse her lord of his fault; for such a course, alas! could never restore lost love. There could, indeed, be but one proper way to act. She must possess her soul in patience and prudent dissimulation; and, while affecting ignorance of what she saw and heard, must strive by kindness and attention to win back some, if not all, of the true affection of former days.

Thus sorrowfully reflecting, she left the room, not with any especial intent, but simply to avoid the presence of the Greek, who, she could not help feeling, was all the while, beneath the disguise of that demure expression, closely watching her. Passing into another apartment, she saw that Sergius had there sauntered in, and had thrown himself down upon a lounge at the open window, where, with one hand resting behind his head, he lay half soothed into slumber by the gentle murmur of the courtyard fountain. Stealing up gently behind him, with a strange, commingling of affectionate desire to gain his attention, and morbid dread of bringing rebuke upon herself by awakening him,

Ænone stooped down and lightly touched his forehead with her lips.

"Ah, Leta!" he exclaimed, starting up as he felt the warm pressure. Then, perceiving his mistake, he lowered his eyes with some confusion, and perhaps a slight feeling of disappointment, and tried to force a careless laugh; which died away, however, as he saw how Ænone stood pale and trembling at receiving a greeting so confirmatory of all her apprehensions.

"It is not Leta—it is only I," she murmured at length, in a tone of plaintive sadness, which for the moment touched his heart. "I am sorry that I awakened you. But I will go away again."

"Nay, remain," he exclaimed, restraining her by the folds of her dress, and, with a slight effort, seating her beside him upon the lounge. "You are not—you must not feel offended at such a poor jest as that!"

"Is it all a jest?" she inquired. "Can you say that the greeting you gave me did not spring inadvertently from the real preoccupation of your mind?"

"Of the mind? Preoccupation?" said Sergius. "By the gods! but it is a difficult question to answer. I might possibly, in some dreamy state, have been thinking carelessly of that Greek girl whom you keep so constantly about you. Even you cannot but acknowledge that she has her traits of beauty; and if so, it is hard for a man not to admire them."

"For mere admiration of her, I care but little," she responded. "But I would not that she should learn to observe it. And what could I do, if she, perceiving it, were to succeed in drawing your love from me? What then would there be for me to do, except to die?"

"To die? This is but foolish talk, Ænone," he said; and he fastened an inquiring gaze upon her, as though wishing to search into her soul, and find out how much of his actions she already knew. Evidently some fleeting expression upon her countenance deceived him into believing that she had heard or seen more than he had previously supposed, for, with another faint attempt at a careless laugh, he continued:

"And if, at the most, there has been some senseless trifling between the girl and myself—a pressure of the hand, or a pat upon the cheek, when meeting by any chance in hall or garden—would you find such fault with this as to call it a withdrawal of my love from you? To what, indeed, could such poor, foolish pastime of the moment amount, that it should bring rebuke upon me?"

To nothing, indeed, if judged by itself alone, for that was not the age of the world when every trivial departure from correctness of conduct was looked upon as a crime; and had this been all, and the real affection of his heart had remained with her, Ænone would have taken comfort. But now she knew for certain that, in uncomplainingly enduring any familiarities, Leta could not, at all times, have maintained her customary mien of timorous retirement, and must, therefore, to some extent, have shown herself capable of acting a deceitful part; and that even though the deceit may have stopped short of further transgression, it was none the less certain that in future no further trust could be reposed in her. Gone forever was that frail hope to which, against all warnings of instinct, Ænone had persisted in clinging—the hope that in the Greek girl she might succeed in finding a true and honest friend.

Seeing that she remained absorbed and speechless, Sergius believed that she was merely jealously pondering upon these trivial transgressions, and endeavored, by kind and loving expressions, to remove the evil effects of his unguarded admission. Gathering her closer in his arms, he strove once more, by exerting those fascinations which had hitherto so often prevailed, to calm her disturbed fancies, and bring back again her confidence in him. But now he spoke almost in vain. Conscious, as Ænone could not fail to be, of the apparent love and tenderness with which he bent his eyes upon her, and of the liquid melody of his impassioned intonations, and half inclined, as she felt at each instant, to yield to the impulse which tempted her to throw her arms about his neck and promise from henceforth to believe unfalteringly all that he might say, whatever opposing evidences might stand before her, there was all the while the restraining feeling that this show of affection was but a pretence wherewith to quiet her inconvenient reproaches—that at heart he was playing with deceit—that the husband was colluding with the slave to blind her eyes—and that the love and friendship of both lord and menial had forever failed her.

"But hold to your own suspicions, if you will," he said, at length, with testy accent, as he saw how little all his efforts had moved her. "I have spoken in my defence all that I need to speak, even if excuse were necessary; and it is an ill reward to receive only cold and forbidding responses in return."

"Answer me this," she exclaimed, suddenly rousing into action, and looking him earnestly in the face; "and as you now answer, I will promise to believe you, for I know that, whatever you may have done, you will not, if appealed to upon your honor, tell me that which is not true. About the trivial actions which you have mentioned I care little; but is there in your heart any real affection for that girl? If you say that there is not, I will never more distrust you, but will go out from here with a soul overflowing with peace and joy as when first you came to take me to your side. But if, on the contrary, you say that you love her, I will—"

"Will do what?" he exclaimed, seeing that she hesitated, and almost hoping that she would utter some impatient threat which in turn would give him an excuse for anger.

"Will pass out from this room, sad and broken hearted, indeed—but not complaining of or chiding you; and will only pray to the gods that they may, in their own time, make all things once more go aright, and so restore your heart to me."

Sergius hesitated. Never before had he been so tempted to utter an untruth. If he now did so, he knew that he would be believed, and that not only would she be made once more happy, but he would be left unwatched and unsuspected to carry on his own devices. But, on the other hand, he had been appealed to upon his honor, and, whatever his other faults, he had too much nobility of soul to lie. And so, not daring to confess the truth, he chose the middle path of refusing any direct response at all.

"Now is not this a singular thing," he exclaimed, "that no man can ever let his eyes rest upon a pretty face without being accused of love for it? While, if a woman does the same, no tongue can describe the clamor with which she repels the insinuation of aught but friendly interest. Can you look me in the eye and tell me that mine is the only voice you ever listened to with love?"

"Can you dare hint to me that I have ever been unfaithful to you, even in thought or word?" cried Ænone, stung with sudden anger by the imputation, and rendered desperate by her acute perception of the evasiveness of his answer. "Do you not know that during the months which you so so lately passed far away from me, there was not one person admitted here into society with me who would not have had your firm approval—and that I kept your image so lovingly before my eyes, and your memory so constant in my heart, as to become almost a reproach and a sarcasm to half who knew me?"

"But before that—before I came to you—can you say that no other eyes had ever looked lovingly into yours, and there met kindred response?"

"Have you the right to inquire into what may have happened before you met me? What young girl is there who, some time or other, has not modestly let her thoughts dwell upon innocent love? Is there wrong in this? Should there have been a spirit of prescience in my mind to forewarn me that I must keep my heart free and in vacant loneliness, because that, after many years, you were to come and lift me from my obscurity?"

"Then, upon your own showing, you acknowledge that

there was once another upon whom your eyes loved to look!" he cried, half gladdened that he had found even this poor excuse to transfer the charge of blame from himself. "And how can I tell but that you have met with him since?"

"I have met him since," she quietly answered, driven to desperation by the cruel insinuation.

In his heart attaching but little importance to such childish affections as she might once have cherished, and having had no other purpose in his suggestion than that of shielding himself from further inquiry by inflicting some trifling wound upon her, Sergius had spoken hesitatingly, and with a shamefaced consciousness of meanness and self-contempt. But when he listened to her frank admission—fraught, as it seemed to him, with more meaning than the mere naked words would of themselves imply, an angry flush of new-born jealousy overspread his features.

"Ha! You have met him since?" he exclaimed. "And when and where? And who, then, is this fortunate one?"

Ænone hesitated. Now, still more bitterly than ever before, she felt the sad consciousness of being unable to pour out to her husband her more secret thoughts and feelings. If she could have told, with perfect assurance of being believed, that in so lately meeting the man whom she had once imagined she loved, she had looked upon him with no other feeling than the dread of recognition, joined to a friendly and sisterly desire to procure his release from captivity and his restoration to his own home, she would have done so. But she felt too well that the once-aroused jealousy of her lord might now prevent him from reposing full and generous trust and confidence in her—that he would be far more likely to interpret all her most innocent actions wrongly, and to surround her with degrading espionage—and that, in the end, the innocent captive would probably be subjected to the bitterest persecutions which spite and hatred could invent.

"I have met him," said she at length, "but only by chance, and without being recognized or spoken to by him. Nor do I know whether I shall ever chance to meet him again. Is this a crime? Oh, my lord, what have I done that you should thus strive to set your face against me? Do you not, in your secret soul, know and believe that there is no other smile than yours for which I live, and that, without the love with which you once gladdened me, there can be no rest or peace for me on earth? Tell me, then, that all this is but a cruel pleasantry to prove my heart, and that there has nothing come between us—or else let me know the worst, in order that I may die."

Sliding down, until her knees touched the floor, and then winding one arm slowly about his neck, she hid her face in his breast, and, bursting into tears, sobbed aloud. It was not merely the reactionary breaking down of a nervous system strung to the highest point of undue excitement. It was the half consciousness of a terrible fear lest the day might come in which, goaded by injustice and neglect, she might learn no longer to love the man before her—the wail of a stricken soul pleading that the one to whom her heart had bound her might not fail in his duty to her, but, by a resumption of his former kindness and affection, might retain her steadfastly in the path of love.

Touched by the spectacle of her strong agony—aroused

for the moment to the true realization of all the bitterness and baseness of his unkindness towards her—moved, perhaps, by memories of that time when between them there was pleasant and endearing confidence, and when it was not she who was obliged to plead for love—Sergius drew his arm more closely about her, and, bending over, pressed his lips upon her forehead. If at that moment the opportunity had not failed, who can tell what open and generous confessions might not have been uttered, unrestrained forgiveness sealed, and future miseries prevented? But at the very moment when the words seemed trembling upon his lips, the door softly opened, and Leta entered.

CHAPTER VIII.

RAISING himself with an assumed air of careless indifference, in the hope of thereby concealing the momentary weakness into which his better feelings had so nearly betrayed him, Sergius strolled off, humming a Gallic winesong. Ænone also arose; and struggling to stifle her emotion, confronted the new-comer.

Leta, upon her part, stood silent and impassive, appearing to have heard or seen nothing of what had transpired, and to have no thought except that of fulfilling the duty which had brought her thither. But Ænone knew that the most unobservant person, upon entering, could not have failed at a glance to comprehend the whole import of the scene—and that therefore any such studied pretence of ignorance was superfluous. The attitude of the parties, the ill-disguised confusion of Sergius, her own tears, which could not be at once entirely repressed—all combined to tell a tale of recrimination, pleading, and baffled confidence, as plainly as words could have spoken it. Apart, therefore, from her disappointment at being interrupted at the very moment when her hopes had whispered that the happiness of reconciliation might be at hand, Ænone could not but feel indignant that Leta should thus calmly stand before her with that pretence of innocent unconsciousness.

"Why do you come hither? Who has demanded your

presence?" Ænone cried, now, in her indignation, caring but little what or how she spoke, or what further revelations her actions might occasion, as long as so much had already been exposed.

"Do I intrude?" rejoined the Greek, raising her eyes with a well-executed air of surprise. "I came but to say that in the antechamber there is—"

"Listen!" exclaimed Ænone, interrupting her, and taking her by the hand. "Not an hour ago you told me about your quiet home in Samos—its green vines—the blue mountains which encircled it—the little chamber where your mother died, and in which you were born—and the lover whom you left weeping at your cruel absence. You spoke of your affection for every leaf and blade of grass about the place—and how you would give your life itself to go back thither—yes, even your life, for you would be content to lie down and die, if you could first return. Do you remember?"

"And now?"

"Now, you shall return, as you desired. You have been given to me for my own; and whether or not the gift be a full and free one, I will claim my rights under it and set you free. In the first ship which sails from Ostia for any port of Greece, in that ship you may depart. Are you content, Leta?"

Still holding her by the hand, Ænone gazed inquiringly into the burning black eyes which fastened themselves upon her own, as though reading the bottom of her soul. She could not as yet believe that even if the Greek had actually begun to cherish any love for Sergius, it could be more than a passing fancy, engendered by foolish compliments or ill-judged signs of admiration, and therefore she did not doubt that the offer of freedom and restoration would be gratefully received. Her only uncertainty was with regard to the manner in which it would be listened to—whether with tears of joy or with loud protestations of gratitude upon bended knees; or whether the prospect of once again visiting that cottage home and all that had so long been held dear, would come with such unpremeditated intensity as to stifle all outward manifestations of delight, except perhaps, that trembling of the lip or ebb and flow of color which is so often the surest sign of a full and glowing heart.

For a moment Leta stood gazing up into the face of her mistress, uttering no word of thanks, and with no tear of joy glistening in her eye, but with the deepened flush of uncontrollable emotion overspreading her features. And yet that flush seemed scarcely the token of a heart overpowered with sudden joy, but rather of a mind conscious of being involved in an unexpected dilemma, and puzzled with its inability to extricate itself.

"My mistress," she responded at length, with lowered gaze, "it is true that I said I would return, if possible, to that other home of mine. But now that you offer me the gift, I would not desire to accept it. Let me stay here with you."

Ænone dropped the hand which till now she had held; and an agony of mingled surprise, suspicion, disappointment, and presentiment of evil swept across her features.

"Are you then become like all others?" she said with bitterness. "Has the canker of this Roman life already commenced to eat into your soul, so that in future no memory of any thing that is pure or good can attract you from its hollow splendors? Are thoughts of home, of freedom, of friends, even of the trusted lover of whom you spoke—are all these now of no account, when weighed against a few gilded pleasures?"

"Why, indeed, should I care to return to that home?" responded the girl. "Have not the Roman soldiers trodden down those vines and uprooted that hearth? Is it a desolated and stricken home that I would care to see?"

"False—false!" cried Ænone, no longer regardful of her words, but only anxious to give utterance—no matter how rashly—to the suspicions which she had so long and painfully repressed. "It is even more than the mere charms of this imperial city which entice you. It is that you are my enemy, and would stay here to sting the hand that was so truly anxious to protect you—that for your own purposes you would watch about my path, and ever, as now, play the spy upon my actions, and—"

"Nay, nay!" cried the Greek, her flashing eye and erect attitude in strong contrast with the softened tone in which, more from habit than from prudence, she had spoken. "When have I played the spy upon you? Not now, indeed, for I have come in, not believing that I was doing harm, but simply because my duty has led me hither. I came to tell you that there is a stranger—an old man—standing in the court below, and that he craves audience with you. Is this a wrong thing for me to do? Were I to forbear performance of this duty, would not my neglect insure me punishment?"

Ænone answered not, but, by a strong effort, kept back the words that she would have uttered. Still angry and crushed with the sense of being deceived, and yet conscious that it was not a noble or dignified thing to be in disputation with her own slave, and that there was, moreover, the remote possibility that the girl was not her enemy, and might really dread returning to a desolated and devastated home, what could she say or do? And while she pondered the matter, the door again opened.

"And this is he of whom I spoke. Do you doubt me now?" exclaimed the Greek, in a tone in which a shade of malicious triumph mingled with soft reproach. And she moved away, and left the room, while Ænone, lifting her eyes, saw her father standing before her.

"A plague take the wench who has just left you!" he muttered. "Did she not tell you that I was below? I sent word by her, and here she has left me for half an hour kicking my heels together in the courtyard. And I might have stayed there forever, if I had not of myself found my way up. Even then, there were some who would have stopped me, deeming me, perhaps, too rough in appearance to be allowed to ascend. But I told them that there was a time when members of the house of Porthenus did not wait in antechambers, but stood beside the consuls of the old republic, and I touched the hilt of my dagger; and whether it was the one argument or the other which prevailed, here I am."

With a grim smile the centurion then threw himself down upon a settee near the door, arranged as properly as possible the folds of his coarse tunic, drew his belt round so as to show more in front his dagger with richly embossed sheath—the sole article of courtly and ceremonious attire in which he indulged—and endeavored to assume an easy and imposing attitude. For an instant he gazed around the room, observantly taking in its wealth of mosaic pavement, paintings, statuary, and vases. Then, as he began to fear lest he might be yielding too much of his pride before the overbearing influence of so much luxury, he straightened himself up, gathered upon his features a hard and somewhat contemptuous expression, and roughly exclaimed:

"Yes, by the gods, the Portheni lived with consuls and proconsuls long before the house of Vanno began to rise from the dregs and become a house at all. And the imperator knows it, and is jealous of the fact, too, or else he would the better acknowledge it. What, now, is that?" he added, pointing to the central fresco of the ceiling.

"It is—I know not for certain, my father—but I think—"

"Nay, but I know what it is. It is the old story of the three brothers of the house of Vanno overcoming the five Cimbri at the bridge of Athesis. No great matter, nor so very long ago, even if it were true. But why did he not paint up, instead, how the founder of the Portheni, with his single arm, slew the ten Carthaginians under the aqueduct of Megara? Is not now your family history a portion of his own? His jealousy prevented him, I suppose; though I doubt not that, when in his cups with his high associates, he often boasts of his connection with the house of Porthenus. And yet he would let the only relic of the family starve before assisting him."

Ænone stood as in a maze of confusion and uncertainty. Were the trials of the day never to end? First her unsatisfactory strife and pleading with her husband; then the undignified contest with her own slave into which she had been betrayed; and now came this old man—her father, to be sure—but so much the more mortifying to her as his vulgarity, querulous complaining, and insulting strictures were forced upon her ears.

"Are you not comfortable? What more can he or I do for you?" she said, with some impatience.

"Ay, ay, there it is," growled the centurion. "One person must have all luxuries—paintings, silver, and the like; but if the other has only mere comforts, an extra tunic, perhaps, or a spare bit of meat for a dog, what more can he want? But I will tell you what you can do. And it is not as a gift, I ask it. Poor and despised as he may be, no one can say that the centurion Porthenus is a beggar. It is as a fair matter of business that I offer it."

"Well, my father?"

"It is this: I have two slaves, and can afford to keep only one of them, particularly as but one can be of use to me. Will the imperator purchase the other? I will give it for a fair price, and therefore no one can say that I have asked for any thing beyond a proper trade, with which either side should be well satisfied."

Ænone listened with a blush of shame for her father overspreading her face. It did not occur to her that the slave rejected as useless could be any other than the hunchback, whom her husband had bestowed upon the centurion a few days before; and for the receiver to try to sell back a gift to the giver was a depth of meanness for which no filial partiality or affection could find an excuse.

"I will show him to you," cried the centurion, losing a little of his gruffness in his eagerness to effect a transaction, whereby, under the thin guise of a simple trade, he could extort a benefit. "I have brought him with me, and left him below. You will see that he is of good appearance, and that the imperator will be pleased and grateful to me for the opportunity of possessing him."

So saying, Porthenus strode to the head of the stairway, and issued his commands in a stern voice, which made the vaulted ceilings of the palace ring. A faint, weak response came up in answer, and in a moment the slave entered the room.

"Is this the one of whom you spoke?" faltered Ænone, unable for the moment to retain her self-possession as she beheld, not the angular, wiry form of the hunchback, but the care-worn and slim figure of Cleotos. "I thought—indeed —I thought that you spoke of the inferior of the two."

"Ay, and so I do," responded her father. "Of what use to me can this man be? The other one, indeed, is of tenfold value. There is no slave in Rome like unto him for cleaning armor or sharpening a weapon, while to run of an errand or manage any piece of business in which brains must bear their part, I will trust him against the world. But as for this man here, with his weak limbs and his simple face—do you know that I did but set him to polish the rim of a shield, and in his awkwardness he let it fall, and spoiled the surface as though a Jewish spear had stricken it."

Ænone remained silent, scarcely listening to the words of her father, while, in a troubled manner, she again mentally ran over, as she had done hundreds of times before, the chances of recognition by the man who stood before her.

"But listen to me still further," continued the centurion, fearful lest his disparaging comments might defeat the projected sale. "I only speak of him as he is useful or not to me. To another person he would be most valuable; for, though he cannot polish armor, he can polish verses, and he can write as well as though he were educated for a scribe. For one favored of fortune like the imperator Sergius Vanno," and here again the centurion began to roll the high-sounding name upon his tongue with obvious relish, "who wishes an attendant to carry his wine-cup, or to bear his cloak after him, or to trim his lamps, and read aloud his favorite books, where could a better youth than this be found?"

Ænone, still overpowered by her troubled thoughts, made no response.

"Or to yourself," eagerly continued the centurion, "he would be most suitable, with his pale, handsome face, and his slender limbs. Have you a page?"

"I have my maidens," was the answer.

"And that amounts to nothing at all," asserted her father. "A plebeian can have her maidens in plenty, but it is not right that the wife of a high and mighty imperator should not also have her male attendants. And the more so when that wife has been taken from an ancient house like that of Porthenus," he added, with a frown in derogation of any tendency to give undue importance to her present position. "But with this Cleotos—come forward, slave, and let yourself be seen."

Cleotos, who, partly from natural diffidence, and partly from being abashed at the unaccustomed splendor about him, had, little by little, from his first entrance, shrunk into a corner, now advanced ; and Ænone, once more resolutely assuring herself that, with the changes which time, position, difference of place and costume had thrown about her, she could defy recognition, summoned all her courage, and looked him in the face. It may have been with an unacknowledged fear lest, now that she saw him so freely in the broad daylight, some latent spark of the old attachment might burst into a flame, and withdraw her heart from its proper duty ; but at the first glance she felt that in this respect she had nothing to dread. In almost every particular, Cleotos had but little changed. His costume was but slightly different from that which he had always been accustomed to wear ; for the centurion, in view of the chance of effecting a profitable sale, had, for that occasion, made him put on suitable and becoming attire. The face was still youthful—the eye, as of old, gentle, expressive, and unhardened by the ferocities of the world about him. As Ænone looked, it seemed as though the years which had passed rolled back again, and that she was once more a girl. But it also seemed as though something else had passed away—as though she looked not upon a lover, but rather upon a quiet, kindhearted, innocent friend—one who could ever be dear to her as a brother, but as nothing else. What was it which had so flitted away that the same face could now stir up no fire of passion, but only a friendly interest? Something, she could not tell what; but she thanked the gods that it was so, and drew a long breath of relief.

But it was none the less incumbent upon her, for the sake of that present friendship and for the memory of that old regard, to cast her protection over him. For an instant the thought flashed across her that it would be well to purchase him, not simply for a page, but so that she could have him in the way of kind treatment and attention until some opportunity of restoring him to his native land might occur. But then again was the danger that, if any great length of time should meanwhile elapse, unconsidered trifles might lead to a recognition. No, that plan could not be thought of. She must keep a protecting eye upon him from a distance, and trust to the future for a safe working out of the problem.

"It cannot be," she murmured, in answer, half to her father, half to her own suggestion.

"'Tis well," muttered the centurion, rising with an air of displeasure which indicated that he thought it very ill. "I supposed that it would be a kindness to the imperator or to yourself to give the first offer of the man. But it matters little. The captain Polidorus will take him any moment at a fair price."

"You will not send him to the captain Polidorus?" exclaimed Ænone in affright. For at once the many atrocities of that man towards his slaves rose in her mind— how that he had slain one in a moment of passion—how that he had deliberately beaten another to death for attempting to escape to the catacombs—how that stripes and torture were the daily portion of the unfortunates in his power—and that, not by reason of any gross neglect of their duty, but for the merest and most trifling inadvertencies. Better death than such a fate.

"Pah! What can I do?" retorted Porthenus, skilfully touching the chord of her sympathies, as he saw how sensitive she was to its vibrations. "It is true that Polidorus is no fawning woman, and that he greets his slaves with the rod and the brand, and what not. It is true that he thinks but little of sending one of them to Hades through the avenue of the fish-ponds. But that, after all, is his affair, and if he chooses to destroy his property, what should it matter to me? Am I so rich that I can afford to lose a fair purchaser because he may incline to hang or drown his bargain? Such self-denial may suit the governor of a province, but should not be expected of a poor centurion."

Ænone trembled, and again the impulse to make the purchase came upon her. Better to risk any thing for herself —recognition, discovery, suspicion, or misconstruction—than that her friendship should so far fail as to allow this poor captive to fall into the hands of a brutish tyrant. There was a purse of gold in the half-opened drawer of a table which stood near her; and, in sore perplexity, she raised it, then let it fall, and again lifted it. As the centurion listened to the ring of the metal, his eyes sparkled, and he prepared to apply new arguments, when Cleotos' himself sprang forward.

"I know nothing about this Polidorus of whom they

speak," he said, dropping upon one knee at her feet. "And it is not to save myself from his hands that I ask your pity. There is much that I have already suffered, and perhaps a little more might make no difference, or, better yet, might close the scene with me forever. It is for other reasons that I would wish to be in this house —even as the lowest, meanest slave of all, rather than to live in the halls of the Emperor Titus himself. There is one in this house, from whom I have long been cruelly separated, and who—what can I say but that if, when I was a free man, she gave me her love, now, in my abasement, she will not fail with that love to brighten my lot?"

Ænone started. At hearing such words, there could be but one thought in her mind—that he had actually recognized her, and that, without waiting to see whether or not she had forgotten him, and certainly knowing that in any event her position towards him had become changed, he was daring to covertly suggest a renewal of their old relationship. But the next words reassured her.

"We lived near each other in Samos," he continued. "I was happy, and I blessed the Fates for smiling upon us. How was I then to know that she would be torn away from me upon the very day when I was to have led her to my own home?"

"You say that she is here? Is it—do you speak of Leta?" cried Ænone.

"Leta was her name," he responded, in some surprise that his secret had been so promptly penetrated before he had more than half unfolded it. "And she is here."

There was to Ænone perhaps one instant of almost unconscious regret at learning that she had been forgotten for another. But it passed away like a fleeting cloud—banished from her mind by the full blaze of happiness which poured in upon her at the thought that here at last was what would counteract the cruel schemes which were warring against her peace, and would thereby bring sure relief to her sorrow.

"And she is here," repeated Cleotos. "When at the first she was torn from my side, I would have died, if I could, for I did not believe that life had any further blessing in store for me. But, though the Roman armies were cruel, the Fates have been kind, and have again brought us near. It was but a week ago that, as I looked up by the moonlight at these palace walls, I saw her. Can it be, that after so long a time, the gods meant I should be brought near, to have but this one glimpse of happiness and then again be sundered from it?"

"It cannot be—it was not meant to be!" exclaimed Ænone, with energy; and again lifting the purse of gold, she placed it in the centurion's hand. "There, I will purchase your slave," she said. "Take from this his proper price, and leave him with me."

CHAPTER IX.

THE centurion received the purse with ill-dissembled joy. Had he been fully able to control himself, he would doubtless have maintained a quiet air of dignified self-possession, befitting one giving full value for what he had received, and therefore not expected to exhibit any peculiarly marked or lively satisfaction. But the affair had been concluded so suddenly, and with such a liberal confidence in his discretion, that for the moment his hands trembled with excitement, and his face shone with avaricious pleasure.

Then he began to count out the gold pieces, gleefully dropping some into his pouch, and reluctantly putting others back into the purse. From the first he had established in his own mind the valuation which he would place upon the slave; and he had taken care to make his calculation upon such a liberal scale that he could well afford to consent to a large reduction, if it were required of him. But now he reasoned that, as his child had merely told him to take out what was proper, there could be no impropriety in paying' himself at the highest possible price. She would never mind, and there were many comforts which he needed, and which an extra gold piece or two would enable him to procure for himself.

Then, as he weighed the purse and pondered over it,

numerous wants and requirements, which he had hardly known until that time, came into his mind. He might supply them all, if he were not too timid or scrupulous in availing himself of an opportunity such as might never come to him again. Had even his first valuation of the slave been a sufficient one? He ought certainly to consider that the man could read and write, and was of such beauty and grace that he could be trained to a most courtly air; and it was hardly proper to sell him for no more than the price of a couple of gladiators, mere creatures of bone and brawn. And, in any event, it was hardly probable that Ænone knew the true value of slaves, or even remembered how much her purse had contained.

Thus meanly reflecting, the centurion dropped more of the gold pieces into his pocket, all the while eyeing the slave with keen scrutiny, as though calculating the market value of every hair upon his head. Then, with a sigh, he handed back the purse, most wofully lightened of its contents, and turned from the room, endeavoring to compose his features into a decent appearance of sober indifference, and muttering that he would not have allowed himself to be betrayed into giving up such a prize so cheaply had it not been that he had an especial regard for the imperator Sergius Vanno, and that the house of Porthenus had never nourished mere traders to wrangle and chaffer over their property.

In one of his conjectures he had been correct. It was little that Ænone knew or cared about the price she was paying. Had the purse been returned to her entirely empty, she would have thrown it unheedingly into the drawer, and have never dreamed but that all had been rightly done. There was now but one idea filling her heart. She thought not about money nor any imprudence which she was committing, nor yet upon the chance of recognition. She only reflected that the day of her triumph had come—that at the sight of the long-absent lover, Leta would abandon the wrong path in which she had been straying, would throw herself into his arms, would tell him how, through the loss of him, she had become reckless, and had allowed her suffering mind to become perverted from the right—but that now all was again well; and thus confessing and being forgiven, would, in the ever-present joy of that forgiveness, lead for the future a different life, and, instead of a rival, become to her mistress a friend and ally.

Glowing with this bright hope, Ænone scarcely noticed the shuffling departure of the centurion, but fixing her eyes upon the captive, keenly scrutinized his appearance. Not that it was likely that Leta, in the first flush of her joy at meeting him, would notice or care in what guise he was presented, so long as the soul which had so often responded to her own was there. But it was well that there should be nothing neglected which, without being directly essential to the production of a proper impression, might be tributary to it.

The inspection was satisfactory. Not only was the dress of the captive clean, neat, becoming, and suitable to his station, but his appearance had undergone visible improvement since Ænone had last seen him. The rest and partial composure of even the few intervening days had sufficed to restore tone to his complexion, roundness to his cheeks, and something of the old merry smile to his eyes.

And though complete restoration was not yet effected, enough had been accomplished to show that there was much latent beauty which would not fail to develop itself under the stimulant of additional care and kindly treatment.

"Go in, thither," said Ænone, pointing to the adjoining room, in which Leta was occupied. "When you are there, you will—it will be told you what you are to do."

Cleotos bowed low, and passed through into the other room; and Ænone followed him with a glance which betrayed the longing she felt to enter with him and witness the meeting of the two lovers. But a sense of propriety outweighed her curiosity and restrained her. It was not right, indeed, that she should intrude. Such recognitions should be sacred to the persons directly interested in them. She would therefore remain outside, and there await Cleotos' return. And as she took into her hands a little parchment ode which lay upon her table, and nervously endeavored to interest herself in it, she delightedly pictured the sudden transport of those within the next apartment, and the beaming look of joy with which, hand in hand, they would finally emerge to thank her for their newly gained happiness.

In the mean time, Leta, having delivered her message, and received her rebuke for the interruption, had retired to the other room, and there, as usual, resumed her daily task of embroidery. Bending low over the intricate stitches and counting their spaces, her features, at a casual glance, still bore their impress of meek and unconscious humility, so far did her accustomed self-control seem to accompany her even when alone. But a more attentive scrutiny would have detected, half hidden beneath the fringed eyelids, a sparkle of gratified triumph, and in the slightly bent corners of the mouth, a shade of haughty disdain; and little by little, as the moments progressed, these indications of an inner, irrepressible nature gained in intensity, and as though her fingers were stayed by a tumult of thought, her work slowly began to slip from her grasp.

At length, lifting her head, and, perhaps, for the first time realizing that she was alone and might indulge her impulses without restraint, she abruptly threw from her the folds of the embroidery, and stood erect. Why should she longer trifle with that weak affair of velvet and dyes? Who was the poor, feeble, and tearful statue in the next room, to order her to complete those tasks? What to herself were the past deeds of the house of Vanno, that they should be perpetuated in ill-fashioned tapestry, to be hung around a gilded banquet-hall? By the gods! she would from that day make a new history in the family life; and it should be recorded, not with silken threads upon inanimate velvet, but should be engraved deeply and ineffaceably upon human hearts.

Standing motionless in the centre of the room, with one foot upon the half-completed tapestry, she now, for the first time, and in a flash of inspiration, gave shape and comeliness to her previous confusedly arranged ideas. Until the present moment she had had but little thought of accomplishing any thing beyond skilfully availing herself of her natural attractions so as to climb from her menial position into something a little better and higher. If, in the struggle to raise herself from the degradation of slavery, she were obliged to engage in a rivalry with her mistress, and by robbing her of the affection naturally belonging to her, were to crush her to the earth, it was a thing to be deplored, but it must none the less be done. She might, perhaps, pity the victim, but the sacrifice must be accomplished all the same.

But now these vague dreams of a somewhat better lot, to be determined by future chance circumstances, rolled away like a shapeless cloud, and left in their place one bright image as the settled object of her ambition. So lofty, so dazzling seemed the prize, that another person would have shrunk in dismay from even the thought of striving for it, and even she, for the moment, recoiled. But she was of too determined a nature to falter long. The higher the object to be attained, the fewer would be the competitors and the greater the chance of success to unwearying determination. And if there were but one chance in a thousand, it were still worth the struggle.

This great thought which stimulated her ambition was nothing less than the resolution to become the wife of the imperator Sergius. At first it startled her with its apparent wild extravagance; but little by little, as she weighed the chances, it seemed to become more practicable. There was, indeed, nothing grossly impossible in the idea. Men of high rank had ere now married their slaves, and the corrupted society of Rome had winked at mesalliances which, in the days of the republic, would not have been tolerated. And she was merely a slave from accidental circumstances— being free-born, and having, but a month before, been the pride and ornament of a respectable though lowly family.

Once let her liberty be restored, and the scarcely perceptible taint of a few weeks' serfdom be removed from her, and she would be, in all social respects, fully the equal of the poor, trembling maid of Ostia, to whom, a few years before, the patrician had not been ashamed to stoop.

This bar of social inequality thus removed, the rest might be in her own hands. Sergius no longer felt for his wife the old affection, under the impulse of which he had wedded her; and the few poor remains of the love which he still cherished, more from habit than otherwise, were fast disappearing. This was already so evident as to have become the common gossip of even the lowliest slaves in the household. And he loved herself instead, for not only his actions, but his words had told her so. A little more craft and plotting, therefore—a little further display of innocent and lowly meekness and timid obedience—a few more well-considered efforts to widen the conjugal breach—a week or two more persistent exercise of those fascinations which men were so feeble to resist—jealousy, recrimination, quarrels, and a divorce—and the whole thing might be accomplished. In those days of laxity, divorce was an easy matter. In this case there was no family influence upon the part of the wife to be set up in opposition —but merely an old centurion, ignorant and powerless. A few writings, for form's sake—and the day that sent the weeping wife from the door might install the manumitted and triumphant slave in her place.

All aglow with the ravishing prospect—her eager hopes converting the possible into the probable, and again, by a rapid change, the probable into the certain—the Greek stood spurning the needle-work at her feet. Then glancing around, the whim seized upon her to assume, for a moment in advance, her coming stately dignity. At the side of the room, upon a slightly elevated platform, was a crimson lounge—Ænone's especial and proper seat. Over one arm of this lounge hung, in loose folds, a robe of purple velvet, with an embroidered fringe of pearls—a kind of cloak of state, usually worn by her upon the reception of ceremonious visits. To this lounge Leta strode, threw herself upon it, drew the velvet garment over her shoulders, so that the long folds fell down gracefully and swept the marble pavement at her feet, and there, half sitting, half reclining, assumed an attitude of courtly dignity, as though mistress of the palace.

And it must be confessed that she well suited the place. With her lithe, graceful figure thrown into a position in which the gentle languor of unembarrassed leisure was mingled with the dignity of queenly state—with her burning eyes so tempered in their brilliancy that they seemed ready at the same instant to bid defiance to impertinent intrusion, and to bestow gracious condescension upon suppliant timidity—with every feature glowing with that proper pride which is not arrogance, and that proper kindliness which is not humility—there was probably in all Rome no noble matron who could as well adorn her chair of ceremony. Beside her, the true mistress of the place would have appeared as a timid child dismayed with unaccustomed honors; and in comparison, an empress might not fill her throne in the palace of the Cæsars with half the grace and dignity.

Then, as she there sat, momentarily altering her attitude

to correspond the better with her ideas of proper bearing, and gathering into newer and more pleasing folds the sweeping breadths of the velvet mantle, the door was slowly swung open, and there glided noiselessly in, clad in its neat and coarse tunic, the timid figure of her old lover Cleotos.

For an instant they remained gazing at each other as though paralyzed. Cleotos, who had looked to see her in her simple white vestment as as of old, and had expected at her first glance to rush to her arms, and there be allowed to pour forth his joy at again meeting her, never more to part—beheld with dismay this gorgeously arrayed and queenly figure. This could not be the Leta whom he had known; or, if so, how changed! Was this the customary attire of slaves in high-placed families? Or could it be the token of a guilty favoritism? His heart sank within him; and he stood nervously clinging against the door behind him, fearing to advance, lest, at the first step, some terrible truth, of which he had already seemed to feel the premonitions, might burst upon him.

And she, for the moment, sat aghast, not knowing but that the gods, to punish her pride and ambition, had sent a spectre to confront her. But being of strong mind and little given to superstitious terrors, she instantly reasoned out the facts of his simultaneous captivity with herself and coincidence of ownership; and her sole remaining doubt was in what manner she should treat him. They had parted in sorrow and tears, and she knew that he now expected her to fall into his arms and there repeat her former vows of constancy and love. But that could not be. Had he come to her but an hour before, while her dreams of the future were of a vague and unsatisfactory character, she might have acted upon such an impulse. But now, a glorious vision of what might possibly happen had kindled her ambition with brighter fires than ever before; and could she surrender all that, and think again only upon starving freedom in a cottage home?

"Is it thou, Cleotos? Welcome to Rome!" she said at length, throwing from her shoulder the purple cloak, and approaching him. As she spoke, she held out her hand. He took it in his own, in a lifeless and mechanical sort of way, and gazed into her face with a strange look of inquiring doubt, which momentarily settled into an expression of deeper apprehension. The blackness of despair began to enter into his soul. Now that she was divested of her borrowed riches, she looked more like herself, and that was surely her voice uttering tones of greeting; but somehow her heart did not seem to be in them, and, for a certainty, this had not been her wonted style of welcome.

"I thought," she continued, "that thou wert slain. Certainly when I parted from you ere you fled into the mountains—"

"You know that I fled not at all," he interrupted, the color mounting into his temples. "Why do you speak so, Leta? I retired to the mountains to meet my friends there, and with them carry on the defence; and previous thereto, I conducted you to what I believed to be a place of safety. And I fought my best against the foe, and was brought nigh unto death. This I did, though I can boast of but a weak and slender frame. And it is hard that the first greeting of one so well loved as you should be a taunt."

"Nay, forgive me," she said. "I doubt not your valor. It was but in forgetfulness that I spoke. I meant it not for a taunt." And in truth, she had not so meant it. It was but the inadvertent expression of a feeling which the sight of his feeble and boyish figure unwittingly produced upon her—an incapacity to connect deeds of valor with apparent physical weakness. But this very inability to judge of his true nature by the soul that strove to look into her own rather than by material impressions, was perhaps no slight proof of the little unison between her nature and his.

"Sit down here," she continued, "and tell me all that has happened to you." And they sat together, and he briefly told her of his warlike adventures, his wound, his captivity, his recognition of herself, and his successful attempt to be once more under the same roof with her. And somehow it still seemed to him that their talk was not as of old, and that her sympathy with his misfortunes was but weak and cheerless; and though he tried to interweave the customary words of endearment with his story, there was a kind of inner check upon him, so that they came not readily to his lips as of old. And she sat, trying to listen, and indeed keeping the thread of his adventures in her mind; but all the while finding her attention fail as she speculated how she could best give that explanation of her feelings which she knew would soon be demanded of her.

"And here I am at last, Leta—as yourself, a slave!" he concluded.

"Courage, my friend!" was her answer. "There are very many degrees and fates reserved for all in this old Rome, and much for every man to learn. And many a one who has begun as a slave has, in the end, attained not only to freedom, but to high honor and station."

"If the gods were to give me honor and station, far be it from me to refuse the gift," he said. "But that, of itself alone, would not content me, unless you were there to share the good with me. And with yourself I would crave no other blessing. We are slaves here, Leta, but even that fate may have its mitigations and happiness for us."

She was silent. How could she tell it to him? But his suspicions, at first vague, were now aroused by her very silence into more certainty.

"Tell me," he cried, again taking her hand, "tell me my fate; and if sorrow is to come upon me, let it come now. It seems as though there were indeed evil tidings in store for me. The blight of anticipated evil even weighed upon me ere I passed yonder hall, and when I knew no reason why I should not find you loving of heart and humble of desire as in other days. Is it all gone? Are you no longer the same? This tawdry velvet in which I found you arrayed—is it the type of a something equally foreign to your nature, and which imperial Rome has thrown about you to aid in crushing out the better feelings of your heart?"

"My friend, my brother," she said at length, with some real pity and some false sorrow, "why have we again met?

Why is it now forced upon me to tell you that the past must always be the past with us?"

He dropped her hand, and the tears started into his eyes. Much as the words and gestures of the last few minutes had prepared him for the announcement, yet when it came, it smote him as though there had been no premonition of it; so lovingly had his heart persisted in clinging to the faint hope that he might have been mistaken. A low wail of anguish burst from his lips.

"And this is the end of all?" he sobbed.

"Think only," she said, "think only that I am not worthy of you."

"The old story—the old story which has been repeated from the beginning of the world," he cried, stung into life by something of heartlessness which he detected in her affected sympathy. "The woman weaves her toils about the man—gilds his life until there is no brightness which can compare with it—fills his heart with high hopes of a blissful future—so changes his soul that he can cherish no thought but of her—so alters the whole tenor and purpose of his existence that he even welcomes slavery as a precious boon because it brings him under the same roof with her. And then—some other fancy having crossed her mind—or an absence of a week or two having produced forgetfulness—she insults him with a cruel mockery of self-unworthiness as her sole apology for perfidy."

"Nay," she exclaimed, half glad of an excuse to quarrel with him. "If you would rather have it otherwise, think, then, that I have never loved you as I should, even though I may have imagined that I did."

"Go on," he said, seeing that she hesitated.

"I know," she continued, "that in other days you have had my words for it, uttered, indeed, in sympathy and truth, as I then felt them. But I was a simple girl then, Cleotos. The sea before me and the mountains behind bounded all my knowledge of the world. The people whom I saw were but few. The tastes I had were simple. Is it wonderful that I should have listened to the first one who spoke to me of love, and should have imagined that my heart made response to him? But now—now, Cleotos—"

"Now, what?" he exclaimed. "Would you say that now you have seen the world better and think differently? What is there in all that you have since known that should change you? Is it that the sight of war and tumult—of burning towns and bleeding captives—of insolent soldiers and cruel taskmasters can have made you less in favor with our own native, vine-covered retreat, with its neighborhood of simple peasantry? Or would you say that since then you have met others whom you can love better than me? Whom, indeed, have you seen but weary prisoners like myself, or else unpitying conquerors whose love would be your shame? You blush, Leta! Pray the gods that it be not the latter! Struggle sternly with yourself to realize that you are merely for the moment fascinated by the unaccustomed splendors of this swarming city; and that after its first brightness has worn off from your dazzled eyes, your soul may return to its native, pure simplicity and innocence, and—and to me."

"Speak not so, Cleotos," she responded. "My eyes are not dazzled with any splendors; but for all that, our ways now and forever lie in different directions. We are slaves, and can give little heed to our affections. Our only course must be for each to strive to rise above this serfdom ; and if, in thus striving, either can help the other, it must be done —but in friendship, not in love. To you, through good conduct, there may open, even in slavery, many posts of influence and profit ; and, in so much, of better worth than our own boasted liberty with poverty. And as for me—I see my destiny already beckoning me to a position such as many a free Roman woman might envy."

Speaking thus obscurely of her anticipated grandeur—to be gained, perhaps, by abasement, but none the less in her mind certain to end in such legitimate position as might sanctify the previous steps thereto—her face again lit up with a glow of pride, as though she were already the powerful patrician's wife. And revelling in such dreams, she saw not the agony which overspread her listener's face as he read her thoughts partly awrong, and believed her content to throw herself away forever, in order to gain some temporary exaltation as a wealthy Roman's plaything.

"And when that day does come," she continued, "if, for the memory of our old friendship, I can help to elevate you to some better sphere—"

"Enough ! No more !" he cried bitterly ; and starting from her, he fled out of the room. It were hard enough that he should lose her, harder yet that he should hear her marking out for herself a life of ruin for some temporary gain, but harder than all, that she should dare to mistake his nature, so far as to insult him with the promise of advancing his prosperity through such an influence.

"Let me go hence!" he cried, in his agony, to Ænone, who, still radiant with the whisperings of her newly discovered hope, met him at the door. "Send me to the captain Polidorus—anywhere—only let me leave this house!"

CHAPTER X.

But though Ænone's sanguinely conceived plan for Cleotos' happiness had so cruelly failed, it was not in her heart to yield to his passionate, unreflecting demand, and send him away from her, even to a kinder home than he would have found at the house of the captain Polidorus. It would but increase his ill fortune, by enforcing still greater isolation from every fount of human sympathy. Though the affection of the wily Leta had been withdrawn from him, her own secret friendship yet remained, and could be a protection to him as long as he was at her side; and in many ways she could yet extend her care and favor over him, until such time as an outward bound vessel might be found in which to restore him to his native country.

Whether there was any instinct at the bottom of her heart, telling her that, in the possibility of trying events to come, his friendship might be equally serviceable to her, and that, even in the mere distant companionship of a slave with his mistress, she might feel a certain protecting influence, she did not stop to ask. Neither did she inquire whether she wished to retain him for his own benefit alone, and without thought of any happiness or comfort to be derived by her from his presence. Had she been accustomed closely to analyze her feelings, she might have perceived, perhaps, that in her growing isolation, it was no unpleasant thing to look upon the features and listen to the tones which carried her memory back to her early days of poverty, when, except for a short interval, her life had been at its happiest. But had she known and acknowledged all this, it would not have startled her, for she would have felt that, in her heart, there was not the slightest accompanying shade of disloyalty. Her nature was not one to admit of sudden transfers of allegiance. It was rather one in which a real love would last forever. When the first romantic liking for Cleotos had consumed itself, from the ashes there had sprung no new passion for him, but merely the flowers of earnest, true-hearted friendship. And it was her misfortune, perhaps, that the real love for another which had succeeded would not in turn consume itself, but would continue to flourish green and perennial, though now seemingly fated to bask no longer in the sunshine of kindly words and actions, but only to cower beneath the chill of harsh and wanton neglect.

Cleotos therefore remained—at first passing weary days of bitter, heart-breaking despondency. His lost liberty he had borne without much complaint, for it was merely the fortune of war, and hundreds of his countrymen were sharing the same fate with him. But to lose that love upon which he had believed all the happiness of his life depended, was a blow to which, for a time, no philosophy could reconcile him—the more particularly as the manner in which that loss had been forced upon him seemed, to his sensitive nature, to be marked by peculiar severity. To have had Leta torn from him in any ordinary way—to part with her in some quarrel in which either side might be partially right, and thenceforth never to see her again—or to be obliged to yield her up to the superior claims of an open generous rivalry—any of these things would, in itself, have been sufficient affliction. But it was far worse than all this to be obliged to meet her at every turn, holding out her hand to him in pleasant greeting, and uttering words of welcoming import; and all with an unblushing appearance of friendly interest, as though his relations with her had never been other than those of a fraternal character, and as though, upon being allowed her mere friendship, there could be nothing of which he had a right to complain.

At first, in the agony of his heart, he had no strength to rise above the weight which crushed him, and to obey the counsels of his pride so far as to play before her a part of equally assumed indifference. To her smiling greetings he could return only looks of bitter despair or passionate entreaty—vainly hoping that he might thereby arouse her better nature, and bring her in repentance back to him. And at first sight it seemed not impossible that such a thing might take place; for, in the midst of all her change of conduct and wilful avoidance of allusion to the past, she felt no dislike of him. It was merely her love for him that she had suppressed, and in its place there still remained a warm regard. If he could have been content with her friendship alone, she would have granted it all, and would have rejoiced, for the sake of olden times, to use her influence with others in aid of his upward progress. Perhaps there were even times when, as she looked upon his misery and thought of the days not so very far back, in which he had been all in all to her, her heart may have been melted into something of its former affection. But if so, it was only for a moment, nor did she ever allow the weakness to be seen. Her path had been taken, and nothing now could make her swerve from it. Before her enraptured fancy gleamed the state and rank belonging to a patrician's wife; and as she wove her toils with all the resources of her cunning, the prize seemed to approach her nearer and nearer. Now having advanced so far, she must not allow a momentary weakness to imperil all. And therefore unwaveringly she daily met her former lover with the open smile of friendly greeting, inviting confidence, mingled with the same indescribable glance, forbidding any renewal of love.

And so days passed by, and Cleotos, arousing from his apathetic despair, felt more strongly that, if the lapse of love into mere friendship is a misfortune, the offer of friendship as a substitute for promised love is a mockery and an insult; and his soul rebelling at being made a passive party to such a bargain, he began himself to play the retaliatory part which a wronged nature naturally suggests to itself. Like Leta, he learned to hold out the unresponsive hand in careless greeting, or to mutter meaningless and cold compliments, and, in any communication with her, to assume all the appearances of indifferent acquaintanceship. At first, indeed, it was with an aching heart struggling in his breast, and an agony of wounded spirit tempting him to cast away all such studied pretences, and to throw himself upon her mercy, and meanly beg for even the slightest return of her former affection. But gradually, as he perceived how vain would be such self-abasement, and how its display would rather tend to add contempt to her indifference, his pride came to rescue him from such a course; and he began more and more to tune the temper of his mind to his actions, and to feel something of the same coldness which he outwardly displayed.

Not but that for awhile such a disposition was forced and unnatural; and however steadily composed he felt, and strongly fortified in his stubborn pride, a look or a word from her would have brought him again a willing slave to her feet. But that look or word was not given. Perhaps, in her eager struggle after the glittering prize which she had held out before herself, she disdained the love which had once delighted her; perhaps, actuated by a purer and less selfish motive, her friendship for Cleotos forbade her, in mere wanton pride, to keep open the wound which she had made. Whatever the reason, the withdrawal of the fascinations which had once attracted him, gave his mind leisure and opportunity to reason with itself in more quietude and composure than could have been expected. And, as he more and more began to realize how closely she was wrapped up in her ambition, to the exclusion of any gentler feeling, and how, under the stimulant of her infatuated hopes, she was allowing herself each day to act with less guarded resolution, there were times when he found himself asking whether she had indeed changed from what she had been; or whether, on the contrary, she had not always, at heart, been the same as now, and his conception of her true character been at fault.

But, in proportion as the veil of error seemed lifted from his soul, letting calm content once more shine in upon him, so, on the other hand, did a night of despair slowly settle upon Ænone. By no reasoning could she longer urge upon herself the belief that the neglect with which her lord treated her could be traced to any inoffensive cause. Claims of court—urgency of military duties—exactions of business might easily account for transitory slights, but not for long-sustained periods of indifference, unbroken by a single word of kindness. And as days passed by and this indifference continued, until at times seeming ready to give place to openly expressed dislike, and her ears became more and more accustomed to words of hasty petulance, and Sergius grew still deeper absorbed in the infatuation which possessed him, and less careful to conceal its influences from her, and the Greek girl glided hither and thither, ever less anxious, as she believed her triumph more nearly assured, to maintain the humble guise which she had at first assumed, Ænone felt that there had indeed come upon herself a sorrow from which there could be no escape. And as again she pondered upon the few projects for relief which suggested themselves to her agitated mind, and laid one after another aside, with the conviction that it would but aggravate the evil, it seemed at last as though the only course left to her was to lie down in her sorrow and die.

It was no uncommon thing then, as now, for the husband to neglect his wife. All Rome rang with the frequent story of marital wrong. But those were days in which the matron did not generally accept her desertion with meekness. Brought up in a fevered, unscrupulous society, she had her own retaliatory resources; and if no efforts were sufficient to bring back the wandering affection, she could recompense herself elsewhere for its loss, secure that her wrongs would be held as a justification, and that her associates, equally aggrieved and avenged, would applaud her course. But with Ænone, brought up in a provincial town, under the shelter of her own native purity and innocence, no such idea could find countenance. Even the thought which sometimes dimly presented itself, that by some harmless coquetry she might perhaps excite her husband's jealousy, and thereby chance to win back his love, was one which she always stifled in its beginning as weak and unworthy.

But the recompenses of friendship were still left to her, and it was surely doing no wrong to accept them. Therefore, the more she realized that her source of real happiness was becoming estranged from her, so much the more did she feel naturally drawn towards the society of Cleotos. To her, of course, he was not a mere slave, but rather a person of equal birth with herself, who had been beaten down by the same fate which had elevated her. And in conversation with him, it was easy to carry her mind back to her early home, and for a little while forget her present misery. And he, in turn, having been repulsed where he had placed his highest hopes of happiness, and embittered by the disappointment, was not at all loth to transfer, in all innocence, his devotion to one who extended such kindly condescension towards him. It therefore happened that the two were naturally drawn much together, and, for a time, without attracting invidious notice. Those were days in which the association between master and slave was often of an intimate character. To the lower class of slaves, indeed, there could be no familiar approach. It was sufficient for them that at times they could look upon the faces of their owners from a distance. But above these, were converging circles, each rising in rank and responsibility, until there were those who stood at their owners' right hands, more in the position of friends and confidants than of menials. Of these was Cleotos, whose winning face and graceful mien, joined to his natural abilities and his valued accomplishments, would have insured him a higher position than that of most captives, even if he had not been assisted by the partiality of his mistress.

It was his duty to announce her guests, to trim the lamps at which she read, to read to her when she felt indisposed to do so for herself, to indite her correspondence—and generally to superintend all those little elegancies and demands of social life which require grace or mental ability in their execution. These offices naturally kept him near her during much of each day—and when Ænone and he were alone, and no task was before him requiring immediate completion, it was but to be expected that a mingling of curiosity and friendly interest should lead her to question him upon his past life, his home, his associates, even his thoughts. And often it as naturally happened that, while he spoke, the music of his voice lulled her into forgetfulness of all but the past, and she would find herself unconsciously relaxing from the somewhat frigid dignity which she felt called upon to assume, until her features must have glowed with some expression of her former familiar kindness. For she would be suddenly startled back into her forced propriety by a strange and troubled look of puzzled thought flitting across his face—a look which she could read and analyze better than he could; for it told her that, without any real suspicion of the truth, he was wondering at the likeness of that beaming face which bent over him to something which he had seen elsewhere in the past.

There was one morning that he sat before her by a little table where he had been writing a letter at her dictation. The letter was folded and sealed, and then ensued one of those vacant intervals when each, having no pressing task at hand, remains for a few moments listlessly thinking what shall be done next. At that instant Leta passed through the room—bowing low as she moved before her mistress, and throwing out towards Cleotos from the corner of her dark eye one of those aggravating looks in which friendly interest in him and pleasure at his sight were mingled with a certain cruel warning against any renewal of past memories. Cleotos retorted with a similar careless greeting, expressive of simple friendliness, unconscious of any warmer emotion. But he had not yet perfectly learned his part; for, as Leta passed out of the room, the quiver of his lips showed how difficult had been the task of mastering his forced smile even for that moment.

"Poor boy!" said Ænone, as she witnessed the effort. "You have not yet learned not to love her."

"Alas, not yet, indeed," he responded. "But it seems as though I knew the task better than last week, and would know it still better a week hence. What can I say? It is not to be thought that I should lapse in a moment into real indifference, even though I may find out that she is unworthy of love. There cannot but be an interval during which the heart will struggle against the judgment, and lead to foolish longings after what has passed."

"True, indeed," said Ænone.

"And still, in my heart, I sometimes almost think that I have never loved her," he continued in a reflective, dreamy tone;—"that I have been under a spell—have been made the slave of certain outward fascinations, which have fettered my judgment. Can it be that one will think he loves and yet does not?"

"It is indeed hard to answer, I suppose."

"It must be hard; for wherein, after all, is the difference between being and thinking to be? But yet it seems as though there were times, even long passed and before this captivity, when, being in our own land, and with nothing to disturb us or make us doubtful of the future, I looked upon her with a strange kind of fear—wondering whether, though I loved her with so strong a passion, it might not rather be the passion of an unlasting, unsatisfying slavery of thought, than of a calm, lifelong trustfulness. And now it seems to me that if I ever had this feeling—for I cannot certainly tell whether I ever had or only now imagine it —it seems to me as though it were an inner instinct warning me against evil; for day by day I see more clearly that there has been some veil over my soul, hiding it from a clear perception of what was suitable for it."

"And you begin to dislike her?" inquired Ænone.

"Not so," he said. "Nor do I know whether I ought to do so, if I could. I believe now that she does not, and perhaps never has loved me; but I must forgive her for all that. She may have tried to do so, and for a time have thought that she did, and the true blame may all the while have rested with me alone. With her strong, unbending temperament, fearless of correction, and jealous of all control, how, indeed, could she long cling to one of such a tranquil and yielding nature as myself? That she loved me not, proves not that she could love no one; and though she now seems so coldly heartless and so rashly heedless of her fame, yet who knows what she might have been if fettered by the love of a spirit more imperious than her own? Who can tell but that the great good that is within her might then have conquered the evil, and her soul have spurned its present headstrong course, and gloriously aroused itself to its sole great duty of love and innocent trustfulness?"

"These, indeed, are very far from being words of dislike," said Ænone; "and they only prove that you still love her, or you would not so readily excuse her."

"Neither have I denied that I love her yet," he said. "But it is not with as blind an affection as before. Her touch, her words, her smile—if given with real love—would still please me as of old; and yet I should feel that there was something gone from me forever. Even if we were restored to our own isle, with no enemy near or rival to interrupt us, I could not but henceforth feel that destiny had not meant her for me, so much would her stronger nature be ill assorted with my own. And sometimes—"

"Well?"

"Sometimes—now that this thraldom of my spirit is passing off—there comes back to me the memory of another face, a gentle, loving face—which, if it were possible ever to see it again, I have too long forgotten, but which, if I may not see it more, I should, for my own sake, have forgotten long ago. But all this, honored mistress, can be of no interest to you, and therefore it were foolish to mention it."

"Nay, speak to me of it," murmured Ænone; and, struggle as she would, the telltale blood began to flow up into her face. "Is there any woman who does not care to listen to a love story?" she added, as though in excuse for her curiosity.

"It is but a common love tale," he said, "and the more so that nothing came of it. A few stolen interviews—a few promises exchanged—and then a parting forever. That is all."

"But where and when was this?"

"Six years ago, at Ostia. For, though a Greek, I have been in this land before now. I was a sailor then, and in that port I met her. Met her and loved her, and promised to return again. And for a while I meant to do so; but on the passage back our ship was wrecked. I could not at once find place upon another, and so took employment on the shore—none the less, however, intending some day to come back and claim her. What shall I say? It is the old story. The sea is wide, and I could interchange no tidings with her. Ill success followed me, and I could not return to Ostia. Then, little by little, as the months drifted past, and I believed her lost to me, her image began to fade from my memory. And then I saw Leta; and under the spell of that new charm, it seemed to me as though the other one had lost all grasp upon my mind. Not altogether, though, for even at the height of my later love, I have always borne about me the last keepsake that she had given me."

"Let me see it—what is it like?" said Ænone, faintly; and in obedience to her command, and perhaps wondering a little that she should take such interest in so simple a story, Cleotos drew from beneath his tunic a thread with a coin dangling at the end.

The tears struggled into Ænone's eyes as she gazed upon the token. It was a poor little silver coin of the time of the first Cæsars—one of the few curiosities of her father's family—and which she had given to her lover as the most precious thing belonging to her. She remembered that when, in that last stroll by the shore, she had hung it about his neck with her own hands, and had made him promise always to keep it, she had received from him a similar token—a bright silver piece of Vespasian, and had placed it near her heart, while murmuring similar vows. He had kept his word, and she had not kept hers. For the moment, she felt even guilty of bad faith, forgetting that when she afterwards gave her more mature affection to Sergius, it was only her duty to lay aside all that even whispered of past promises.

"I could not bear to part with it," he said; "for it still spoke to me of her friendship, if not of her love. And a superstitious thought came into my mind that I might some day see her again, and that, though we should not meet as lovers, yet she might, perhaps, be pleased to learn that I had not entirely forgotten her. Would she not be so, do you think?"

"She does—that is, it surely should so move her," said Ænone.

"So have I still worn it," he continued. "And somehow each day brings back the recollection of her more faithfully to me. Whether it is because this other absorbing love is passing from my heart, and leaving to me greater freedom of thought—or whether it is that Ostia is now so near to me that I daily hear of it and see its costumes in the streets, and thus my recollection of the place is kindled anew—or whether it is—"

"Is what?" said Ænone, encouragingly.

"I know not how to dare say it," he stammered. "It is a presumption, indeed, but I mean it not for such. I would say that there is something in your own face,—a look —a flash of thought—a glance of the eye—a something I know not what, which reminds me of her whom I knew so many years ago. So that sometimes, were it not for the difference of dress and all else around you, so much at variance with what had been her state, I could almost forget the lapse of years, and imagine that—Pardon, most noble mistress! I meant not to offend!"

For she had arisen; and now, drawn to her full height, was looking down upon him with all the coldness of patrician dignity that she could summon to her aid. He, too, arose, and stood trembling opposite her. For a moment they remained gazing upon each other; he aghast at the apparent consequences of his remark, reproaching himself for having so inconsiderately raised her anger by daring to compare, even in feature, a lowly country girl with her, and despairingly asking himself what he should do to restore himself to her favor—she more and more wrapping herself in a disguise of outward pride and haughty bearing, lest by some chance his unsuspecting eyes might detect the truth, and yet inwardly bleeding at the heart to think that she could not reveal herself to him and promise him her friendship, in full confidence that his love for her would not return and bring new distress upon them. Then suddenly, while each stood wondering what course to take, a light step was heard in the outer hall, and the poet Emilius

CHAPTER XI.

At the interruption, Ænone hastily reseated herself; while Cleotos, in obedience to a quick and significant motion of her finger, remained in the room, and resuming his position at the table, prepared to continue his writing. The poet Emilius could not, of course, fail to notice this somewhat confused alteration of posture, but no suspicion of having intruded upon an embarrassing scene crossed his mind. He merely saw a proudly erect mistress and a cowering slave; and it was no unusual thing to interrupt a Roman lady in the act of giving even corporeal correction to her attendant, nor did the stranger's entrance always cause the punishment to cease.

"Has the caitiff been insolent?" he exclaimed, in gallant tone, as he approached and seated himself before her. "Has he dared to look too rebelliously upon so charming a mistress? If so, permit that I may chastise him for you. It is not fit that such fair hands should be obliged to wield the rod."

"Nay, it is nothing," she said. "Nothing, indeed, needing much reproof; and it is all past now. And wherefore have we lately seen so little of you?"

"Commands of court—the claims of Parnassus—these alone have withheld me from heretofore giving to beauty its proper meed of admiration and worship. To speak more plainly, I have undertaken, by order of our emperor, the not ungrateful task of weaving a few poetical sentiments to be recited at the opening of our new amphitheatre. And in order that the results of my labor might not lessen my already acquired fame, I judged it most prudent to seclude myself for the past few days from the gaieties of the world, and give myself up to study and meditation. Though, after all, I could not deny, if closely questioned, that my seclusion was but little productive of results ; for, upon being tempted out one evening, sorely against my judgment, to a feast at the house of the comedian Bassus, the true poetic inspiration overtook me at the end of my third goblet, and, calling for papyrus, I there accomplished, in one short hour, the greater portion of my task."

"Then, I presume that your ode, unlike your other works, will be of a cheerful and lively character, more especially as it is written for such a festive occasion."

"Scarcely, perhaps, what the world would call altogether lively, though here and there a thread of playful thought may gleam upon the more sober texture of the basis. I have rather judged it proper that, for the due celebration of an event of such wondrous magnificence, I should give utterance to deeper and more lasting sentiments, so as to fit the minds of the spectators for a higher comprehension of its true significance. But, if you wish, I will read aloud a few of my thoughts ; and be assured that so far no eye has seen the scroll, not even the august eye of the Emperor Titus himself.

Ænone inclined her head in assent, and he drew from the

breast of his tunic a small roll of parchment, carefully wrapped in a covering of embroidered silk.

"I commence, of course, by an address to the emperor, whom I call the most illustrious of all the Cæsars, and liken unto Jove. I then congratulate the spectators not only upon living in his time, but also upon being there to bask in the effulgence of his majesty ; his countenance being the sight most to be desired, and the games and combats being merely accessory thereto. After which, I speak to the gladiators and captives ; and prove to them how grateful they should be to the gods for allowing them the privilege of dying in such an august presence."

"Is it such a privilege, do you think ?" inquired Ænone.

"Perhaps not a privilege, but certainly no great hardship. The trained gladiators surely cannot complain, for they have voluntarily assumed the risks ; and as for the captives, the most of them will some day die a violent death of some kind or another, and, therefore, why not now, attended by the decent observances of the games and the applause of all the Roman people ? But to proceed. From thence I speak of death—its pleasures and its recompenses ; showing that, if there be a future life, the gods have done wisely to withhold its exact nature from us, and that, whatever uncertainties may exist in other respects, nothing can be more true than that those who now die in the arena will, in another world, find their highest felicity in the privilege of looking up from a distance at the loved emperor in whose honor they perished, and beholding him enjoying, through adoption, the society of the inhabitants of Olympus. I then —but it is useless to detail all the argument. I will read the poem itself; or rather, if you so permit, I will let this scribe of yours read it for me. Perhaps, upon hearing it from another's mouth, I may be led to make still further corrections."

Handing the manuscript with all care to Cleotos, the poet leaned back with eyes closed in delicious revery, now and then arousing himself to correct some defective emphasis or unsatisfactory intonation, the tolerance of which, he imagined, would mar the proper effect of the production; or, with persistent desire for praise, momentarily calling closer attention to such passages as appeared to him deserving of especial commendation—and generally omitting no opportunity of exacting that entire admiration to which he believed his genius entitled him. Apart from a somewhat extravagant display of high-strained metaphor, the poem had merit, being bold in scope, sonorous and well rounded in tone, and here and there gracefully decked with original and pleasing thoughts. Throughout the whole, however, the singular propensity of the author for indulgence in morbid and gloomy reflection found its usual development, while every line was laden with lofty maxims of moral philosophy, mingled with urgent incentives to the adoption of a virtuous career;—all, in themselves, both unexceptionable and praiseworthy, but, nevertheless, having a strange sound in the ears of those who recognized them as the utterances of one whose conversation was always flippant and puerile, and whose daily life, in the enormity and uninterrupted persistency of its profligacy, rendered him the acknowledged leader of all that was most disreputable and contaminating in Roman society.

At length, the reading having been fully completed, and the listener's powers of flattery exhausted, the author carefully rewrapped his poem in its silken cover and carried it away, to read it, in turn, to other noble matrons, with the same transparent pretence of giving exclusive hearing of it to each. For a few moments Ænone remained in thoughtful silence, with her head bowed upon her hand; recalling the scattered fragments of the sonorous verses, and wondering why it was that, when each line had seemed so perfect in itself, and every thought so pure and noble in its purport and conception, the whole should have left upon her mind such an undefinable impress of dissatisfaction.

Cleotos, with unobtrusive scrutiny, seemed to read her thoughts, for, at the first intimation of her perplexity, he said:

"It is because the author of those verses has not sincerely felt the full meaning of what he has there written. For, with whatsoever display of ingenious and artistic skill fair sounding maxims of morality may be expressed, yet, if they come not from the heart, their utterance must seem hollow and unreal. I do not know this author—how or where he lives. It may be that in his daily life he is outwardly all that could be desired. But I know this—that he has written about virtue and death, not because he loves the one and fears not the other, but simply because, by a display of well-toned periods, he may more surely hope to gain the applause of the arena and the smiles of the court."

"But why should not these sentiments, though called into being by personal ambition alone, give equal pleasure as if springing directly from the heart? Are they not, after all, as true?"

"Nay, honored mistress, neither are they true. This is again where they fail to please ; for in your soul there is an instinct, though you may not know of it, which forbids that such cold and unsatisfactory reasoning should bring you comfort. He speaks of death : is it cheering to be told that, though the gods have appointed death to every person, they have given it, not as a veiled mercy, but rather as a dreadful fate—that there is no certainty about our future condition, but that, if we are destined to live again, it may be with the same evils encompassing us which bind us now—and that the slave may then still be a slave, destined forever to look up to and worship the high and mighty ones who trampled on him here ?"

"That is, in truth, no comfort," said Ænone. And she bowed her head upon her hands, and sadly thought how worthless to her would be the gift of eternal life, if her present sorrows were to follow her. "But what can we do? If it were possible to discover and believe in some other fate, telling us that death, instead of being a dreaded pang, is a boon and relief to the sick and weary and oppressed—"

"There is a book," said Cleotos—and for a moment he hesitated, as though fearful of proceeding—"there is a book which I have read, and which tells us all this. It says that death is not merely a fate, but is a source of blessing ; since it leads to a world where the sufferings of this life shall be recompensed with abundant joy, not to the rich merely, but more especially to the poor and lowly."

"Where is that book?" cried Ænone, with sudden energy, as the wondrous depth and power of the sentiment flashed upon her. "Where can I see and read it? He who can talk like that, must surely have said still more?"

"I have not that book," answered Cleotos. "I have only this little copy of a small portion of it;" and he hesitatingly drew from beneath his tunic a single small leaf of discolored parchment, closely filled with Greek characters. "But being at Corinth, a year ago, I was permitted to see the book itself, and to hear portions of it read. It was written to a Christian church there, by one Paul, a leader of that sect."

At the word "Christian" the first impulse of Ænone was to shrink back, not knowing but that even the presence of one who had ever come into contact with any of that despised sect might be injurious to her. For at once she began to recall many of the tales which she had heard to its discredit—its members hiding as outcasts in the caves and dens of the earth—their repeated insults to the gods—their proud and unaccountable worship of a malefactor—their sacrifice of infants—and other exaggerations and calumnies, begotten in malice or ignorance, and thence widely spread, making it not hard to believe that the only fate fit for those to whom they related was a life of persecution and a cruel death in the arena.

But only for a moment did this instinctive horror control her. The single doctrine which she had just heard advanced already began to bear its fruits. It seemed, indeed, not unlikely that one who could write such truths, and those, his disciples, who could so gratefully treasure them up, might not, after all, be wantonly wicked, but, at the worst, might be merely victims of mistaken zeal. And then, in turn, she thought of much that had been related to her in their favor. During her life at Rome, indeed, she had heard no mention of the Christian sect, unless accompanied with sneers or contempt. But she remembered how that in Ostia, while she was yet a very young girl, she had heard it sometimes whispered that the Christians were kind and loving to all the world, and free from many sins in which other men openly exulted, and that, through their great love for their founder, they organized charities which had never before been even thought of—and how that once, when she had been very sick, a strange woman had nursed her into health and refused all payment for it, alleging that her religion bade her give herself up to such tasks —and how that she had once seen pass by, one who was pointed out to her as a holy man among the sect,—whose name indeed she could not remember, but whose mild and serene expression yet lived in her recollection. It was hardly possible that one whose face was so radiant with universal love and benevolence as to impress itself thus lastingly upon the heart of a young child could have been very wicked. Nor did it seem likely that Cleotos, whose greatest weakness was that his life had been almost too innocent and trusting, could speak well of a sect which worthily ought to be persecuted. And then again she thought upon that little book to the sect at Corinth, and she bade Cleotos read a verse or two. He did so. At another time she might have listened as she had listened to the moral maxims of the poet Emilius—judging well of it, perhaps, for the beauty of its words, but, beyond that, regarding it simply as some new and more original expression of long-accepted philosophy. But now, in her trouble, she felt that there was something in it beyond all known philosophy—a new development of faith, appealing to the heart, and speaking comfort to all who were in misery. It surely could not be that such words were the emanations of an evil influence.

"Art thou—answer me, Cleotos—art thou one of the sect of Christians?" she inquired.

"How can I tell?" he responded. "I have so often asked that question of my heart, and yet have not been able to understand what it has said to me. There are times when I think that I must pray only to the gods of Olympus, and that all I have heard or read about other gods must be untrue. And again, when I read this little parchment of mine, and remember other like things that have been told to me, and see how they all speak of death as a relief to the sorrowing, and of another life in which the down-trodden and the captive shall be recompensed for what they have suffered here, and know that I am one of those who need such recompense—then I think that perhaps the only true God is the God of the Christians. But I can learn so little about it all, that I cannot, from my own judgment, determine which must be right."

"Perhaps," thoughtfully responded Ænone, "it may be that if you tell me all you know about it, I may be able to assist your conclusions. Who knows what light I myself need, or how much of good we may borrow from this new religion? It cannot be wrong to examine for one's self, and the gods will not be angry if we gain good doctrine even from wrong sources, so long as it may make us better. To-morrow, therefore, let us begin."

Upon the morrow, therefore, and for many succeeding days, the mistress and the slave spent stolen moments in groping after the truth of that faith which makes the high and the low equal. It was a blind search, for neither of them had any definite comprehension of the history and doctrine upon which the new religion had been founded. Cleotos had enjoyed the best opportunities of acquainting himself with it, having naturally, in his wanderings about the East, and in his contact with the poor and enslaved of many lands, heard much respecting the Christian churches and their belief; but having had no instructor, a great portion of what he had thus received came to him in but distorted and puzzling array. And Ænone could not comprehend how, when the gods ruled Rome, and Rome had scattered the Jews, one whom the Jews had had the power to slay could be greater than all. But between them, for their study, lay the leaf of parchment, closely covered with writing, beside which the proudest and choicest philosophy of Rome seemed mockery; and though they could not understand its full meaning, they knew that it spoke such good words that, at the least, though it may have come from erring men, it was no less worthy to have come from a God. Whatever the real nature of the faith itself, here was certainly a proof that among its attributes were mercy and peace and brotherly love towards all.

What might have been the consequences if Ænone had been free to pursue the investigation as far as she wished

—to send for other books to aid her—to consult more learned teachers, who, though perhaps hiding in secret shelter, were yet attainable with proper search, cannot be known. It is not improbable that, in the end, one more might have been added to the list of those few Roman women of high degree who even then gave up all their rank and state in order to share the persecutions of the Nazarenes. But it was otherwise ordered. Already indications, each slight in itself, but altogether of important bearing, began to present themselves before her, warning her that jealous eyes were watching her, and that, if she would avoid the consequences of misconstruction, she must bring her feeble investigations to a close.

Until now, Leta, in her struggle to alienate the husband from the wife, had been actuated simply by the exigencies of her ambitious policy. Bearing in her heart no especial hatred against her mistress, she would willingly have spared her, had not the circumstances of the case seemed to require the ruin of the one preliminary to the exaltation of the other. But now, other incentives to her efforts were added. First in her mind came jealousy of Cleotos; for though she had cast him off, and bade him stifle the yearnings of his heart, and, by the cool exercise of intellect and craft alone, seek a better fortune for himself, it was hardly natural that she should feel pleased to have him so soon appear to take her at her word. She would have better liked to see him display more prolonged sorrow for her loss. Then came jealousy of Ænone, who had apparently been able to console him so early. And mingled with all this, there began to press upon her a startling thought—one which she at first contemned as unlikely and absurd—but which, though continually driven away, so obstinately returned and commended itself to her attention with newer plausibility, that at last she began to give bitter and anxious heed to it. What if this constant communication between Ænone and Cleotos were to result in a mutual love? It was no uncommon thing in those days for the high-born lady to cast her eyes upon the slave. How mortifying to herself, then, if, while she had been exerting all her powers of fascination, taxing the utmost resources of her intellect, and making of her whole existence one labored study for the purpose of gaining an undue influence over the lord, Cleotos, without art or disguise or apparent effort, or any advantage other than that afforded by his simple-hearted, trusting nature, should have quietly won from the other side of the house a victory of almost equal importance! And further than this—what if the lord were to perish in some brawl or by the hired assassin of a rival house; and Ænone, released from her thraldom, and despising conventional scruples—as again was not uncommon among the Roman ladies of that day—were to exalt her favorite with legal honors, and thus make herself, Leta, his slave? This, to be sure, was an improbable chance; but a mind as active as her own did not disdain to foresee and provide against all contingencies.

Then, in addition to every thing else, she became absorbed in the one overwhelming and bitter reflection, that after all her sacrifice and labor, the anticipated success might be escaping her. It is true that, thanks to her efforts, the distance between Sergius and Ænone had widened, until it seemed that there could never be a perfect reunion; but all this, if the state of partial neglect which had existed in the beginning could be relied upon as an indication, was a consequence which might easily, in time, have come of itself. It is true that Sergius had yielded himself a willing victim to the unlawful fascinations thrown around him; but yet Leta could not avoid seeing that he regarded her not with the deep, earnest love which she had hoped to inspire, but rather with the trifling carelessness of one giving himself up to the plaything of the hour. Not having, from the very first, been chary of the sidelong glance and the winning smile, and whatever grace of style or manner could tempt him to pursuit, as an illusive appearance of success seemed to beckon her onward, her heart at times grew desperate with the apprehension that all had been in vain. For Sergius, content that the wife whom he neglected did not disturb his repose with idle complaints, had no thought of inflicting any deeper injury upon her, being well satisfied to have her remain and confer honor upon him by the grace with which she maintained the dignity of his house. And though well pleased to sun himself in Leta's smile, there never came to him the thought that the slave could be worthy of any exaltation, or that her highest ambition could prompt her to desire more than a continuance of the companionship with which he honored her. All this Leta began to dimly see; and there were times when, strive to hide it from her heart as she would, it seemed as though he might be even growing weary of her.

Thus tormented with doubt and jealousy and the constantly increasing suspicion of baffled ambition, how was she to act? To accept her situation as a decree of fate, to fawn upon the mistress like a patient slave, and, if the lord were to tire of her in the end and give himself up to other captivations, to submit unmurmuringly to the unavoidable necessity? All this some might consent to do ; but surely not one like herself, gifted with indomitable will, and stung to desperation with the sense of great and irreparable sacrifices. To her there could be but one course. She must abandon her slow and cautious policy, and seek the earliest opportunity to urge the matter to its crisis. If, by sparing no watchfulness or ingenuity, or by the exercise of bold and vigorous manœuvring, she could produce a quarrel and final separation between Sergius and his wife, it might not be impossible for her to impress upon him how much she was necessary to his happiness, and thereby elevate herself into the vacant place. And if unsuccessful, at the least she would be but sharing a ruin which would fall like an avalanche upon all alike.

CHAPTER XII.

A WEEK passed away. It was towards the end of a bright and cloudless day, and Rome was gradually arousing itself from its wonted siesta. The heat had at no time been oppressive, for during the whole morning a cool breeze had been gambolling across the Campagna from the sea; so that even during the small hours of the day, the streets had not been kept free from moving masses of life. Now that the atmosphere became still further tempered, fresh throngs poured forth from all the smaller passages and alleys, until the greater arteries of the city swarmed with eager, animated crowds.

More now than at any other time during the few weeks that had just elapsed; for upon the morrow was to commence the dedication of the great amphitheatre of Titus, and thousands of strangers had already poured into Rome to witness the games, combats, and pageantry. From the surrounding towns and villages—from the cities of the south—from the confines of the Alps—even from the fathermost provinces, countless throngs had assembled to greet an occasion second only to the grand triumphal entry with the spoils of Jerusalem.

From her window overlooking the streets, Ænone surveyed the panorama of life spread out before her. Upon the battlements and towers of the Cæsars' house, in full sight over against the Palatine Hill, floated the imperial banners, gently waving their folds in anticipation of the splendors of the ensuing days; and round about stood crowds of strangers, wondering at the magnificence of the palace architecture, and the vast compass of its walls, and straining their eager gaze in the hope of being able to catch a chance glimpse of the emperor himself. Further down was the now completed Colosseum, around which other thousands stood watching the pigmies who, in dark clusters upon the top and along the edge, laboriously erected the poles on which, in case of need, to stretch the protecting velarium. This was the last outward preparation of all; and when that was done, every thing would be ready. As one of these poles was being elevated, he who had hold of the lower end of it lost his balance, and fell to the ground. He was lifted up outside, dead—a shapeless, gory mass. The crowd shuddered to see that helpless body falling from such a height; but, at the next moment, all sympathy passed away. The man wore a slave's dress, and was recognized as belonging to the prætorian lieutenant Patrocles. Upon the morrow, if he had lived, he was to have appeared in the arena as a retiarius—he would then most likely have been conquered and slain—it was merely a day sooner—a victim outside the walls instead of within —he had clambered up to overlook the ground upon which he was to have fought, and need not thus recklessly have volunteered to aid the regular laborers—it was his fate— *Deus vult*—what more could be said?

Ænone had not witnessed the fall, for she had not been looking at palace or amphitheatre, both of which were too familiar with her to attract her attention. The one had been for years the centrepiece of her view—and the other had grown up arch by arch and tier by tier so steadily before her eyes that it seemed as though she could almost count its stones. Her gaze was now fixed upon the open space beneath her window, where the Sacred and Triumphal Ways joined—a space always at that hour gay with phantasmagoria of shifting life, and at this time more than ever provocative of curiosity and attention. Its bordering palaces, already being hung with lively tapestries for the morrow—its sparkling fountains—its corners decked with arches—its pavement thronged with carriages and horsemen—the crowds of slaves beginning in advance to take their holiday, and affording pleasing contrasts as they wound their way in slender currents through the openings in the throng of their betters—the soldiery passing here and there in large or small detachments—where else in the world could such a varied scene of life and animation be presented?

First before her eyes passed a number of the prætorian guard, with martial music, cutting the crowd asunder like a wedge in their steady march towards the imperial palace. Then came the chariot of the African proconsul, with liveried footmen in front, and Nubian slaves, in short tunics and silver anklets, running beside the wheels. After that a covered van, toilsomely dragged along by tired horses and guarded by armed slaves in livery. The imperial cipher was emblazoned upon the dusty canvas screen thrown over the top, and from within, at intervals, came half-smothered growls and roars. It was some wild beast arriving at this late hour from Nubia—a contribution from some provincial governor—a booty which had cost pounds of gold, and perhaps the lives of many slaves, and which was now destined to perform, in the sanded arena, the combats of the jungle. The crowd, which had let the African proconsul pass by with but a careless glance of uninterested scrutiny—for dignitaries were too common to excite much curiosity—pressed tumultuously and with frantic eagerness around 'the heavy cage, exulting in each half-stifled roar from within as though it were a strain of sweet music—and thus followed the van until it arrived at the amphitheatre and passed out of sight through one of the deep, low arches leading to the tiers of grated stone cages, already well filled with the choicest forest spoils of every tributary country.

Then came a black-bearded horseman. The trappings of his steed were marked with the insignia of distinction; and footmen, with staves, ran before him to clear the way. He sat with proud and haughty mien—as one who felt his power and immunity, and yet with the expression of one aware that all his rank and state could not protect him from secret scorn and hate. Not many looked at him; for, in that thronging display of wealth and power, a single gayly caparisoned horse and two liveried footmen counted for almost nothing. One or two, however, of those few who study men for their deeds alone, turned and gazed scrutinizingly after him, for he had already taken rank as one of the historians of the age. And as he passed further along, a group of slaves, whose marked features denoted Jewish descent, suffered expressions of aversion to break from them; some turning their backs—some gazing up with faces inflamed with the fiercest intensity of hate—while one, less cautious, clenched his fist and hurled after the rider a handful of dust and volleys of heavy Hebrew curses. And so the apostate Josephus passed on, and was gradually lost to view.

After him, slowly wending his way on foot through the crowds, occasionally moving aside to allow others, more urgent, the privilege of passing him, and constantly careful not to excite the impatient wrath of those nearest to him by a too lively pressure, yet all the time making sure progress along his chosen path, came a single figure—a white-bearded man, in plain, coarse tunic and well-worn sandals. Few regarded him or even seemed to know that he was there, except when in their hurry they found it expedient to jostle him one side. But in his face gleamed an intelligence far beyond what could be expected from one in his humble attire; and as Ænone watched him, a suspicion crossed her that the poor beggarly garb and the quiet yielding mien were assumed to baffle observation. Soon another person in similar dress but of fewer years met him. The two joined hands and looked earnestly into each other's eyes, and the older one appeared to mutter a word or two. What was that word, at which the younger bent his head with reverent gesture? Was it a command or a blessing? Whatever it was, in a second it was all said. The hands then unclasped—the bended head raised with a startled glance around, as though with a fear that even such a mere instant of humble bearing might have betrayed something which should be kept secret; and then the two men parted, and were swallowed up in different sides of the concourse.

"I know that person," said Cleotos. He had been gazing, for the past minute, out at the same window with Ænone; and while attracted by the humble figure of that old man, he had noticed that she had been equally observant.

"You know him, Cleotos?"

"They call him Clemens, noble lady. He is a leader of the Christian sect, and a person of influence among them. It was at Corinth that I first saw him, and it was he who let me copy the good words which are written upon my little leaf of parchment. That was two years ago, but I still recognize him. What does he here? Why should he thus peril his life in public?"

"Give me that little scroll, Cleotos," said Ænone. "Let me have it for my own."

Cleotos gazed at her for a moment in dismay. Was she about to use her authority, and take away from him by force those few lines, which, though he understood them so little, had often served to cheer his heart with their promises of future rest and joy? If so, he must submit; but of what avail, then, was all her previous kindness?

"I ask it not as mistress, but as friend," she said, reading his thoughts. "I ask it because, when you are away, I shall need some memory of what have been happy days, and because I may then often wish to apply those same words of comfort to my own soul. You can make another copy of the same, and, in your own land, I doubt not, can find, with proper search, many more words of equal value."

"In my own land?" Cleotos repeated, as in a dream. But, though her meaning did not as yet flash upon him, he knew that she spoke in kindness, and that she would not ask any thing which he would not care to grant; and he drew the little stained parchment from beneath his tunic, and handed it to her.

"Close, now, the window, Cleotos, and shut out from sight that giddy whirl, for I have something to say to you."

He closed the window with its silken blind; and then, in obedience to her motion, glided away from before it. She seated herself upon her lounge, and he upon his accustomed stool in front of her.

"Think not, Cleotos," she said, after a moment's silence, "that I first brought you hither to become a mere slave. It was rather done in order that, when the proper time came, I might set you free. Had she—Leta—but shown herself worthy of you, the day might have come when I could have managed to free her also, and send you both home again together. But that cannot be. You must go alone, Cleotos, but not, I hope, despairingly. Once again in your own loved Samos, I know that, sooner or later, there will be found some other one to make you forget what you have suffered here."

He could no longer doubt her meaning—she was about to give him to liberty again. At the thought the blood rushed to his heart, and he gasped for breath. For the moment, as he gazed into her face and saw with what sisterly sympathy and compassion she looked upon him, the impulse came into his mind to refuse the proffered freedom, and ask only to remain and serve her for life. But then came such floods of memories of his native place, which he had never expected to see again—and its hills and streams and well-remembered haunts seemed to approach with one bound so near to him—and the faces of the loved ones at home began once again to look so tenderly into his own— and the thought of throwing off even the light, silken chains which he had been wearing, and of standing up in the sight of heaven a free man again, was so grateful to his soul—what could he do but remain silent and overpowered with conflicting emotions, and wait to hear more?

"Think not to refuse your liberty," she said, as she read his doubts and perplexities. "It must not be. No man has the right to suffer degradation when he can avoid it. And though I might continue kind to you, who can answer for it that I should live to be kind to the end? No, no; from this instant be a free man again. And, for the few moments that remain to us, strive to think of me only as your equal and your friend."

Still silent. What, indeed, could he say? She knew that he was grateful to her, and that was enough. But why should he, of all slaves in Rome, find such kindly treatment? What had he ever done to deserve it? And —as often before—that puzzled look of wondering inquiry came over his face while he gazed into her own. She noticed it, but now made no attempt to disguise herself by any forced and unnatural assumption of haughty pride. Were he at last to learn the truth, there could surely no harm come of it.

"You must depart to-night," she said, "and before it becomes known that I am sending you away ; lest, knowing it, others might claim authority to delay or prevent you. Take this little purse. It contains a few gold pieces, which you may need. And here is a written pass which will lead you to Ostia. There you will go to the tavern of the Three Cranes, and inquire for one Pollio, who has a vessel ready to sail for Samos. In that vessel your passage is paid. Show him this ring. It will be a token for him to know you by. And keep the ring ever afterwards, as a sign that you have a friend left here, who will often think of you with pleasure and interest."

"My mistress," he said, taking the ring and placing it upon his finger, "what have I done that you should be thus kind to me?"

"Nay; no longer mistress, but friend," she said, with a melancholy smile. "As such alone let us converse during the hour that remains, for you must soon leave me. It may be that when you arrive at Ostia, the vessel will not be ready to set sail, nor yet for a day or two, for its owner spoke to my messenger concerning possible delays. If so, there will be time for you to look around you, and think of the days when you wandered along the shore, hand in hand with your chosen one. You will, perhaps, go over those wanderings again—along the sands leading past Druse's olive-grove to the altar of Vesta, or to the—"

"How know you about Druse's grove?" he cried with a start; and again that look of keen inquiry came into his face. It was but a single step now—he stood upon the very border of the truth. Should she repress him?

It were hardly worth the while. So she let him gaze, and, if any thing, softened her features yet more into the old familiar expression.

"Past Druse's Grove, Cleotos—or to the smooth rock which the waves washed at Cato's Point. Do you remember, Cleotos, how often we there sat, you holding me with your arm while I slid down the sloping side, the better to dip my naked feet into the water?"

With a wild sob he seized her hand, and threw himself at her feet. Near to the truth as he had been standing, it seemed at the last to burst upon him with as much force as though even a suspicion of it had been a thing before impossible. And yet, at the same time, it appeared to him as though he must have known it all the while; for how could he comprehend his past blindness?

"Ænone," he cried, "send me not away! Let me stay here to serve you forever!"

"Oh, speak not thus!" she said, touching his lips lightly with her finger. "Had you not been about to go from here, you should never have recognized me. Forget, now, all that has ever passed between us; or rather, strive to remember it only as a pleasant dream which left us in its proper time. If the Fates separated us, it was only because they were wiser than ourselves. Those bright anticipations of our youthful love could never have been fully realized; and if persisted in, might have led only to sorrow and despair. Let me not blush now at having revealed myself to you. Think, for the few minutes that remain to us, of friendship and of duty alone."

Raising him up, she placed him beside her, and there

they talked about the past and its pleasant recollections. How the cross miller, who had never been known to do a kindness to any one else, had sometimes let them ride upon his horse—how they had once rowed together about the bay, and he had taken her aboard his ship—how she had stolen away from home each pleasant evening to meet him, and with what feeble excuses—and the like. As the shades of afternoon deepened and shut out from sight the gilded cornices and costly frescoes, and all else that could remind them of present wealth, and as, each instant, their thoughts buried themselves still further in the memories of the past, it seemed to them, at last, as though they were again wandering hand in hand upon the beach, or sitting upon the wave-washed rock at Cato's Point.

With something wanting, however, No force of illusion could bring back to either of them, in all its former completeness, that sense of mutual interest which had once absorbed them. Whatever dreams of the past might, for the moment, blind their perceptions, there was still the ever-present consciousness of now standing in another and far different relation to each other. Though Ænone musingly gazed upon his face and listened to his voice, until the realities of the present seemed to shrink away, and the fancies of other years stole softly back, and, with involuntary action, her hand gently toyed with his curls and parted them one side, as she had once been accustomed to do, it was with no love for him that she did it now. He was only her friend—her brother. He had been kind to her, and perhaps, if necessary, she might even now consent to die for him; but, with all that, he was no longer the idol of her heart. Another had taken that place, and, however unworthy to hold it, could not now be dispossessed. And though Cleotos, likewise, as he looked at her and felt the gentle pressure of her hand upon his forehead, seemed as though transported into the past, until he saw no longer the matron in the full bloom of womanhood, but only the young girl sparkling with the fresh hue and sunshine of early youth, yet to him still clung the perception that there was a barrier between them. What though the form of the treacherous Leta may then have faded from his memory as completely as though he had never seen her? What though Ænone's pleasant and sympathetic tones may have again melted into his heart as warmly as when first whispered at Ostia? The smile upon her face—the winning intonation of her voice—all might seem the same; but he knew that he must hide within his own heart whatever he had thus felt anew, and be content with the offered friendship alone, for that not merely her duty but her altered inclination had separated her from him forever.

At last the brief hour came to an end, and Ænone arose. The sun had set, and the darkness of night had already begun to shroud the city. Here and there, from some of the more wealthy neighborhoods, faint glimmers of lamp-light shone out and marked the scenes of solitary study or of festive gathering, but as yet these indications were few. Already the chariots and horsemen who had thronged the Appian Way had dispersed—a single rider here and there occupying the place where so lately gay bands had cantered, disputing each available empty space of pavement.

The walks were yet crowded with loiterers, but of a different class. Patricians and fair ladies had departed, and left the course to the lower orders of citizens and to slaves, who now emerged from the arches and alleys, and, anticipative of the morrow's holiday, swarmed in dusky crowds hither and thither in search of rude pastime.

"You must go now," said Ænone, dropping the curtain which she had lifted for a moment in order to peer into the street. "Stay not for any thing that belongs to you, for I would not that you should be hindered or delayed. You have been here as mine own property; and yet, how do I know that some pretence of others' right might not be urged for your detention, if it were known that you were departing? Go, therefore, at once, Cleotos, and may the gods be with you!"

She held out her hand to him. He took it in his own, and, for the moment, gazed inquiringly into her face. Was this to be their only parting? Nay, need there be a parting at all? A flush came into his countenance as he felt one wild thought and desire burning into his soul. What if he were to yield to the impulse which beset him, and should throw himself at her feet, and ask her to forget the years which had separated them, and the trials which had beset them, and to give up all else, and depart with him? Alas! only one result could follow such an appeal as that! In the vain attempt to gain her love, he would lose her friendship also. She would part from him as an enemy who had taken advantage of her sisterly affection to inflict an insult upon her. He knew that this would surely be the consequence; but yet, for the moment, he could scarce resist the maddening impulse to thus forfeit all while striving to attain impossibilities.

"Shall we never meet again?" he said, at length, after the hard struggle to command himself.

"It may be, in after-years; who can tell?" she answered. "And yet, let us rather look the truth in the face, and not delude ourselves with false hopes. The world is very wide, and the way from here to your home is far, and the fatalities of life are many. Dear Cleotos, let us rather make up our minds that this parting is for ever; unless it may be that the gods will let us look upon each other's faces again in some future state. But there may be times when you can write to me, or send some message of good tidings; and then—"

"Talk not to me of the gods!" he interrupted, in a storm of passionate exclamation. "What have they ever done for us, that we should worship or pray to them? Why look to them for blessings in a future state, when they have done us such evil in the present life? Here we were poor and lowly together; and have they not dragged us apart? And will they, then, in another life, be the more disposed to let us see each other's faces—you one of the nobles of the earth, and I one of its meanest plebeians? Is it written in the temples or by the priests and oracles, that when the Cæsars are throned in Olympus, their lowly subjects shall be permitted to approach them any nearer than when here? How, then, could we meet each other better hereafter than now? Away with all talk about the gods! I believe not in them! If we part now for this world, it is for eternity as well!"

"Oh, say not that!" she exclaimed. "And still pray to the gods as of old, for they may yet bring good out of all that now seems to us so obscure. Remember that to the best of us, this world offers little but what is mingled with unhappiness. Take not, therefore, away from yourself and me a belief in something better to come."

"Take, then, with you, a belief in the God about whom I learned in Greece, for He it is who tells of comfort hereafter for the poor and oppressed, and He is the only one who does so," Cleotos doggedly answered.

"It may be—it may be," she said. "Who can tell which is right? We have so often talked about it, and have not yet found out. They may all, both yours and mine, be the true gods—they may neither of them be. Ah, Cleotos, my brother, let us not doubt. It is pleasanter and safer, too, that we should believe, even if we extend our faith to a belief in both. Choose, then, your own, as I will mine. I must not abandon the gods in whose worship I have been brought up; but when I pray to them, I will first pray for you. And you—if you adopt the God of the Christians, who speaks so much better comfort to your soul—will always pray to Him for me. And thereby, if either of us is wrong, the sin may perhaps be pardoned, on account of the other, who was right. And now, once more—and it may be forever—dear Cleotos, farewell!"

"Farewell, Ænone, my sister!" he said. And he raised her hand and pressed it to his lips, and was about turning sorrowfully away, when the door flew open, and Sergius Vanno burst into the room.

CHAPTER XIII.

WITH Sergius there was seldom any interval between impulse and action. Now, without giving time for explanation, he made one bound to where Cleotos stood; and, before the startled Greek had time to drop the slender fingers which he had raised to his lips, the stroke of the infuriated master's hand descended upon his head, and he fell senseless at Ænone's feet, with one arm resting upon the lounge behind her.

"Is my honor of so little worth that a common slave should be allowed to rob me of it?" Sergius exclaimed, turning to Ænone in such a storm of passion that, for the moment, it seemed as though the next blow would descend upon her.

Strangely enough, though she had ever been used to tremble at his slightest frown, and though now, in his anger, there might even be actual danger to her life, she felt, for the moment, no fear. Her sympathy for the bleeding victim at her feet, of whose sad plight she had been the innocent cause, and whose perils had probably as yet only commenced—her consciousness that a crisis in her life had come, demanding all her fortitude—her indignation that upon such slight foundation she should thus be accused of falsity and shame—all combined to create in her an unlooked-for calmness. Added to this was the delusive impression that, as nothing had occurred which could not be explained, her lord's anger would not be likely to prolong itself at the expense of his returning sense of justice. What, indeed, could he have witnessed which she could not account for with a single word? It was true that within the past hour she had innocently and dreamily bestowed upon the Greek caresses which might easily have been misunderstood; and that all the while, the door having been partly open, a person standing outside and concealed by the obscure gloom of the antechamber, could have covertly witnessed whatever had transpired within. But Ænone knew that whatever might be her lord's other faults, he was not capable of countenancing the self-imposed degradation of espionage. Nor, even had it been otherwise, could he have been able, if his jealousy was once aroused by any passing incident, to control his impatient anger sufficiently to await other developments. At the most, therefore, he must merely, while passing, have chanced to witness the gesture of mingled emotion and affection with which Cleotos had bidden her farewell. Surely that was a matter which would require but little explanation.

"Do you not hear me?" cried Sergius, glaring with wild passion from her to Cleotos and back again to her. "Was it necessary that my honor should be placed in a slave's keeping? Was there no one of noble birth with whom you could be false, but that you must bring this deeper degradation upon my name?"

Ænone drew herself up with mingled scorn and indignation. His anger, which at another time would have crushed her, now passed almost unheeded; for the sense of injury resulting from his cruel taunt, and from his readiness, upon such slight foundation, to believe her guilty, gave her strength to combat him. The words of self-justification and of reproach towards him were at her lips, ready to break forth in unaccustomed force. In another moment the torrent of her indignant protestations would have burst upon him. Already his angry look began to quail before the steadfast earnestness of her responsive gaze. But all at once her tongue refused its utterance, her face turned ghastly pale, and her knees seemed to sink beneath her.

For, upon glancing one side, she beheld the gaze of Leta fixedly fastened upon her over Sergius' shoulder. In the sparkle of those burning eyes and in the curve of those half-parted lips, there appeared no longer any vestige of the former pretended sympathy or affection. There was now malice, scorn, and hatred—all those expressions which, from time to time, had separately excited doubt and dread, now combining themselves into one exulting glance of open triumph, disdainful of further concealment, since at last the long-sought purpose seemed attained. Ænone felt, with a sickening, heart-breaking pang, that she was now lost indeed. It was no mystery, any longer, that the slave girl must have listened at the open door, and have cunningly contrived that her master should appear at such time as seemed most opportune for her purposes. And how must every unconscious action, every innocent saying have been noted down in the tablets of that crafty mind! What explanation, indeed, could be given of those trivial caresses now so surely magnified and distorted into evidences of degrading criminality?

Faint at heart, Ænone turned away—unable longer to look upon that face so exultant with the consciousness of a long-sought purpose achieved. Rather would she prefer to encounter the angry gaze of her lord. Terrible to her as was his look, she felt that, at the last, pity might be found in him, if she could only succeed in making him listen to and understand the whole story. But what mercy or release from jealous and vindictive persecution could she hope to gain from the plotting Greek girl, who had no pity in her heart, and who, even if she were so disposed, could not, now that matters had progressed so far, dare to surrender the life-and-death struggle? Alas! neither in the face of her lord could she now see any thing but settled, unforgiving pitilessness; for though, for an instant, he had quailed before her gaze, yet when she had, in turn, faltered at the sight of Leta, he deemed it a new proof of guilt, and his suspended reproaches broke forth with renewed violence.

"Am I to have no answer?" he cried, seizing her by the arm. "Having lost all, are you now too poor-spirited to confess?"

"There is nothing for me to confess. Nor, if there had been, would I deign to speak before that woman," she answered with desperation, and pointing towards Leta. "What does she here? How, in her presence, can you dare talk of sin—you who have so cruelly wronged me? And has all manliness left you, that you should ask me to open my heart to you in the presence of a slave; one, too, who has pursued me for weeks with her treacherous hate, and now stands gloating over the misery which she has brought upon me? I tell you that I have said or done nothing which I cannot justify; but that neither will I deign to explain aught to any but yourself alone."

"The same old excuse!" retorted Sergius. "No harm done—nothing which cannot be accounted for in all innocence; and yet, upon some poor pretence of wounded pride, that easy explanation will not be vouchsafed! And all the while the damning proof and author of the guilt lies before me!"

With that he extended his foot, and touched the senseless body of Cleotos—striking it carelessly, and not too gently. The effect of the speech and action was to arouse still more actively the energetic impulses of Ænone—but not, alas! to that bold display of conscious innocence with which, a moment before, she had threatened to sweep aside his insinuations, and make good her justification. She was now rather driven into a passion of reckless daring—believing that her fate was prejudged and forestalled—caring but little what might happen to her—wishing only to give way to her most open impulses, let the consequences be what they might. Therefore, in yielding to that spirit of defiance, she did the thing which of all others harmed her most, since its immediate and natural result was to give greater cogency to the suspicions against her. Stooping down and resting herself upon the lounge, she raised the head of the still senseless Cleotos upon her lap, and began tenderly to wipe his lips, from a wound in which a slight stream of blood had begun to ooze.

"He and I are innocent," she said. "I have treated him as a brother, that is all. It is years ago that I met him first, and then he was still more to me than now. He is now poor and in misery, and I cannot abandon him. Had he been in your place, and you in his, he would not thus, without proof, have condemned you, and then have insulted your lifeless body."

For a moment Sergius stood aghast. Excuse and pleading he was prepared to hear. Recriminations would not have surprised him, for he knew that his own course would not bear investigation, and nothing, therefore, could be more natural than that she should attempt to defend herself by becoming the assailant in turn. But that she should thus defy him—before his eyes should bestow endearments upon a slave, the partner of her apparent guilt, and with whom she acknowledged having had an intimacy years before, was too astounding for him at first to understand. Then recovering himself, he cried aloud:

"Is this to be borne? Ho, there, Drumo! Meros! all of you! Take this wretch and cast him into the prison! See that he does not escape, on your lives! He shall feed the lions to-morrow! By the gods, he shall feed the lions! Bear him away! Let me not see him again till I see his blood lapped up in the arena. Away with him, I say!"

As the first cry of Sergius rang through the halls, the armor-bearer appeared at the door; and before many more seconds had elapsed, other slaves, armed and unarmed, swarmed forth from different courts and passages, until the antechamber was filled with them. None of them knew what had happened, but they saw that, in some way, Cleotos had incurred the anger of his master, and lay stunned and bleeding before them. To obey was the work of a moment. The giant Drumo, stooping down, wound his arm around the body of Cleotos, hoisted him upon his broad shoulder, and stalked out of the room. The other slaves followed. Ænone, who, in the delirium of her defiance, might have tried to resist, was overpowered by her own attendants, who also had flocked in at Sergius' call, and now gently forced her from the room. And in a moment more, Sergius was left alone with Leta.

She, crouching in a dark corner of the room, awaited her opportunity to say the words which she dared not say while he was in this storm of wild passion ; he, thinking himself entirely alone, stalked up and down like a caged tiger, muttering curses upon himself, upon Ænone, upon the slave, upon all who directly or indirectly had been concerned in his supposed disgrace. Let it not be forgotten that, though at first he had acted hastily and upon slight foundation of proof, and had cruelly wounded her spirit by abhorrent insinuations, without giving time or opportunity for her to explain herself, she had afterwards given way to an insane impulse, and had so conducted herself as to fix the suspicion of guilt upon herself almost ineffaceably. What further proof could he need ? While with false lips, she had denied all, had she not, at the same time, lavished tender caresses upon the vile slave?

Then, too, what had he not himself done to add to the sting of his disgrace ? Convinced of her guilt, he should have quietly put her away, and the truth would have leaked out only little by little, so as to be stripped of half its mortification. But he had called up his slaves ! They had entered upon the scene, and would guess at every thing, if they did not know it already! The mouths of menials could not be stopped. To-morrow, all Rome would know that the imperator Sergius, whose wife had been the wonder of the whole city for her virtue and constancy, had been deceived by her, and for a low-born slave ! Herein, for the moment, seemed to lie half the disgrace. Had it been a man of rank and celebrity like himself—but a slave! And how would he dare to look the world in the face—he who had been proud of his wife's unsullied reputation, even when he had most neglected her, and who had so often boasted over his happy lot to those who, having the name of being less fortunate, had complacently submitted themselves to bear with indifference a disgrace which, at that age, seemed to be almost the universal doom !

Frantically revolving these matters, he raged up and down the apartment for some moments, while Leta watched him from her obscure corner. When would it be time for her to advance and try her art of soothing? Not yet; for while that paroxysm of rage lasted, he would be as likely to strike her as to listen. Once he approached within a few feet of her, and, as she believed herself observed, she trembled and crouched behind a vase. He had not seen her, but his eye fell upon the vase, and with one blow he rolled it off its pedestal, and let it fall shattered upon the marble floor. Was it simply because the costly toy stood in his way? Or was it that he remembered it had been a favorite of Ænone? One fragment of the vase, leaping up, struck Leta upon the foot and wounded her, but she dared not cry out. She rather crouched closer behind the empty pedestal, and drew a long breath of relief as, after a moment, he turned away.

At last the violence of his passion seemed to have expended itself, and he sank upon the lounge, and, burying his face in his hands, abandoned himself to more composed reflection. Now was the time for her to approach. And yet she would not address herself directly to him, but would rather let him, in some accidental manner, detect her presence. Upon a small table stood a bronze lamp with a little pitcher of olive-oil beside it. The wicks were already in the sockets, and she had only to pour in the oil. This she did noiselessly, as one who has no thought of any thing beyond the discharge of an accustomed duty. Then she lighted the wicks and stealthily looked up to see whether he had yet observed her.

The lamp somewhat brightened the obscurity of the room, sending even a faint glimmer into the further corners, but he took no notice of it. Perhaps he may have moved his head a little towards the light, but that was all. Otherwise there was no apparent change or interruption in his deep, troubled thought. Then Leta moved the table with the lamp upon it a few paces towards him, so that the soft light could fall more directly upon his face. Still no change. Then she softly approached and bent over him.

What could he be thinking of? Could he be feeling aught but regret that he had thrown away years of his life upon one who had betrayed him so grossly at the end? Was he not telling himself how, upon the morrow, he would put her away, with all ceremony, forever? And might he not be reflecting that, Ænone once gone, there would be a vacant place to be filled at his table? Would he not wish that it should be occupied without delay, if only to show the world how little his misfortune had affected him? And who more worthy to fill it than the one whose fascinations over him had made it empty? Was not this, then, the time for her to attract his notice, before other thoughts and interests could come between her and him?

Softly she touched him upon the arm; and, like an unchained lion, he sprang up and stared her in the face. There was a terrible look upon his features, making her recoil in dismay. Was that the affectionate gaze with which she had expected to be greeted? Was that the outward indication of the pleasing resolves with which her eager fancy had invested his mind?

Never had she been more mistaken than in her conceptions of his thoughts. In them there was for herself not one kindly impulse; but for the wife whom he had deemed so erring, there was much that was akin to regret, if not to returning affection. The violence of his passion had been so exhausting, that something like a reaction had come. A new contradiction seemed developing itself in his nature. This man, who a few minutes before had prejudged her guilty, because he had seen the lips of a grateful slave pressed against her hand, now, after having seen her so aroused and indifferent to reputation as to defend that slave in her arms, and claim him for at least a friend and brother, began to wonder whether she might not really be innocent. She had confessed to nothing—she had asserted her blamelessness—she had never been known to waver from the truth; might she not have been able to explain her actions? With his regret for having, in such hasty passion, so compromised her before the world that no explanation could henceforth shield her from invidious slander, he now began to feel sorrow for having so roughly used her. Whether she was false or not—whether or not he now loved her—was it any the less true that she had once been constant and loved by him, and did the memories of that time, not so very long ago, bring no answering emotion to his heart? Who, after all, had ever so worshipped him? And must he now really lose her? Might it not be that he had been made the victim of some conspiracy, aided by fortuitous circumstances?

It was just at this point, when, in his thoughts, he was stumbling near the truth, that the touch of Leta's hand aroused him; and in that instant her possible agency in the matter flashed upon him like a new revelation. She saw the tiger-like look which he fastened upon her, and she recoiled, perceiving at once that she had chosen an inopportune moment to speak to him. But it was now too late to recede.

"Well?" he demanded.

"I have lighted the lamp," she faltered forth. "I knew not that I should disturb you. Have you further commands for me?"

Still his fierce gaze continued fixed upon her; but now with a little more of the composure of searching inquiry.

"It is you who have brought all this destruction and misery upon me," he said at length. "From one step unto another, even to this end, I recognize your work. I was a weak fool not to have seen it before."

"Is it about my mistress that you speak?" she responded. "Is it my fault that she has been untrue?"

"If she is false, what need to have told me of it? Was it that the knowledge of it would make me more happy? And did I give it into the hands of my own slaves to watch over my honor? Is it a part of your duty that for weeks you should have played the spy upon herself and me, so as to bring her secret faults to light?

She stood silent before him, not less amazed at his lingering fondness for his wife than at his reproaches against herself.

"How know I that she is guilty at all?" he said, continuing the train of thought into which his doubts and his better nature had led him. "I must feel all this for certain. How do I know but what you have brought it about by some cunning intrigue for your own purposes? Speak!"

For Leta to stop now was destruction. Though to go on might bring no profit to her, yet her safety depended upon closing forever the path of reconciliation towards which his mind seemed to stray. And step by step, shrouding as far as possible her own agency, she spread out before him that basis of fact upon which she so well knew how to erect a false superstructure. She told him how the intimacy of Ænone and Cleotos had led her to keep watch—how Ænone had once confessed having had a lover in the days of her obscurity and poverty—how that this Greek was that same lover—and how improbable it was that he could have been domiciled in that house by chance, or for any other purpose than that of being in a situation to renew former intimacies. She told how, after long suspicion, she had settled this identity · of the former lover with the slave—and how she had seen them, in the twilight of that very day, standing near the window and addressing each other endearingly by their own familiar names. As Sergius listened, the evident truthfulness of the facts gradually impressed themselves upon him; and no longer doubting his disgrace, he closed his heart against all ·further hope and charity and affection. The pleasant past no longer whispered its memories to his heart—those were now stifled and dead.

"And what reward for all this do you demand?" he hissed forth, seizing Leta by the arm. "For of course you have not thus dogged her steps day after day, without expectation of recompense from me."

Did he mean this—that she was capable of asking a reward? Or was he cunningly trying her nature, to see whether she might prove worthy of the great recompense which she had promised herself? It was almost too much now to expect; but her heart beat fast as she saw or fancied she saw some strange significance in the gaze which he fastened upon her. Babbling incoherently, she told how she did not wish reward—how she had done it all for love of him—how she would be content to serve him for life, with no other recompense than his smile— and the like. Still that gaze was fastened upon her with penetrating power, more and more confusing her, and again she babbled forth the same old expressions of disinterested attachment. How it was that at last he understood her secret thoughts and aspirations, she knew not. Certainly she had not spoken, or even seemed to hint about them. But whether she betrayed herself by some glance of the eye or tremor of the voice, or whether some instinct had enabled him to read her, of a sudden he burst into a wild hollow laugh of disdain, threw her from him, and cried, with unutterable contempt:

"This, then, was the purpose of all! This is what you dreamed of! That you, a slave—an hour's plaything—could so mistake a word or two of transient love-making as to fancy that you could ever be any thing beyond what you are now! Poor fool that thou art!—Oho, Drumo."

The giant entered the room, and Leta again drew back into the closest obscurity she could find, not knowing what punishment her audacity was about to draw upon her. But worse, perhaps, than any other punishment, was the discovery that Sergius had already forgotten her; or rather, that he thought so little about her as to be able to dismiss her and her pretensions with a single contemptuous rebuke. He had called his armor-bearer for another purpose than to speak of her. A new phase had passed over his burdened and excited mind. He could not endure that solitude, with ever-present disagreeable reflection. And since his disgrace must sooner or later be known, he would brave it out by being himself the first to publish it.

"Is it not to-morrow that the games begin?"

"Yes, master," responded the armor-bearer.

"And does it not—it seems to me that I promised to my friends a banquet upon the previous night. If I did not, I meant to have done so. Go, therefore, and bid them at once come hither! Tell the poet Emilius— and Bassus—and the rest. You know all whom I would have. Let them understand that I hold revel here, and that not one must dare to stay away! Tell my cooks to prepare a feast for the gods! Go! Dispatch!"

The giant grinned his knowledge of all that his master's tastes would require, and left the room to prepare for his errand. And in a moment more Sergius also departed, without another thought of the Greek girl, who stood shrinking from his notice in the shadow of the furthest corner.

CHAPTER XIV.

IN an hour from that time the banqueting hall of the palace was prepared for its guests. Silken couches had been drawn up around the table. Upon it glittered a rich array of gold and silver. Between the dishes stood flasks of rare wines. Upon the buffet near by were other wines cooling in Apennine snow. Tall candelabras in worked and twisted bronze stood at the ends and sides of the table, and stretched overhead their arms hung with lamps. From the walls were suspended other lamps, lighting up the tapestries and frescoes. At one end of the hall, richly scented spices burned upon a tripod. With a readiness and celerity for which the Vanno palace was famous, a feast fit for the emperor had been improvised in a few minutes, and nothing was now wanting except the guests.

These now began to drop in one by one. The poet Emilius—the comedian Bassus—the proconsul Sardesus—others of lesser note ; but not one who had not a claim to be present, by reason of intimate acquaintance or else some peculiarly valuable trait of conviviality. In collecting these, the armor-bearer had made no mistake ; and knowing his master's tastes and intimates, he had made up the roll of guests as discreetly as though their names had been given him. One he had met in the street—others he had found at their homes. None to whom he gave the invitation was backward in accepting it upon the spot, for there were few places in Rome where equal festal gratification could be obtained. To have been called to the house of Sergius Vanno and not to have gone there, was to have lost a day to be forever regretted. None, therefore, who had been spoken to, among that club of congenial spirits, was absent. Of those who did not come, one was sick and two were at their country villas. These, however, were lesser lights, valuable by themselves, perhaps, but of no account in comparison with others who had come; and therefore their absence was scarcely noticed.

Sergius stood at the door receiving his guests as each arrived. He had arrayed himself in his most festive costume, and had evidently resolved that whatever might happen on the morrow, that night at least should be passed in forgetfulness and unbridled enjoyment. Even now his face was flushed with the wine he had taken in anticipation, in the hope of giving an artificial elation to his spirits. But it seemed as though for that time the wine had lost its accustomed charm. Although at each greeting he strove to wreathe his face in smiles, yet it was but a feeble mask, and could not hide the more natural appearance of care and gloom which rested upon his features; and while his voice seemed to retain its old ring of joyous welcome, there was an undertone of sad discordance. As the guests entered and exchanged greetings with their host, each, after the first moment, looked askant at him, with the dim perception that, in some way, he was not as he was wont to be; and so, in a little while, they sank, one by one, into a troubled and apprehensive silence. He, too, upon his part, looked furtively at them, wondering whether they had yet heard the thing that had befallen him. It was but a short time ago, indeed, and yet in how few minutes might the unrestrained gossip of a slave have spread the ill tidings! For the moment, Sergius recoiled from the difficult task of entertainment which he had taken upon himself. Why, indeed, had he called these men around him? How could he sit and pledge them in deep draughts, and all the time suspect that each one knew his secret, and was laughing about it in his sleeve? And if they knew it not, so much the worse, for then he must tell the tale himself. Was it not partly for this purpose that he had assembled them? Far better to speak of it himself—to let them see how little he regarded the misfortune and the scandal—to treat it as a brave jest—to give his own version of it—than to have the matter leak out in the ordinary way, with all conceivable distortions and exaggerations. But how, in fact, could he tell it? Was there one among them who would not, while openly commiserating him, laugh at him in the heart? Did there not now sit before him the lieutenant Plautus, who, only a month before, had met with a like disgrace, and about whom he had composed derisive verses? Would not the lieutenant Plautus now rejoice to make retaliatory odes? Would it not be better, then, after all, to forbear any mention of the matter, and, letting its announcement take the usual chance course, to devote this night, at least, to unbroken festivity? But what if they already knew it?

Thus wandering in his mind from one debate to another,

and ever, in a moment, coming back to his original suspicion, he sat, essaying complimentary speeches and convivial jests, and moodily gazing from face to face, in a vain attempt to read their secret thoughts. He was wrong in his suspicions. Not one of them knew the reason of the burden upon his mind. All, however, perceived that something had occurred to disturb him, and his moody spirit shed its influence around, until the conversation once again flagged, and there was not one of the party who did not wish himself elsewhere. The costliest viands and wines spread out before them were ineffective to produce that festive gaiety upon which they had calculated.

"By Parnassus!" exclaimed the poet Emilius, at length, pushing aside his plate of turbot, and draining his goblet. "Are we to recline here, hour after hour, winking and blinking at each other like owls over their mice? Was it merely to eat and drink that we have assembled? Hearken! I will read to you that which will raise your spirits, to a certainty. To-morrow the games and combats commence in the arena of the new amphitheatre. Well; and is it known to you that I am appointed to read a dedicatory ode before the emperor and in honor of that occasion? I will give you a pleasure, now. I will forestall your joy, and let you hear what I have written. And be assured that this is no small compliment to your intelligence, since no eye hath yet looked upon a single verse thereof."

With that the poet dragged from his breast his silken bundle, and carefully began to unwind the covering.

"You will observe," he said, as he brought the precious

parchment to light, and smoothed it out upon the table before him, "you will observe that I commence with an invocation to the emperor, whom I call the most illustrious of all the Cæsars, and liken to Jove. I then congratulate the spectators, not only upon the joy of living in his time, but also upon being there to bask in the effulgence of—"

"A truce to such mummery!" cried Sergius, suddenly arousing from his spiritual stupor and bursting into a shrill laugh. "Do we care to listen to your miserable dactyls? Is it not a standing jest through Rome that, for the past month, you have daily read your verses to one person after another, with the same wretched pretence of exclusive favoritism? And do we not know that no warrant has ever been given to you to recite a single line before the emperor, either in or out of the arena? We are here to revel, not to listen to your stale aphorisms upon death and immortality. Ho, there, more wine! Take off these viands, which already pall upon us! Bring wine—more wine!"

The guests were not slow to respond to the altered mood of their host; for it was merely the reflection of his sullen gravity that had eclipsed their own vivacity. The instant, therefore, that he led the way, the hall began to resound with jest and laughter. The poet, with some humiliation, which he endeavored to conceal beneath an affectation of wounded dignity, commenced rolling up his manuscript, not before a splash of wine from a carelessly filled flagon had soiled the fair-written characters. More flasks were placed upon the table by ready and obedient hands—and from that moment the real entertainment of the evening commenced.

Faster than any of his guests, as though care could be the better drowned by frequent libations, Sergius now filled and refilled his flagon; and though the repeated draughts may not have brought forgetfulness, yet, what was the nearest thing, they produced reckless indifference. No longer should the cloud which he had thus suddenly swept away from his brow be suffered to remain. Was he not master in his own house? If woman deceives, was that a reason why man should mourn and grow gray with melancholy? What though a random thought might at times intrude, of one who, in the next room, with her head against the wall, lay in a half stupor, listening to the ring of goblets and the loud laugh and jest? Had she not brought it all upon herself? He would fill up again, and think no more about it! And still, obedient to his directing tone, the guests followed him with more and more unbridled license, until the hall rang with merriment as it had never rung before.

Then, of course, came the throwing of dice, which, at that time, were as essential a concomitant of a roystering party as, in later centuries, cards became. Nor were these the least attraction of the feasts of Sergius; for though the excellence of his viands and wines was proverbial, the ease with which he could be despoiled at the gambling table was not less so. Already he was known to have seriously crippled his heritage by continued reverses, springing from united ill luck and want of skill; but it was as well understood that much still remained. And then, as now, the morality of gambling was of a most questionable character—invited guests not thinking it discreditable to unite in any combinations for the purpose of better pillaging their host. This seemed now the general purpose; for, leaving each other in comparative freedom from attack, they came forward one by one and pitted their purses, great and small, against Sergius, who sat pouring down wine and shaking the dicebox, while he called each by name, and contended against him. The usual result followed; for, whether owing to secret signs among the players, or to superior skill, the current of gold flowed but one way, from the host to his guests. For a while he bore the continued ill luck with undiminished gaiety, deeming that in meeting their united prowess he was doing a brave thing, and that, whatever befell him, he should remember that in character of host he must consent to suffer. But at length he began to realize that his losses had been carried far enough. He had never suffered so severely in any one evening before. Even his duty to them as their host did not demand that he should completely ruin himself, and he began to suspect that he had half done so already. With a hoarse laugh he pushed the dice away, and arose.

"Enough—quite enough for one night," he exclaimed. "I have no more gold; nor, if I had, could I dare to continue, with this ill run against me. Perhaps after another campaign I may meet you again, and take my revenge; which, if the Fates are just, must one day or another be allotted me. But not now."

He thought that he was firm in his refusal, but his guests had not yet done with him. It needed but gentle violence to push him back again upon his couch, and to replace the dicebox in his hand.

"Art weary, or afraid to continue?" said the prætorian captain. "Well, let there be one more main between us, and then we will end it all. Listen! I have won this night two hundred sestertia. What is the worth of that quarry of yours to the south of the Porta Triumphalis?"

"Three hundred sestertia—not less," responded Sergius.

"Nay, as much as that?" rejoined the captain, carelessly throwing down his own dice. "Then it is useless to propose what I was about to. I had thought that as the quarry had been well worked already, and was now overrun with fugitive slaves and Nazarenes, and the like, to ferret out whom would require half a legion, I could offer to put the two hundred sestertia against it, so that you might chance to win them back. But it is of little consequence."

Sergius sat for the moment nervously drumming upon the table. He knew that the other was purposely disparaging the property and trying to tempt him into an unequal stake; and yet he suffered himself to be tempted. The luck might this time be with him. It were worth while to try it, at least. If he lost, it would be but one more buffet of fortune. And if he won, how easily would those two hundred sestertia have been regained, and what a triumph over the one who had enticed him! And therefore they threw—five times apiece; and after a moment of breathless excitement, the play was decided in favor of the captain.

"The quarry is mine, therefore," he said, endeavoring to

assume a nonchalant air of indifference. "Would you still win it back, Sergius? And the sestertia also? Well, there is that vineyard of yours on the slope of Tivoli, which—"

"Stay!" exclaimed the proconsul Sardesus, who, of all the party, had not as yet touched the dicebox. "Let this be enough. Will you plunder him entirely? Have you no regard for my rights over him? Do you not know that to-morrow, at the amphitheatre, Sergius and I are to match gladiators against each other for a heavy wager, and that I expect to win? How, then, will I get this money, if you now strip him of all that he owns?"

Probably the proconsul felt no fear about collecting what he might win, and spoke jestingly, and with the sole intention of putting a stop to a system of pillage which seemed to him already too flagrant and unscrupulous. But his words were too plain spoken not to give offence at any time, more particularly now that all present were heated with excitement; and the usual consequence of disinterested interference ensued. The other guests, in no measured language, began to mutter their displeasure at the insinuations against themselves; while the host, for whose benefit the interruption had been intended, resented it most strongly of all. He needed no counsel, but was well able to take care of himself, he intimated. And he remembered that he had entered into some sort of a wager about the result of a gladiatorial combat, and he had supposed that no one would have doubted his ability to pay all that he might lose therein. It was proper, at least, to wait until there had been some precedent of the kind proved against him. No one, so far, had found him wanting. And the like.

"And yet," he continued, as after a moment of reflection he began to realize the value of the wager, and how inconvenient it would be to lose, and that he had not yet succeeded in making any preparation for the contest, "when I tell you that I have not yet found a gladiator to my mind, you will not force this match upon me to-morrow? You will forbear that advantage, and will consent to postpone our trial to another time?"

The proconsul shrugged his shoulders.

"Was it in the bond," he said, "that one should await the convenience of the other? Has there not been time enough for each to procure his man? This wager was made between us months ago, Sergius—before even you went into the East."

"And it was while I was there," exclaimed Sergius eagerly, "that I found my man—a Rhodian, with the forehead, neck, and sinews of a bull. He could have hugged a bull to death, almost. Having him, I felt safe, for whom could you obtain to stand up against him? But in an evil hour, not over a month ago, this play-actor here—this Bassus—by a stupid trick gained him from me. What, then, have I been able to do for myself since? I have sought far and near to replace him, but without success; and had made up my mind, if you would not postpone the trial, to pay up the forfeit for not appearing, and think no more about it. But, by the gods! I will, even at this late hour, make one more attempt. Harkee, Bassus! Whenever I have asked you about this Rhodian, you have said that you have sold him; and, for some low reason, you have refused to tell who owns him now. Tell me, now, to whom you sold him, so that I can purchase him at once ? Tell me, I say; or there will be blood between us!"

"What can he say," interrupted the proconsul, "but that he sold his Rhodian to me, the day thereafter? You do well to praise him, Sergius. Never have I seen such a creature of brawn and muscle. And with the training I have given him, who, indeed, could overcome him? You will see him to-morrow, in the arena. You will see how he will crush in the ribs of your gladiator, like an egg-shell."

Sergius gave vent to a groan of mingled rage and despair.

"And you will not postpone this trial?" he said. "Will you, then, take up with an offer to play off that Rhodian against ten of my slaves? No? Against twenty, then? What else will tempt you? Ah, you may think that I have but little to offer to play against you, but it is not so. I have no gold left, and my last quarry is gone. But I have my vineyards and slaves in plenty. What say you, therefore?"

"Tush! Beseech him not!" interrupted Emilius, to whom the mention of vineyards and slaves gave intimation of further spoils. "Do you not see that he shakes his head? And do you not know his obstinacy? You could not move him now were you to pay him in full the amount of the forfeit. It is not the gold that he longer cares for, but the chance to distinguish himself by the exhibition of the slave of greatest strength and prowess. So let that matter go for settled. Rather strive, in some other manner, to win the money with which to pay your forfeit. This, with good luck, you may do—a little here and a little there—who knows? Perhaps even I can help you. Have I not won fifty sestertia from you? I will now wager it back against a slave."

"Against any slave?"

"By Bacchus, no! I have enough of ordinary captives to suit me, and care but little for any accession to the rabble of them. But you have one whom I covet—a Greek of fair appearance and pleasing manners—fit not for the camp or the quarries, but of some value as a page or cupbearer. It was but lately that I saw him, writing at your wife's dictation, and I wished for him at once. Shall we play for him?"

"No! a thousand times, no!" exclaimed Sergius, striking the table so heavily with his open hand that the dice danced and the flagons shook. "Were you to offer me thrice his value—to pay off my forfeit to Sardesus to the last sestertium—to gain me back my quarry and my vineyards—all that I have lost—I would not give up that slave. My purpose is sweeter to me than all the gold you could offer, and I will not be cheated out of it. That slave dies to-morrow in the amphitheatre—between the lion's jaws!"

"Dies? In the arena?" was the astonished exclamation.

"Is there aught wonderful in that?" Sergius fiercely cried. "Have you never before known such a thing as a master giving up his slave for the public amusement? And let no man ask me why I do it. It may be that I wish revenge, hating him too much to let him live. It may be that I seek to be a benefactor like others, and furnish entertainment to the populace at my own expense. It is sufficient that I choose it. Will not any other slave answer, Emilius?"

"Nay, no other will do," remarked the poet, throwing himself carelessly back, with the air of one dismissing a fruitless subject from his mind. "This was the only one whom I coveted. For any other I would not care to shake the dicebox three times, though I might feel sure to win."

"Will you offer the same to me, Sergius?" eagerly cried the comedian. "I also have won heavily from you. Will you play any other slave than this page against fifty sestertia?"

For his only answer, Sergius seized the dice, and began impatiently to rattle them. The eyes of Bassus sparkled with anticipated victory.

"You hear?" he cried, to all around him. "Against my fifty sestertia he will stake any of his slaves excepting this Greek page?"

"They all hear the terms," retorted Sergius. "Now throw!"

"Whether male or female?" continued Bassus, still looking around to see that all understood.

"Are they fools? Can they not hear? Will you throw or not?" shouted Sergius.

In a wild delirium of excitement, the comedian began the game, and in a few minutes it was concluded. Then he leaped from his couch, crying out :

"I have won! And there can be no dispute now! You

all heard that he gave the choice of his slaves, whether male or female?"

"Fool!" sneered Sergius, throwing himself back, "what dispute can there be? Do you think that I would deny my word? And do you suppose I did not know your aims, cunningly as you may think you veiled them? Would I have given up Leta to you, if she had been of any further value to myself? By the gods! had you waited a while, I do not know but what I would have made her a present to you; not, however, to oblige you, but to punish her!"

The comedian listened in chopfallen amazement. Already it seemed to him that his prize had lost half its value.

"Be at rest, though," Sergius continued, in a contemptuous tone. "I have merely tired of her, that is all. Her eyes are as bright and her voice as silvery as ever. She may not ever come to love you much, but she will have the wit to pretend that she does; and if she makes you believe her—as you doubtless will—it will be all the same thing to you. Who knows, too, with what zeal she may worm herself into your affection, under the guidance of her ambition? For, that she has ambition, you will soon discover. By Bacchus! since you have no wife or household to fetter your fancies, it would not surprise me were you to succumb to her wiles, and to make of her your wife. You may recline there and smile with incredulity; but such things have been done before this, and by men who would not condescend to look upon one in your poor station. Yes, I will wager that, in the end, you will make of her your wife. Well, it would be no harm to you. She will then deceive you, of course; but what of that? Have not better men submitted to that inevitable lot? Yes, she will deceive you ; and then will smile upon you, and you will believe her word, and be again deceived. But you will have only yourself to blame for it. I have warned you in advance."

CHAPTER XV.

As the shouts of laughter elicited by the host s remark rang through the hall, drowning the muttered response of the comedian, Leta glided softly and rapidly from behind the screen of tapestry which veiled the open doorway. There, crouching out of sight, she had remained concealed for the last hour—watching the revellers through a crevice in the needlework, and vainly hoping, either in the words or face of Sergius, to detect some tone or expression indicative of regretful thought or recollection of herself When at last her name had been mentioned, for a moment she had eagerly held her breath, lest she might lose one syllable from which an augury of her fate could be drawn. Then, repressing, with a violent effort, the cry of despair which rose to her lips, upon hearing herself thus coolly and disdainfully surrendered as the stake of a game of dice, and with less apparent regret than would have been felt for the loss of a single gold piece, she drew the fold of her dress closely about her and passed out.

Out through the antechamber—down the stairway—and into the central court; no other purpose guiding her footsteps than that of finding some place where she could reflect, without disturbance, upon the fate before her. In that heated hall she must have died; but it might be that in the cool, open air, she could conquer the delirium which threatened to overwnelm her, and could thus regain her self-control. If only for five minutes, it might be well. With her quick energy and power of decision, even five minutes of cool, deliberate counsel with herself might suffice to shape and direct her whole future life.

Hardly realizing how she had come there, she found herself sitting upon the coping of the courtyard fountain. The night was dark, for thick clouds shut out the gleam of moon and stars. No one could see her, nor was it an hour when any one was likely to be near. From one end to the other the court was deserted, except by herself. No light, other than the faint glow from the windows of the banquet hall upon the story above her. No sound beyond the sullen splash of the water falling into the marble basin of the fountain. There was now but little to interfere with deliberate reflection.

What demon had possessed the Fates that they should have brought this lot upon her? It could not be the destiny which had been marked out for her from the first. That had been a different one, she was sure. Her instinct had whispered peace and success to her. Such were the blessings which should have been unravelled for her from off the twirling spindle ; but some malignant spirit must have substituted another person's deserved condemnation in place of her more kindly lot.

That she had failed in attaining the grand end of her desires was not, of itself, the utmost of her misfortune. She had aimed high, because it was as easy to do that as to accept a lower object of ambition. She had taken her course, believing that all things are possible to the energetic and daring, but at the same time fully realizing the chances of failure. But to fail had simply seemed to her to remain where she was, instead of ascending higher—to miss becoming the wife of the imperator, but to continue, as before, the main guide and direction of his thoughts, impulses, and affections.

And now, without previous token or warning, had come upon her the terrible realization that she had not only gained nothing, but had lost all, and that the fatal chance which had fettered her schemes, had also led to her further degradation. Thrown aside like a broken toy—with a jeering confession that she had wearied her possessor—with a cool, heartless criticism upon her character, and with cruel prophecies about her future—gambled for with one whose sight filled her with abhorrence—and, when won, made over to him as a bone is tossed to a dog—what more bitterness could be heaped upon her?

But there was now no use in mourning about the past. What had been done could not be altered. Nor could she disguise from herself the impossibility of ever regaining her former position and influence. Those had passed away forever. She must now look to the future alone, and endeavor so to shape its course as to afford herself some relief from its terrors. Possibly there might yet be found a way of escape.

Should she try to fly? That, she knew, could not be done—at least, alone. The world was wide, but the arm of the imperial police was long; and though she might, for a little while, wander purposelessly hither and thither, yet before many hours the well-directed efforts of a pursuer would be sure to arrest her. She could die—for in every place death is within reach of the resolute; but she did not wish to die. For one instant, indeed, she thought of the Tiber, and the peace which might be found beneath its flow —but only for an instant. And she almost thanked the gods in her heart that it had not yet gone so far with her as that.

Burying her face in her hands, she sat for a moment, endeavoring to abstract her thoughts from all outward objects, so as the more readily to determine what course to adopt. But for a while it seemed as though it was impossible for her to fix her mind aright. Each instant some intruding trifle interfered to distract her attention from the only great object which now should claim it. A long-forgotten incident of the past would come into her mind—or perhaps some queer conceit which at the time had caused laughter. She did not laugh now, but none the less would she find herself revolving the merits of the speech or action. Then, the soft fall of the water into the fountain basin annoyed her, and it occurred to her that it might be this which prevented undivided reflection. Stooping over, therefore, and feeling along the edge of the basin, she found the vent of the pipes, and stopped the flow. At once the light stream began to diminish and die away, until in a moment the water was at rest, except for the few laggard drops which one by one rolled off the polished shoulders of the bronze figures. These gradually all trickled down, and then it seemed as though at last there must be silence. But the murmur of the evening breeze among the trees intervened; and, far more exasperating than all, she could now hear the bursts of merriment which rang out from the banqueting room overhead. Therefore, once more putting her hand into the basin, she turned on the flow, and the gentle stream again sprang from the upstretched beak of the stork and fell down, deadening all lesser sounds.

Then Leta looked up at the sky, overspread with its thick pall of clouds, and wondered vacantly whether there would be rain upon the morrow; and if so, whether the games appointed for the new amphitheatre would take place. But she recovered herself with a start, and again buried her face in her hands. What were games and combats of that kind to her? She was to enter upon a different kind of struggle. She must reflect—reflect!—and when she had reflected, must act!

For ten minutes she thus remained; and now, indeed, seemed to have gained the required concentration of thought. No outward sound disturbed her. Once a Nubian slave, who had heard the stoppage of the fountain's flow, emerged from beneath an archway, as though to examine into the difficulty. Finding that the water was still playing as usual, he imagined that he must have been mistaken, gave utterance to an oath in condemnation of his own stupidity, slowly walked around the basin, looked inquiringly at Leta, and, for the moment, made as though he would have accosted her—and then, changing his mind, withdrew and walked back silently into the house. Still she did not move.

At length, however, she raised her head and stood upright. Her eyes now shone with deep intensity of purpose, and her lips were firmly set. Something akin to a smile flickered around the corners of her mouth, betraying not pleasure, but satisfaction. She had evidently reflected to some purpose, and now the time for action had arrived.

"Strange that I should not have thought of it before," she murmured to herself. Then stepping under the archway which led from the courtyard into the palace, she reached up against the wall and took down two keys which hung there. Holding them tightly, so that they might not clink together, she glided along, past the fountain—through the clump of plane-trees—keeping as much as possible in the deeper shadows of arch and shrubbery—and so on along the whole length of the court, until she stood by the range of lower erections which bounded its further extremity. Then, fitting one of the keys into an iron door, she softly unlocked it.

Entering, she stood within a low stone cell. It was the prison-house of the palace, used for the reception of new slaves, and for the punishment of such others as gave offence. It was a long, narrow apartment, paved with stone and lighted by a single grated aperture set high in the wall upon the courtyard side. The place was of sufficient dimensions to hold fifty or sixty persons, but, in the present case, there was but one tenant—Cleotos. Not even a guard was with him, for the strength of the walls and the locks were considered amply sufficient to prevent escape.

Cleotos was sitting upon a stone bench, resting his head upon his right hand. At the opening of the door he looked up. He could not see who it was that entered, but the light tread and the faint rustle of a waving dress sufficiently indicated the sex. If it had been daylight, a flush might have been seen upon his face, for the thought flashed upon his mind that it might be Ænone herself coming to his assistance. But the first word undeceived him; and he let his head once more fall between the palms of his hands.

"Cleotos," whispered Leta, "it is I. I have come to set you free."

"It is right," he said, moodily. "All this I owe to you alone. It is fit that you should try to undo your work."

"Could I foresee that it would come to this?" she responded, attempting justification. "How was I to know that my trivial transgression would have ended so sorrowfully for you? But all that is easily mended. You have money, and a token which will identify you to the proper parties. There is yet time to reach Ostia before that ship can sail."

"How knew you that I had gold—or this signet-ring; or that there was a ship to sail from Ostia?" he exclaimed with sudden fierceness. "You, then, had been listening at the door! And having listened, you must have known with what innocence we spoke together! And yet, seeing all this, you called him to the spot and left him to let his eyes be deceived and his heart filled with bitter jealousy, and have played upon his passion by wicked misrepresentation, until you have succeeded in bringing ruin upon all about you! I see it all now, as clearly as though it were written upon a parchment rolled out before me! To think that the gods have beheld you doing this thing, and yet have not stricken you dead!"

"I have sinned," she murmured, seizing his hand and dending over, so that a ready tear rolled down upon it. He felt it fall, but moved not. Only a few days before, her tears would have softened him; but now his heart was hardened against her. He had found out that her nature was cruel and not easily moved to repentance, and that, if emotion was ever suffered to overcome her, it was tolerated solely for some crafty design. The falling tear, therefore, simply bade him be upon his guard against deceit, lest once again she might succeed in weaving her wiles about him. Or, if she really wept with repentance, he knew that it was not repentance for the sin itself, but rather for some baffled purpose.

"Go on," he simply said.

"I have sinned," she repeated, still clinging to his hands. "But, O Cleotos! when I offer to undo my work and set you free, you will surely forgive me?"

"Yes, it is right that you should repair the mischief you have caused," he repeated; "and I will avail myself of it. To-night, since you offer to set me free, and claim that you have the power to do so—to-night for Ostia; and then, then away forever from this ruthless land! But stay! What of our mistress? I will not go hence until I know that she is safe and well."

"She is well," responded Leta, fearful lest the truth might throw a new obstacle before her plans. "And all is again right between her lord and herself, for I have assured him of her innocence."

"Then, since this is so, there is no motive for me to tarry," he said. He believed her, and was satisfied; not that he esteemed her worthy of belief, but because it did not seem to him possible that such a matter as a grateful kiss upon a protecting hand could require much explanation. "I would like well once more to see her and bid her farewell, and utter my thanks for all her kindness; but to what purpose? I have done that already, and could do and say no more than I have already done and said. There remains, therefore, nothing more than to fulfil her commands, and return to my native home. But tell her, Leta, that my last thought was for her, and that her memory will ever live in my heart."

"I cannot tell her this," slowly murmured Leta, "for I shall not see her again. I—I go with you."

Cleotos listened for a moment in perplexed wonderment, and then, for his sole answer, dropped her hand and turned away. She understood him as well as though he had spoken the words of refusal.

"You will not take me with you, then; is it not so?" she said. "Some nice point of pride, or some feeling of fancied wrong, or craving for revenge, or, perhaps, love for another person, tells you now to separate yourself from me! And yet you loved me once. This, then, is man's promised faith!"

"You dare to talk to me of faith and broken vows!" he exclaimed, after a moment of speechless amazement at her hardiness in advancing such a plea. "You, who for weeks have treated me with scorn and indifference—who have plotted against me, until my life itself has been brought into danger—who, apart from all that, cast me off when first we met in Rome, telling me then that I was and could be nothing to you, yes, even that our association from the first had been a mistake and a wrong! Yes, Leta, there was a time when I truly loved you, as man had never then done, or since, or ever will again; but impute not to me the blame that I cannot do so now."

"I was to blame," she said; and it seemed that this night must be a night of confession for her, in so few things could she justify herself by denial or argument. "I acknowledge my fault, and how my heart has been drawn from you by some delusion, as powerful and resistless as though the result of magic. But when I confess it freely, and tell you how I now see my duty and my heart more clearly, as though a veil of error had been drawn away, and when, after all, I find no forgiveness in your heart, said I not truly that man's faith cannot be trusted? Am I not the same Leta as of old?"

"The same as of old?" he exclaimed. "Can you look earnestly and truthfully into your soul, and yet avow that you are the pure-hearted girl who roamed hand, in hand with me only a year ago, in our native isle, content to have no ambition except that of living a humble life with me? And now, with your simple tastes and desires swept away—with your soul buried beneath a love of material pleasures as under a lava crust—wrapt up in longing for Rome's most sinful, artificial excesses—having, for gold or position or power or ambition, or what not, so long as it was not for love, given yourself up a willing victim to a heartless master—do you dare, after this, to talk to me of love, and call yourself the same?"

"And are you one of those who believe that there can be no forgiveness for repentant woman?"

"Of forgiveness, all that can be desired; but of forgetfulness, none. There is one thing that no man can forget; and were I to repulse the admonitions of my judgment, and strive to pass that thing by, who would sooner scorn me than yourself? Let all this end. Know that I love you not, and could never love you again. Your scorn, indifference, and deceit have long ago crushed from my heart all the love it once held. Know further, that if I did still love you, my pride would condemn the feeling, and I would never rest until I had destroyed it, even were it necessary to destroy myself rather than to yield."

"These are brave words, indeed!" she exclaimed, taunted by his rebuke into a departure from her assumption of affection. "But they better suit the freeman upon his own mountain-side than the slave in his cell. Samos is still afar off. The road from here to Ostia has not yet been traversed by you in safety. Even this door between you and the open street has not been thrown back. And yet you dare to taunt me, knowing that I hold in my hand the key, and, by withdrawing it, can take away all hope from you. Do you realize what will be your fate if you remain here—how that on the morrow the lions and leopards of the amphitheatre will quarrel over your scattered limbs?"

"Is this a threat?" he cried. "Is it to assure me that if I do not give my love where my honor tells me it should not be given, I must surely die? So, then, let it be. I accept the doom. One year ago, I would have cheerfully fought in the arena for your faintest smile. Now I would rather die there than have your sullied love forced upon me."

Without another word he sat down again upon the stone bench. Even in that darkness she could note how resolute was his expression, how firm and unyielding his attitude. She had roused his nature as she had never seen it before. She had not believed that a spirit which she had been accustomed to look upon as so much inferior in strength to her own, could show such unflinching determination; and for the moment she stood admiring him, and wondering whether, if he had always acted like that, he might not have bound her soul to his own and kept her to himself through all temptation and trial. Then, taking the other key, she unlocked the door in the rear wall of the cell, and threw it open. The narrow street behind the court was before him, and he was free to go.

"I meant it not for a threat," she said. "However low I may sink, I have not yet reached the pass of wishing to purchase or beg for affection. Why I spoke thus, I know not. It may be that I thought some gratitude might be due me for rescuing you. But I cannot tell what I thought. Or it might have been that words were necessary for me, and that I used the first that came. But let that pass. Know only that your safety lies before you, and that it is in your power to grasp it. And now, farewell. You leave me drifting upon a downward course, Cleotos. Sometimes, perhaps, when another person is at your side, making your life far happier than I could have made it, you will think kindly of me."

"I think kindly of you now, Leta," he said. "Whatever love I can give, apart from the love which I once asked you to accept, is yours. In every thing that brotherly affection can bestow, there will be no limit to my care and interest for you. Nay, more, you shall now go away from hence with me ; and though I cannot promise more than a brother's love, yet with that for your guide and protection, you can reach your native home in peace and security, and there work out whatever repentance you may have here begun."

"And when we are there, and those who have known us begin to ask why, when Cleotos has brought Leta back in safety, he regards her only as a sister and a friend, and otherwise remains sternly apart from her, what answer can be given which will not raise suspicion and scorn, and make my life a burden to me? No, Cleotos, it cannot be. Cruel as my lot may be here, I have only myself to answer for it, and it is easier to hide myself from notice in this whirl of sin and passion than if at home again. And whatever may henceforth happen to me, the Fates are surely most to blame. How can one avoid his destiny?"

"The Fates do not carve out our destiny," he said. "They simply carry into relentless effect the judgments which our own passions and weaknesses have pronounced upon ourselves. O Leta! have you considered what you are resolved upon encountering? Do you not know that some day this master of yours will tire of you, and fling you to a friend of his—a soldier, actor, or what not— that as the years run on and your beauty fades, you will fall lower and lower? Have not thousands like yourself thus gone on, until at last, becoming old and worthless, they are left to die alone upon some island in the Tiber? Pray that you may die a better death than that!"

"It is a sad picture," she answered. "It is not merely possible, but also probable. I acknowledge it all. And yet, if I saw it all unrolled before me as my certain doom, I do not know that I would try to shun it. Already the glitter of this world has changed my soul from what it was, and I am now too feeble of purpose to spend long years in retrieving the errors of the past. There came into my heart a thought—a selfish thought—that you might forget what has gone before; and then it seemed that I might succeed in winning back my peace, and so shun the fate which lies before me. But you cannot forget. I blame you not; you are right. You have never spoken more truly than when you said that I would have despised you if you had yielded. Therefore, that hope is gone; and now I must submit to the destiny which is coming upon me."

"But, Leta, only strive to think that—"

"Nay, what is the use? Rather let me throw all regrets away, and strive not to think at all. Why not yield with a pleasant grace to the current, when we know that in the end, struggle as we may, it will surely sweep us under?"

"Leta—dear Leta—"

"Not a word, dear Cleotos; it must not be. From this hour I banish all human affections from my heart, as I banish all hope. Could you remain here, you would see how relentless and fierce my nature will grow. Plots and schemes shall now be my amusement; for if I must be destroyed, others shall fall with me. This must be the last tender impulse of my life. I know not why it is, but I could now really weep. Cleotos, forgive me! I came hither, loving you not, but hoping to beguile you into receiving me again. I have failed, and I ought to hate you for it; and yet I almost love you instead. It is strange, is it not?"

"But, Leta—"

"How my heart now feels soft and tender with our recollections of other days! Do you remember, Cleotos, how once, when children, we went together and stole the grapes from Eminides' vine? And how, when he would have beaten you, I stood before you, and prevented him? Who would then have thought that, in a few years, we should be here in Rome—slaves, and parting forever? We shall never again together see Eminides' vineyard, shall we?"

"O Leta—my sister—"

"There, there; speak not, but go at once, for some one comes near. Tarry no longer. If at home they ask after me, tell them I am dead. Farewell, dear Cleotos. Kiss me good-by. Do not grudge me that, at least. And may the gods bless you!"

He would still have spoken, would have claimed a minute to plead with her and try to induce her to leave the path she was pursuing, and go with him. But at that instant the voice of some one approaching sounded louder, and the tones of Sergius could be distinguished as he tried to troll forth the catch of a drinking melody. There was no time to lose. With a farewell pressure of her arm about Cleotos' neck, Leta pushed him through the aperture into the dark back street; and then, leaving the keys in the locks, turned again into the garden, and fled towards the house.

CHAPTER XVI.

GLIDING softly through the shrubbery, and beneath one of the side colonnades, Leta gained the house unperceived, passing Sergius, who loitered where she had been sitting, upon the coping of the fountain basin. His friends had departed, bearing away with them his gold and much else that was of value ; and he, with the consciousness of evil besetting him on every side, had morbidly wandered out to try if in the cool air he could compose his thoughts to sobriety. As he sat rocking to and fro, and humming to himself broken snatches of song, Leta stood under one of the arches of the court, glowering at him, and half hoping that he would lose his balance and fall into the water behind. It was not deep enough to drown him, but if it had been, she felt in no mood to rescue him. In a few moments, however, the fresh breeze partially dissipating the fumes of the wine which he had drunk, somewhat revived him ; making him more clearly conscious of his misfortunes, indeed, but engendering in him, for the instant, a new and calmer state of feeling, which was not sobriety, but which differed from either his former careless recklessness or maddening ferocity. And in this new phase of mind, he sat and revolved and re-revolved, in ever-recurring sequence, the things that had befallen him, and his changed position in the world.

Alone now,—for she, Ænone, had left him. Left him for a stripling of a slave—a mere creature from the public market. What was the loss of gold and jewels and quarries to this! And how could he ever hold up his head again, with this heavy shame upon it! For there could be no doubt ;—alas! no. Had he not seen her press a kiss upon the slave's forehead? Had she not tenderly raised the menial's head upon her knee with caressing pity? And, throughout all, had she attempted one word of justification? Yes,—alone in the world now, with no one to love or care for him! For she must be put away from him forever; she must never call him husband more. That was a certain thing. But yet—and a kindly gleam came into his face for the moment—even though guilty she might not be thoroughly and utterly corrupt. If he could, at least, believe that she had been sorely tempted—if he could only, for the sake of past memories, learn to pity her, rather than to hate! And this became now the tenor of his thoughts. In his deep reflection of a few hours before, he had tried to believe that she was innocent. Now, circumstances of suspicion had so overwhelmed her, that he could not think her innocent; but he could have wished to believe her less guilty, and thereby have cherished a kindly feeling towards her.

Rising up, and now for the first time seeing Leta, as she still stood under the archway and watched him, he tottered towards her; and, incited by this new impulse of generous feeling, he pleaded to her—humbling his pride, indeed, but in all else, whether in word or action, clothing himself with the graceful dignity of true and earnest manliness.

"Tell me," he said, "whether you know aught about her

which can calm my soul and give me the right to think better of her. You cannot make me believe that she is innocent—I do not ask it of you. That hope is past forever. But it may be that you can reveal more than you have yet mentioned to me. You have watched her, I know. Perhaps, therefore, you can tell me that she struggled long with herself before she abandoned me. Even that assurance will help me to think more pityingly of her. Remember that there was a time when I loved her; and, for the sake of that time, help me to feel and act generously towards her."

As Leta gazed upon him, and saw how his late imperiousness had given place to earnest, sorrowful entreaty, she hesitated for the moment how to answer him. There is, perhaps, a latent sympathy in the hardest heart; and despite her resolve to become at once lost and unpitying, some sparks of tender feeling, kindled into life by her parting with Cleotos, yet glimmered in her breast. Cleotos having gone away, she felt strangely lonesome. Little as she had regarded him when present, it now seemed as though, in separating from him, she had lost a portion of her own being. Certainly with him had departed the last link that bound her to her native land; and though she never expected to return thither, yet it was not pleasant to feel that she had been cut asunder from all possibility of it. Now, for the moment, she was in the mood to look around her for a friend to lean upon; and it might be that she could find that friend in Sergius, if she would consent to let her vengeance sleep, and would forbear to pursue him with further machinations. His love, to be sure, was gone from her, never to be restored ; but, after all, might it not be better to retain his friendship than to incur his hate? And if she were now to make full disclosure of the past, and ask his pardon, who could estimate the possible limits of the forgiveness and generosity which, in his newly found happiness, he might extend to her? And then, now that her plans had failed, what need of inflicting further misery upon those who, in their former trust, had lavished kindnesses upon her? And once more her thoughts reverted to Cleotos ; and with that feeling of utter loneliness sinking into her heart, and making her crave even to be thought well of by another, she reflected how that friend of her youth would not fail to ask the blessing of the gods upon her, if ever, in his native home, he were to hear that she had acted a generous part, and, by a few simple and easily spoken words, had swept away the web of mischief which her arts had woven.

"What can I say?" she exclaimed, hesitatingly, as she met the pleading look which Sergius fastened upon her.

"Say the best you can ; so, that, though I can never forgive her, I may not think more harshly of her than I ought. Can I forget that I loved her for years before I ever met yourself; and that, but for you, I might be loving her still? Can I forget that it was not for my own glory, but for hers, that I tore myself away from her and went to these late wars, hoping to win new honors, only that I might place them at her feet? Night after night, as I lay in my tent and gazed up at the sky, I thought of her alone, and how that the stars shone with equal light upon us both ; and I nerved my soul with new strength, to finish my task with diligence, so that I might the more quickly return to her side. And then, Leta, then it was that I met yourself; and how sadly and basely I yielded to the fascinations you threw about me, you too well know. It was not love I felt for you; think it not. My passion for you was no more like the calm affection with which I had cherished her, than is the flame which devours the village like the moonlight which so softly falls upon and silvers yonder fountain. But, for all that, it has brought destruction upon me. And now—"

"And now, Sergius?"

"Now I am undone by reason of it. From the first moment your ensnaring glance met mine, I was undone, though I then knew it not. Then was my pure love for her obscured. Then, impelled by I know not what infernal spirit, I began my downward course of deceit, until at last I almost learned to hate her whom I had so much loved, and met her, at the end, with but a simulated affection; caring but little for her, indeed, but not—the gods be thanked!—so far gone in my selfish cruelty as to be able to wound her heart by open neglect in that hour of her joy. Whatever I may have done since then, that day, at least, her happiness was undimmed. How gladly would I now give up all the honors I have gained, if I could but restore the peace and quiet of the past! Remembering all this, Leta, and how much of this cruel wrong is due to you, can you not have pity? I know that she would never have been exposed to this temptation but for my own neglect of her, and but for the fact that you had ambitious purposes of your own to work out. Nay, I chide you not.

Let all that pass and be forgotten. I will be generous, and never mention it again, if you will only tell me how far your arts, rather than her own will, have led her astray. It cannot harm you now to freely utter every thing. The time for me to resent it is past. I have no further power over you, or the will to exercise it if I had."

A moment before, and she had been on the point of yielding to the unaccustomed pity that she began to feel, and so make full disclosure. But now, as, almost unconsciously to himself, Sergius spoke of her baffled hopes and vaguely hinted at her altered position towards himself—a change of which he believed her to be yet ignorant—her fount of mercy became instantly sealed up, and her nearly melted heart again turned to flint. Yes, she had almost forgotten her new destiny. But now at once appeared before her, with all the vividness of reality, the banquet hall, ringing with the shrill laughter of the heated revellers, as, with the dicebox, they decided her future fate. Like a flash the softened smile fled from her face, leaving only cold, vindictive defiance pictured there. And as Sergius, who had been led on from utterance to utterance by the increasing signs of compassion he read in her, saw the sudden and unaccountable change, he paused, in mingled wonderment and dismay; and, with the conviction that his hopes had failed him, he put off, in turn, his own softened mien, and glaring back defiance upon her, prepared for desperate struggle.

"You speak of my new ownership—of the actor Bassus?" she exclaimed.

"You know it, then?" cried he. "You have played the spy upon us?"

"Know it?" she repeated. "When, in your wild revelling, your raised voices told me how heedlessly you were bringing ruin upon yourself with the dice, would I have been any thing but a fool not to have remembered that I too, being your property, might pass away with the rest? Was it not fit, then, that I should have stolen to the screen and listened? You thought to keep it secret, perhaps, until Bassus should send to take me away from here; for you imagined that I might attempt escape. But you do not know me yet. Am I a child, to kick and scream, and waste my strength in unavailing strife against a fate that, in my heart, I feel must sooner or later be submitted to? Not long ago—it matters not how or when—I could have avoided it all, but would not. Now that I have sacrificed that chance, I will go to my doom with a smile upon my lips, whatever heaviness may be in my heart; for, having chosen my path, I will not shrink from following it. Thus much for myself. And as for you, who have tossed me one side to the first poor brute who has begged for me, and even at this instant have taunted me with the story of baffled hopes, does it seem becoming in you to appeal longer to me, as you have done, for comfort?"

No answer; but in the angry, heated glare with which he faced her, could be seen the new fury which was rising within him—all the more violent, perhaps, from the late calm that had possessed him.

"And yet, for the sake of the past, I might even be willing to comfort you, if it were possible," she continued, casting about in her mind for new tortures with which to rack him, and now suddenly struck with an inward joy, as her ever-ready invention came to her aid. "Yes, if I knew aught of good to tell, I would mention it, for the memory of other days. But how can I speak with truth, unless to recapitulate new deceits and wiles which she has practised upon you, and of which, may the gods be my witness! I would have told you before, but dared not? You say that you have never loved me, Sergius Vanno. It is well. But if you had done so, I would have been faithful to you to the end. You say that you loved her, and that, but for your own falsehood, she would not have strayed from you. Poor dupe! to believe that, for all that meek pale face of hers, she cannot resolve, and act, and mask her purposes as cunningly as any of the rest of her sex! Shall I tell you more? Do you dream that, while you have been revelling, she has been idly whimpering in her chamber? Had you watched outside with me, you might have known better. Look above your head, Sergius, to where the prison keys are wont to hang, and tell me where they are now!"

More from mechanical instinct than from any actual purpose of mind—for he did not, at the first instant, fully comprehend her meaning—Sergius followed the motion of her hand, and gazed at the wall above his head; then passed his fingers along until he touched the empty nail—then looked back inquiringly at her.

"The keys are gone, are they not?" she said. "Fool! to lock up one party to a fault, and yet let the other one go free! Do you suppose that during your carousing with your boon companions, she would fail to succor him for whose sake she has already lost so much?"

Still he gazed at Leta with a look of puzzled inquiry,

10

which now began, however, to be disturbed by an expression of painful doubt. Then suddenly, ascertaining that the keys were really gone, her meaning flashed upon him; and dropping his hand with a wrathful exclamation, he turned and strode into the palace. Not, perhaps, with full conviction of the truth of the suggestion so artfully arrayed before him. But he would at least prove its truth or falsity; and, with that suspicion fastened upon his bewildered and unreasoning mind, to doubt was almost to believe, and crossing the antechamber to Ænone's room, he burst in upon her.

She had fallen into a troubled sleep—lying dressed upon the outside of her couch, as, in her agony of mind, she had first thrown herself down. The unspent tears still trembled upon her eyelids. Beside her lay the little folded parchment which Cleotos had given her. She had taken it out to read, hoping, but scarcely believing, that she would now be able to experience the truth of what she had been told about the earnest words there written being divinely adapted to give peace to a troubled heart. But her sorrow was too deep to be healed by phrases whose spirit could, of necessity, be so imperfectly comprehended by her; and the writing had slipped unheeded from her light grasp.

As her husband now entered, she awoke and sat upright, in frightened attitude, not knowing what fate was about to befall her.

"Where is he? What have you done with him?" Sergius cried, seizing her by the arm.

She did not answer, not knowing, of course, wherefore

the question was put to her, or what it concerned. Yet, perceiving that she was again suspected of some act of which she was innocent, she would have asked for mercy and pardon, if time had been given her. But even that was denied her. Hardly, indeed, could she draw a breath, when she felt that a new thread was woven in the web of misconception which surrounded her. For, at that moment, her husband's eye fell upon the forgotten parchment; and picking it up, he opened it, gave one hasty look, and then tossed it aside. What need, now, of further proof? Was not that the slave's writing, recognizable at a glance? Words of love, of course! And she had gone to sleep fondly holding them in her hands, as a treasure from which she could not be parted for an instant. Words not freshly written, either, for the parchment was yellow and discolored. So much the worse, therefore; for did it not prove a course of long-continued deception? Could there be any doubt now? Yes, a long deceit. And this was she for whom, in his simplicity, he had but a moment before been framing excuses, in the effort to convince himself that her fault had been one of impulse, rather than of cool deliberation! This was she in whose behalf he had weakly lowered himself to plead to his own cast-off slave for extenuating evidences! And once more grasping her by the arm, he lifted her from the couch, and, followed by Leta, hurried her across the room into the outer hall, into the courtyard, past the fountain, and so onward until they stood before the prison-house. There, seeing the inner door open, the outer door swinging loosely inward, with the key yet remaining in its lock, and the captive fled, Sergius deemed her new crime fully proved, and again turned madly upon her.

"Where is he? What have you done with him? Am I to be thus balked of my vengeance? Is it to be endured that, while I entertain my friends, you should steal off so treacherously, and thus complete the dishonor you have brought upon me?"

"I have not—done dishonor—to my lord!" she gasped with difficulty, for she was almost speechless from the rapidity with which he had hurried her along, and his close grasp upon her arm pained her. "Let me but speak—I will explain—I know not how—"

"No falsehood—no pleadings to me!" he cried. "It will avail you nothing now. What more proof do I need? Is not the whole story written out plainly before my eyes? Have you not stolen away to release him, preferring his safety and favor to my honor or your own? If not, where is he? Escaped me, by the gods! Escaped me, after all! Fool that I have been, to leave those keys within your meddling reach!"

Overborne by his violence, not of words merely, but of gesture, Ænone had, little by little, shrunk from before him as he spoke, until she had unconsciously passed through the open doorway, and into the narrow street beyond. Leta and he still remained within the building, standing beside the swinging door. There was even now but a single pace between Ænone and himself, and it was scarcely likely that such a trifling distance could reassure her. It was more probably something in his tone or action which now gave her courage to meet his imputation. Whatever the nature of the inspiration, she now suddenly drew herself up, as though endued with new strength, and answered him with something of the same recklessness of spirit with which once before during that day she had cast aside all fear of misconstruction, and, with the sustaining consciousness of innocence and justice, had defied him.

"Escaped you?" she cried; "I thank the gods for it! I did not set him free, but I would have done so, had I known how. He was my friend—my brother. Would I have left him, do you think, to suffer torture and death for simple kindnesses to me, when, with one turn of a key, I could have released him? Would I let the memory of other days so completely pass from my mind as to—"

How, at that instant, happened the door to close? Was it owing to the wind, or to a skilful and concealed touch of Leta's hand, or to some unconscious pressure of Sergius against it? The cause matters little. It was enough that, of a sudden, the loosely hanging door swung round on its creaking hinges into its place, fastening itself securely with a spring-bolt as its edge touched the lintel, and leaving Ænone shut out alone in the dark street upon the other side.

Upon the instant, Sergius sprang forward to reopen the door. Convinced of her perfidy, and madly lashing himself into yet further fury with the consciousness of his wrongs, it was as yet not in his mind that even by accident such a forced separation as this should befall her. His hand was upon the bolt—in another second it would have been drawn back—when his further action was arrested by a few lowly uttered words of Leta.

Not spoken to him, for, in his present state of mind, he was more than ever morbidly jealous of any interference or attempted control, and would most surely have disregarded them. But spoken as though to herself, in a kind of whispered soliloquy, softly muttered, but yet with utterance sufficiently distinct to reach his watchful ear.

"Ah, she will not regard that," were the words, "for of course she will know where to rejoin him."

Sergius started as the new idea impressed itself upon him. Could this be true, indeed? Why not? Was it likely that the wife would have released the slave whom she loved, and not have told him where they could meet again? That, surely, would be too foolish an oversight, for it would be throwing away all the benefits attending the escape. It were hardly possible that any trust could have been reposed in the prospect of future chance interviews, for that would be but a slender hope to lean upon. In that boiling, seething world of Rome, now more than ever disturbed by the inroads of strangers eagerly looking forward to the excitements of the amphitheatre, it would be in vain to make even deliberate and careful search for a lost slave, unless some clew should be left behind. Yes, she must surely have that clew; and doubtless she purposed to use it as soon as daylight came. Let her go now, therefore. It were idle to call her back only for new flight in a few hours hence.

Still with his hand resting upon the bolt as these reflections passed through his mind, Sergius glanced keenly at Leta, as though possessed with some dim suspicion that she had meant her words to be overheard. Then, feeling reassured by her composed attitude, he turned away, muttered something to himself, the import of which she could not catch, dropped his hand from the undrawn bolt to his side, stood for a moment in a kind of maze of confusion, and finally left the prison, and staggered through the garden to the house.

CHAPTER XVII.

STUNNED and confused by her sudden exclusion, and naturally believing that it was the result of deliberate action upon her husband's part, Ænone now felt all her sudden inspiration of courage deserting her, and sank half fainting against the outside wall. For a moment it seemed to her like a dream. She could realize suspicion, harsh language, and even cruel treatment to a certain limit, for these were all within the scope of her late experience; but it was hard to comprehend this unlooked-for and apparently deliberate excess of degradation. But gradually the mist cleared away from her bewildered mind, and she recognized the reality of what had befallen her. Still, however, her thoughts could not at once grapple with the overwhelming sense of the indignity and suffering cast upon her. She could not doubt that she had been expelled from her lord's house—cast out unprotected and friendless in the midst of night, with undeserved reproaches. But, for all that, a delusive hope clung to her. He could not mean that this should last. It was but an impulse of sudden anger. He would repent of it in a moment, and would call upon her to return to him. He would shed tears of bitter shame, perhaps, and would beg that she would forgive him. And she would be foolish enough to do so, she felt, at the very first pleading word from him; though at the same time whispering that her own self-respect should prompt her to show more lasting resentment. If she thus easily forgot the past, what security could she have that, in some future transport of rage, he might not repeat the act? But for all that, she felt that she would weakly too soon forgive him.

Sliding her trembling hand down the damp wall, she found along its foot a ledge of stone more or less projecting in different sections, in accordance with the architectural requirements of the building. Seating herself upon the widest portion of this ledge, she now waited to hear the key again turned in the lock and the door swung open upon its creaking hinges, and to see loving arms extended with repentant words of self-reproach. Once or twice she fancied that she heard the key softly fitted into its place, but it was only the abrasion of two contiguous branches of a plane-tree overhead. Once again she felt certain that she heard the sound of persons approaching through the garden, but it was the voice of men in the street—two slaves coming around the corner and drawing near, speaking some harsh northern dialect which she knew not. As the men approached, she endeavored to shrink out of sight behind a perpendicular projection of the wall, and nearly succeeded. They had passed, indeed, before they noticed her. Then they turned and gazed curiously at her; and one of them made some remark, apparently of a jesting nature, for they both laughed. Then again they turned and moved on out of sight without attempting further molestation.

But the incident alarmed her, and caused her to realize yet more vividly than before the exceeding unprotectedness of her situation. These men had not sought to injure her, but how could she answer for the next who might approach? It was a lonely, dark street, narrow, and comparatively seldom used, and but little built upon, being mainly flanked by garden walls. Upon the side where she sat there were no buildings at all, excepting low prison-houses for slaves, similar to that belonging to the Vanno palace—for the street ran along an inner slope of the Cœlian Mount and parallel to the Triumphal Way, and thus naturally served as a rear boundary to the gardens of the palaces and villas which fronted upon the latter avenue. This very loneliness, therefore, added to her insecurity; for though it was possible that no one else might pass by for hours, there was the equal chance that if any one came with evil intent, she might be murdered before help could be summoned. And at a time when the broadest streets were never entirely safe even for armed men, a weak woman, with tempting jewelry upon her person, might well shudder at being left alone in a narrow alley.

Slowly and painfully—for the night was cool, and she had now been sitting long in one position—Ænone raised herself and stood up, looking hither and thither for some place of refuge. She had now waited more than an hour, and if her lord had been inclined to recall her from her exclusion, his repentance would scarcely have tarried so long.

His anger was generally fierce, but of short duration; could it be that in this case his sense of injury was so great as to make him more unreasoning than usual? Her heart sank yet lower with a new weight of despair; but again hope whispered alleviation. He had been drinking deeply—she said to herself—and had not clearly comprehended what he had done. And afterwards he had probably forgotten all about it, and had fallen off into sleep. Upon the morrow he would be himself again. Perhaps he would not then remember the outrage he had committed against her. Certainly his anger would not still burn when corrected by returning reason. She must therefore endeavor to gain access again to the palace, and there avoid his presence, until the morrow brought to him fresher reflection and a better inclination to listen to explanation.

And accordingly she commenced her departure for her hiding-place, and slowly crept along the blank flanking wall of the little street, hoping soon to gain the palace front. At first it seemed a very easy thing to do so. Though she had never before been in that portion of the city, she knew enough of its geography to feel certain that if she followed the street in either direction, she could not fail to come to some intersecting alley, through which she might reach the Triumphal Way. Once there, the route was familiar to her, and she could arrive at her home in a few minutes. But as she advanced, she found that what had appeared to be an easy stroll, seemed converted into a toilsome and perplexing journey. Confused and terrified, the coolness necessary to pursue in safety even so short a route began to fail her. At times she imagined that she heard strangers approaching, and then it became needful to conceal herself again, as well as she could, behind projections or in recesses of the wall. Then, when once more venturing out, the shadows of the wall itself or of neighboring buildings would terrify her into seeking other concealments. And once, after having resumed her course, she discovered that she had mistaken the direction, and was retracing her steps.

At last, after a journey of nearly an hour, during which she had only advanced as far as a resolute person might have gone in a few minutes, she reached an intersecting street leading to the Triumphal Way. It was a wider passage than that which she was leaving, and this fact added to her dismay. For though she had at first feared the narrower street for its loneliness, yet now that she had so far glided through it in safety, she had begun to feel somewhat reassured, and in turn dreaded the more open channels, since they would naturally be more frequented. It was, therefore, with new trepidation that, upon turning the corner, she saw, in the broader street before her, signs of movement and life. The street happened to be a favorite thoroughfare from the Triumphal Way, across the Cœlian Mount, and, in consequence, was never, perhaps, entirely deserted. Now that the whole city was throbbing with anticipations of the morrow's festivities, there were more persons wakeful and wandering about with feverish expectation than usual. Moreover, it was a street which abounded with drinking-shops, and these were now all open, in spite of the lateness of the hour, and appeared to be thronged with customers. One of these shops stood upon the corner where Ænone had halted. A faint light burned over the doorway to mark the locality; and through the open passage she could see a crowd of ill-conditioned, rough-looking men, appearing, in the dim light, more rough and uncouth than they really were. Here were mingled together artisans of the lower orders, slaves and professional gladiators, all drinking and singing together in close fraternity. For a moment Ænone paused and hesitated, not daring to pass on. If she could reach the further side without attracting observation, it would be but one step gained, for there were many other drinking-shops glimmering in the distance along the whole street, and each one had its special crowd of noisy customers. To escape one peril seemed only to run into another. Then, as she deliberated and alternately put her foot forward and withdrew it again in a fruitless attempt to muster courage to run the gauntlet, two men emerged from the wine-shop, and staggered towards her—a slave and a gladiator, linked arm in arm, and singing a wild song in discordant keys. Both appeared to be under the influence of wine, though in different degrees; for while the former had set no bounds to his license, the latter had somewhat restrained his propensities, in view of the demands upon his strength which the morrow's work would surely make. Seeing these men reel towards her, Ænone turned and fled, without knowing, or, for the moment, caring, in which direction she went. The men had not at first seen her, but, as they now caught sight of her flying figure, they set up a drunken whoop, and attempted to follow. All in vain; for ere they had advanced many paces, their weakened limbs betrayed them, and they sank powerless upon the ground, and, forgetting the pursuit, rolled over lovingly in each other's arms. Meanwhile, Ænone, not daring to look back, and not knowing that the chase had-ended, still fled in wild terror, until at last her breath failed her, and she tottered helplessly into the shade of the nearest wall.

She was now lost, indeed. How long she had been running, or in which direction, how many divergencies she had taken, or how many narrow alleys threaded, she knew not. She simply realized that she was in a portion of the city where she had never been before, and from which extrication seemed impossible, so dark and narrow and winding seemed the passages in every direction. Far narrower and darker, indeed, than the lane behind the palace, and without its protecting solitude. In place of high garden walls, the whole route seemed lined with miserable tenements, the refuge of the lowest of the Roman population. There, crowded together in close communication, were the rabble of poorer slaves and beggars, all equally marked with rags and filth.

In all this there was one comfort. However thronged the tenements along the side might be, the street itself seemed deserted, nor could Ænone any longer hear the sound of pursuit. That, at least, she had escaped, and now again she took partial courage as she reflected that with moderate caution she might yet be able to extricate herself. There must be some outlet to that neighborhood of squalid misery; and take whichever way she might, she could scarcely fail, at the end, to emerge into some more reputable region.

Again the sound of two persons approaching restrained her, and caused her to shrink into a corner until they might pass. Unlike the others, these men had not been drinking, but advanced gravely and steadily, with a slow, deliberate pace, indicative of weighty reflection. These, also, were slaves; and before they emerged into sight from the surrounding darkness, Ænone could distinctly mark the low, plotting whisper with which they spoke, occasionally rising, from excess of emotion, into a louder key. As they came opposite to her, they paused—not seeing her, but simply seeming to be arrested by the vehemence of their debate ; and again their words sank nearly into a whisper.

"Tell me why I should not do so?" hissed the nearest, a man of gigantic proportions and development of strength. "Why should I not leap out of the arena where these men place me to play a fool's part; and scrambling over the ranges of seats, plunge this dagger into his heart? Ye gods ! were I once to begin to clamber up, no force could stop me from reaching him, were he at the very topmost range ! And I will—why not ?"

"You would gain but an instant's revenge," said the other, striving to soothe him, "and you would lose—"

"What ? My life would you say ?" retorted the first. "I know it. I know well that before I could strike him thrice, I would myself be beaten down a corpse. But one blow from me would be sufficient for him. Ay, though I used not my knife at all, but only my hardened fist. Would it not be a fine revenge, say you, thus to kill him ? It was on account of my strength of arm that he laid toils for my capture, and for that alone he most valued me. Why not, then, prove its quality upon himself? With a single blow I could crush in his proud head like an egg-shell. Then let them kill me—I care not."

"And yet the life once lost by you cannot be gained again," responded the other.

"O feeble-minded !" said the first, with disdain. "Have

I ever so dearly cared for life that I should thus guard it at the expense of honor? While I was a free man, in my native Rhodes, with my wife and children around me, did I not then risk my life among the very first? And am I likely to value it the more now that I am a slave, with wife torn from me and sent I know not where, with children slain one by one, as the only means of capturing me, with the accursed livery of the arena placed upon me that I may administer to their gaping appetite for blood? Can all this make me love my life more than I have ever loved it before?"

"But wait—only wait. There will come a time—"

"Ay, ay; there will come a time. It is what all say, and will continue to say, and yet the time comes not. There is never any time like the present. All around me are thousands of men, once free and now chained into slavery—and chained, perhaps, more through their own indolence than by the power of their masters; and yet they lie supine, and call upon each other to wait! And to-morrow there will be a thousand such in the arena, and instead of rising up together in their strength, they will fight only with each other. What might not that thousand accomplish, were they to act together in brave and earnest revolt? What chance would a few hundred pampered prætorians have of staying the flood? There, seated in fancied security upon their benches, will be the emperor, the court, the nobles, and the most wealthy of the empire. In one hour of action, we could sweep these away like chaff, together with all else that is held most worthy of place and power in the whole empire! And yet these thousand slaves will not rise up together with me, and it will not be done!"

The head of the Hercules dropped upon his chest with a gesture of despair.

"You say truly," responded the other. "It will not be done, for they will not act with you. And what can you do alone?"

"Nothing—nothing; I see it all. I am powerless," murmured the first. "Well, I will be patient, and dissimulate. I will do as you request, Gorgo. I will restrain myself. As for this man—this imperator—why should I there wreak my vengeance upon him? It would only be giving to the rest of the people an unlooked-for sight—a newer pleasure, that is all. I will therefore act the part of a good and faithful slave—will kiss the rod held over me—and will duly serve my master by slaying my adversary, whoever he may be, and thus winning that store of gold pieces which have been laid out as the stake of my life. And then—then I will go home to my kennel and my bones. But this I swear, by the immortal gods! that I will follow this man from house to forum, wherever he may go, until I find a proper chance to strike him down in secret like a dog. You were right. I must not lose my life to kill him, when I can so easily slay him and yet live to slay other men as bad as he. My life is for other things. And when the time comes that I can raise the standard of insurrection, will you then—"

"Then I will be with you heart and soul forever, until our freedom is built up on the ruins of this accursed Rome!" cried the other, striking his hand responsively into the outstretched palm before him. And the two men again took up their walk, and passed on until they were swallowed up in the darkness and their voices, growing more and more indistinct, were finally hushed.

CHAPTER XVIII.

LISTENING intently for a moment longer until every sound of voice or footfall had died away, Ænone once more prepared to creep out from her shelter. Most fortunately for her peace, she had not heard all the words that had been spoken before her. But she knew that what she had listened to, was the complaint of two oppressed and overburdened victims of tyranny, bewailing their ill-deserved lot, and crying aloud for vengeance ; and to her other misery was now added the saddest of all emotions that can beset the human heart, the sense of growing disbelief in any thing good and pure and noble and worth living for in the world. Was it everywhere thus? Were the rich all purse-proud and cruel and wedded to arrogance and dissipation? Were the poor always to be cast down into abject hopelessness? Was the blight of slavery to rest forever upon the lives of thousands, until there was nothing left to them but despair or impotent struggling for impossible vengeance? Were truth and justice wholly banished from the world?

Again the narrow street resounded with approaching footsteps, and once more Ænone shrank back with terror into her corner. This time it was but one man ; and as he drew near, he commenced in a deep, harsh, broken voice, the chorus of a camp-song. Unmelodious as was the air and false the rendering, the notes struck upon Ænone's ear with a familiar expression that filled her heart with eager hope. That song, indeed, was no novelty. Whole legions had pealed it forth upon the Rhine and the Danube, and there was now scarcely a child in Rome who could not repeat a line or two of it. But still, with a vague expectation of identifying the singer, Ænone stood peering out from her shelter with eager attitude and quickened breath; and as, at the end of the opening strain, her eager ears detected a familiar false quaver, more excited grew her breathing. And at length, as the man staggering slowly along came into view from out of the surrounding darkness, she tottered forth in a transport of wild joy, and threw herself down before him.

"My father! You are here and I am saved!"

The centurion paused in stupid amazement. Indeed, he could not have passed on without stumbling over the half-fainting form at his feet. For the moment, startled with the sudden surprise, he could not collect his thoughts; for, in common with a large proportion of the population of the city, he had been festively celebrating the approaching games, and his ideas were somewhat confused and scattered. But, after leaning for a moment upon a short stick which he carried before him, he began somewhat to realize the position of matters.

By the brazen helmet of Mars!" he growled forth. "What is all this? You, and at this time of night alone? Speak, Ænone!"

"And Ænone spoke, clasping his knees as though asking pardon for being turned out of her home and losing her way. Then, when the centurion had heard her story, he swore all his strongest oaths in his very deepest tones and lifted her up.

"The dastardly caitiff!" he cried. "The double-dyed villain, worse than Jew or Nazarine! He shall suffer for this! Had you been one of his own miserable race, indeed, it would not have mattered so much, for men will get drunken at times, and will then do things which they will repent of when they are sober again. I myself did once turn out your mother for a night, by reason of some fancied wrong. Ay, and once, when overtaken in my cups, I slew my best friend. Such things will happen; and as your mother and my friend were no more than my equals, if they were even that, what I did was no disgrace to them. But to think of this man, indeed, daring to cast out from before him, in such insulting manner, a member of the house of Porthenus! Now may the gods strike him dead!"

"Nay, father, he is still—"

"Forbear! Still your husband, you would say! I know that old speech by heart, and how ready all you wives are to grant forgiveness. And if you were merely his equal in birth, it might be well, perhaps, to do so. But do you not perceive that in acting as he has done, he has not merely ill-treated you, but has insulted the house from which you have sprung? Ay, not only I, but all of the Portheni, if there should be any of them now left besides ourselves, must feel the indignity. And he shall die for it! By the gods! I will strike him to the heart with this dagger, won long centuries ago by the founder of our family, from a Carthaginian prince ; and I will leave it standing in the wound, so that all shall know how terribly any of the Portheni can resent an injury !"

"Nay, nay, my father ; for this time forego any thoughts of vengeance, and be content with taking me to my home again. It will turn out all a mistake, be assured that it will. Take me, therefore, back to my home, and I—"

"Back to the palace ?" thundered the centurion. "Would you have me to conduct you thither and suffer you to steal in at some low door, like a thief or the lover of a slave, and so appear before him on the morrow with a simper and smile on your lips, as if nothing had happened ? No! You shall this night repair to my own home ; and when the morrow comes, I will myself take you back to him in the full blaze of sunlight, and will force him on his knees to ask your pardon for this insult to yourself and family, and to beg, with tears, that you will consent to return to him."

"Let it be to your house, then, my father," said Ænone. "Anywhere, so long as I find rest and protection."

And clasping his arm to her breast, and feeling greatly comforted for all her troubles at finding herself once more under sure safeguard, she crept along at his side, ready to be guided by him in all future matters, in the full assurance that he would be kind to her after his rude manner, and that she need scarcely apprehend a rigid fulfilment of his terrible threats against her lord.

So, for a few moments, they passed along in silence—through that narrow lane into another, equally dark and desolate—thence into a third street, lined with wine-shops

—thence into still another, wider and fronted with neat villas—and so on, from turning to turning, through an apparently inextricable confusion of passage-ways, until suddenly the route before them opened wider and brighter and they stood in the broad area before the Colosseum.

Ænone could have clapped her hands for joy. Now, indeed, did she once more begin to recognize familiar objects. The very same side of the great amphitheatre upon which she had gazed for so many months from her window, was towards her. Looking up, she could even mark, by the gleam of torches carried by some laborers below, the broken cornice at the corner of one of the lower arches; and she remembered how she had witnessed the cruel chastisement of the slave whose awkward management, while hoisting a stone to one of the upper tiers, had led to the mischief. Upon the further hill-slope was the house of the Cæsars, stretching across and down into the valley. Further along was the Forum, with its graceful lines of stairways and column-crowned terraces. And at her left, in distant perspective, stretched the Triumphal Way. She could almost see where stood her own house; yes, she could quite see it, for, at that moment, the full moon looked out through a broken rift in the clouds and sent down a shimmer of silver light, brightening up the arches of the amphitheatre, the gilded roof of the Cæsars' palace, and the fluted columns of the Forum, and, at the same time, bringing out into full distinctness the two marble fawns which stood, one on each side, at the gateway of the Vanno mansion. To have so much that was familiar to her revealed so suddenly, was as cheering as the sight of land to the lost and bewildered mariner; and for the moment Ænone felt even happy.

"My father, I know now where we are. We are nearly home. We have only to go down this passage to the street of Fabius, and then—"

"And then," muttered the centurion, "we shall be home. But do you think, after all, that it will be best to go on to my house, instead of stopping at once at your own?"

Ænone gazed at him with bewilderment, and her heart sank within her. Many times ere this she had been forced to recognize the readiness with which her father could surrender high and noble resolves, under the stimulant of base policy; and she now too surely gathered from his tone of voice and the sidelong manner with which he glanced at her, and even from his unconsciously meanly crouching attitude, that he was once more about to betray his better nature. In fact, the centurion had already begun to repent of his first sudden outburst of angry pride; and while they had been walking side by side so silently together, and she had been gaining new courage and confidence, he had been slowly reasoning his kindly impulses away and allowing all the selfishness of his nature to regain its control. To be sure, Ænone had been wronged—he reflected—but not a day ever passed during which such matters did not occur, and it were best not to be too morbidly sensitive about them. The imperator had been drinking deeply; what then? Why, on the morrow he would be sober again and would forget all about it. The house of Vanno was beneath the house of Porthenus, to be sure; but then it had lands, and palaces, and slaves by the hundred, while the Portheni had nothing to boast of but their past grandeur, and even this now seemed to be forgotten by all but themselves. They could not live on these recollections alone. And then the centurion thought of his own paltry office and what he should do if he were to lose it, by becoming embroiled with the powerful imperator; and he also thought of the many gold pieces he had from time to time carried out from the Vanno palace, thanks to the filial charity of its mistress.

"You should know," he continued in an apologetic tone, "I have been thinking the matter over anew, and perhaps it were better that you should come before him in the morning as though nothing of especial moment had occurred."

"As you please," she murmured, and half withdrew her hand from his. For though, being far from desirous of obtaining any violent and compelled restoration to her rights, she would, from the very first, have preferred the more quiet reconciliation now suggested, yet she could not fail to feel that her father had proposed the change not as much from a regard for her as from some selfish motive of his own.

"And, Ænone," he faltered forth, "you had better forbear telling him that I had brought you home. Let him rather think that you had found the way yourself."

"You think—is it wrong, therefore, that a father should have rescued his child from almost certain death?" she responded, with increased bitterness of disappointment.

"Nay, I mean nothing wrong. But these quarrels between a man and wife,—surely it is best that no one else should be mingled in them. He might be angry if I did so; and then, what might become of me? And, Ænone, what if he had had a right to be angry with you,—a little angry, only, of course? Not that you could wilfully do any wrong; but at times we all unwittingly commit actions which others could not approve of. And if this handsome slave of yours,—you would not love him, of course, but there are many Roman women who would not refuse some innocent and playful intimacy for the moment, —a kiss upon the lips or a pressure of the hand—and we are all weak, you know, and—Nay, nay, I did not say that it was at all true; only, if it had been—".

He stopped, for he felt that her eye was upon him—not in anger, but in a strange puzzled doubt as to his meaning, mingled with surprise that he should thus speak to her. His words were plain enough, but might there not have been some other sense attached to them than that which first appeared? It seemed, too, impossible that his selfish consideration for himself should lead him to justify neglect of her by imputations of wrong conduct. The moon had again passed under a cloud, shutting out from sight palace and temple; and the centurion could not catch her expression, but could merely see the outline of her form standing before him with the face upraised. But he felt that there was a look upon her features which, if well studied, must abash him, and he hung his head with the consciousness of shame.

"My father, what is it that you mean?" she said.

"Nay, nothing, my child," he muttered. And he made some feeble attempt to remove from her mind the evil impression which he had already produced. But in the end he only deepened it; for while disclaiming any meaning of ill, he seemed, by some perversion of his faculties, to repeat in another form the disparaging thought to which he had first given expression,—alternately mumbling words of self-accusation and denial, and then returning to his original idea and treating it as a matter of little consequence and to be leniently considered. What if such and such a thing had actually happened? What if in some moment of resentment at her lord's neglect of her, she had been tempted into unguarded levities? This, after all, was no great sin, judged from the standard of all around her; and while so many women of noble birth were daily guilty of worse, surely she should not greatly reproach herself for momentary forgetfulness, nor take offence at being spoken to about it. But none the less, of course, would the imperator be privileged to feel incensed upon discovering the fact; and none the less would he vent his anger upon any one who should come between him and his indignation.

"It were best, then," the centurion repeated, "that you should not mention how I had met you and guided you home."

"Can it be that you believe me guilty of this thing?" Ænone exclaimed, beginning more fully to realize the import of his words.

"Guilty? No, not so, my child," he responded. "But if so—not that I could believe it; but if so—"

And then again he ran on in the old train of thought, which, having once possessed his mind, could not thenceforth be ejected. The supposition which he had at first entertained as a mere passing excuse for his selfish avoidance of her interests, now, as he more doggedly fastened upon it, began to be sustained by his suspicious nature as a truth, and he could not shake it off. Camp life and low company had made him naturally distrustful. Was it likely, after all, that the imperator should have thus acted, without proof? And how was Ænone so different from others, that she should be immaculate?

Ænone read his doubts and hesitation. The tears gushed from her eyes, and her whole strength and power of resistance broke down with a wild sob. She had never thought that it could come to this. Even the rough suspicion of her lord she had tried to pardon in her heart, saying to herself that he had been drinking much wine and knew not what he was doing, and that possibly, from her neglect of appearances, she had innocently given him cause for suspicion. But that her father could thus coolly weigh together in his mind the chances of her guilt and innocence, with a lurking doubt in favor of the former, could treat it as a thing to be but little grieved over, and then, instead of taking her to his heart, should be so moved by selfish apprehension as not only to refuse her an entrance into his house, but also to withhold his open countenance and protection from her, choosing rather to let her bear the weight of all coming tribulations alone,—this was a blow beneath which it seemed as though her nature, until then sustained by hope and the consciousness of innocence, must at last break down.

"I will go home," she said, with a wail of despair. "What have I ever done that these misfortunes should come upon me? But I will go home. My lord can but drive me out again. And if he does, it will be no more than what I have already borne. Come not with me. The moon will be out again soon; and besides, I know the way. I would rather go alone. He might see you from a distance, and then might reproach you for having aided your own child when she was in trouble."

"Not so," said the centurion, repenting with shame. "I will go with you. Stay but a moment." And he strove to detain her by her robe. But she eluded his grasp, and ere he could pursue her, they were separated still further by a crowd of men, who, in disorderly array, dashed in between. At their head was one of the most celebrated gladiators of the day, and the most favored by the public; and those who followed were his friends and devoted admirers, who, seeing him patrolling the streets, had joined in his train, gathering accessions at every corner, until the concourse was numbered by hundreds, all leaping and screaming in their efforts to get nearer to the grand idol of the arena. And when the crowd had passed on and the centurion looked for Ænone, she was not to be seen.

He, a man of sturdy muscle, and armed with his short dagger, had escaped without much difficulty; but with Ænone it was different. At first, borne along by the impetuous torrent, she had maintained a position upon the outskirts of the gladiator's train, but as it increased in volume, she found herself insensibly mingled with it. To pause was to be trodden under foot,—to plead for release and urge her weakness was to be treated with derision; there was but one recourse, and that was to still follow the drifting of the mob, and trust to the chance of gradual extrication.

And so, for a moment or two longer, she was hurried along with the current, foot-sore and weary, but still without attracting especial observation. Then an Ethiopian slave alongside took notice of her, at first with curiosity, and then with greed as he marked the gold rings in her ears, and the pin upon her bosom ; and seeing that she appeared unprotected, he watched his opportunity and roughly tore away one of the former. Another slave upon the other side witnessed the action, and sprang forward to obtain his share of the spoils. And in an instant Ænone found herself the centre of a writhing mass of men, each wrestling with those around him in an attempt to obtain a share in the common robbery.

At last she was alone again. In some manner, during the strife over her, she had been thrown towards the outside of the mass, and there been abandoned, every thing valuable having been stripped from her person. Rings, bracelets, and all the ornaments usually worn by a Roman woman of high rank had been torn from her, and she found herself lying faint and weary at the foot of a flight of white marble steps leading upward to the portico of a newly finished temple.

Raising herself with difficulty, she strove to discern her location, but without success. That she had not been left long to herself was evident, for the screams and yells of the gladiator's retinue, as it passed into the distance, could yet be heard. But how far she had come during that struggle, or in which direction, was all a mystery to her. At a distance she could faintly see the towering ellipse of the new amphitheatre, but it was from a point of view which was not familiar to her. All appearance of palace, Forum, or broad Appian Way was now lost.

There were yet two courses left open to her. One was to make another attempt to reach her home ; and she saw that with time and strength she could perhaps do so. She had only to walk forward to the amphitheatre, never losing sight of it, and when she reached the base to creep around its walls until she came to the side with which she was familiar, and from whence she could see the broad street leading to the Vanno palace. But what certainty of succeeding could she have, even in such a short and simple route ? New dangers would be sure to rise at every step, for, however feasible her plans might seem to be, some cruel' fate would be sure to intervene. The other course was the sad one of lying upon that cold white step, and there, if possible, yielding up her life. Wearied and bruised in body, and more cruelly tortured in mind, and not knowing how strongly the spirit will cling to earth even amid the harshest adversities, it seemed to her that it would not only be easy to stay there and die, but that it would be a pleasant and joyful thing to do so. How calmly would her soul pass away in the soft glow of that pure moonlight, now again pouring down through the broken rifts of cloud ! How eagerly could she fly away from the ills and troubles of life to the refuge of the tomb ! Gradually sinking back and gazing up at the snow-white columns which, in pure and chaste Corinthian beauty, rose like light vestal sisters above her head, all aglow with the pleasant contrasts of light and shade which dwelt in cornice and capital and delicately wrought fluting, she felt a strange and unwonted serenity and peace of mind creeping over her, and gently closed her eyes with the sweet belief that her life was at last really passing away.

In was not the grasp of death, however, but merely the kindly soft touch of sleep resting upon her, for the weariness to which her body had been subjected now at length compelled repose. Therefore the troubled thoughts which had beset her, one by one fled away, and her eyelids closed, and bright dreams began to wing their way down to her, and she was about to fall into as gentle a slumber as ever she had enjoyed in her own bed at home, when a new alarm startled her into wakefulness.

Another crowd of midnight wanderers was heard approaching; and, in a moment more, turned the corner into sight. It was no popular gladiator which attracted them, but a huge box or van upon wheels. This was the travelling cage of some choice animal from Africa, arriving at a late period for participation in the games. As the great van, drawn by eight horses, rolled onward towards the amphitheatre, into one of the cells of which the beast would be thrown for a few hours' seclusion, the crowd pressed eagerly around it, giving responsive yells to each sullen roar which came from within.

Ænone stood at the lower step of the portico and watched the passage of the crowd. Fully awakened, she knew now that she was not destined to die yet, but that she must again strive to set out upon her homeward route as soon as this new concourse should have passed. In a moment more the way would have been clear, when suddenly, either from the movement of the horses or from the pressure of the crowd, the van slid off from its wheeled platform and rolled over upon its side. A louder roar burst from within,—the word flew about the startled concourse that the terrified beast was escaping,—men frantically rushed hither and thither in their struggle to evade the impending danger,—numbers of them fled to the portico of the temple as apparently the safest place,—and Ænone, with the instinct of life yet strong within her, caught the contagion of flight, staggered up the steps, and between the columns into the interior, and thence, not staying her course, passed to the other end of the building and fell fainting upon the pavement.

11*

CHAPTER XIX.

Upon a pedestal at the further end of the interior was placed a marble statue of Ceres, in whose honor the temple had been erected. The goddess stood delicately poised, with one foot slightly extended. In her arms were the stalks of corn, and in her hair the fruitful garlands typical of autumnal plenty. The head was balanced upon the shoulders with an air of satisfied serenity, and partially inclined forward, so that the gaze would rest upon the ground at the distance of a few feet in advance. Peace and benignity shone upon the features, mingled with a certain reflective expression of tender solicitude, as though the sculptor had intended to represent her in the act of compassionating the many, who, through poverty or neglect, seldom attained her bounties. At the base of the pedestal glimmered a small bronze lamp with three wicks, casting a faint glow upon the marble and enriching its surface with changing beauties of light and shade, as the jets of flame flickered with the drifting currents of the night air.

This light now also shone upon Ænone, who, with torn garments, lay upon the marble pavement in front of the statue, and in the very spot where the glance of its bended face might be supposed to rest. There was therefore, for the moment, a peculiar significance in that compassionate gaze, for it seemed to speak of the solicitude of the goddess, not merely for distant classes of unknown dependants, but rather for one immediate, present, and living sufferer thrown in agony at her feet. This would have been the natural interpretation given by one having sufficient art and imagination to combine the living figure and the marble statue into one group. And it would scarcely have seemed surprising or unnatural, if the goddess, in her compassion for the helpless victim, should have wrought a miracle and become incarnate, for the purpose of bestowing divine ministration upon her.

And Ænone needed help. It was not mere fatigue that had now overcome her, nor was the insensibility into which she had fallen, at all like the sweet calm sleep which, a few moments before, had been on the point of visiting her. Bruised and suffering, she was now the prey of a deathlike stupor, in which the present was blotted out only to give place to hideous images that revelled in her troubled dreams and threatened to destroy the whole balance of her mind. Weariness and fright and mental torture seemed at last about to complete their work, and to summon to her relief that death which she had before wished for in vain.

But while she lay upon the cold pavement, with one arm thrown behind her head, and moaned with anguish, a single figure appeared crouching at the temple door. Slowly he ventured in, turning his head this side and that, as though dreading interruption, and so glided further and further into the building. Then, seeing the insensible form of Ænone at the foot of the statue, he advanced at a quicker pace, and taking up the little bronze lamp, held it closely over her. And at the next moment, uttering an exclamation of joy, he dropped the lamp, and lifting Ænone, clasped her in his arms. The lamp rolled away from him and the lights went out, but he did not heed that. He needed no further light, for he had found what he sought.

"Ænone,—my own Ænone!" he cried. "Said I not true? We did not part forever, and now the gods have brought us together again!"

"Who calls?" she murmured. "And where am I?"

"In safety, Ænone; with one who will protect you henceforth for life,—with Cleotos!"

"Ah, Cleotos—my brother!" she whispered.

"More than a brother now, Ænone! But let us leave this place at once."

"This place? What is it?" she said; and she raised her head and looked around. Then, as she felt the chill of a great building enveloping her and saw the dim outline of the marble goddess bending over from above, her recollection slowly began to return.

"Yes,—I know it all now," she said. "I came into the temple,—I was weary and frightened and I took refuge here. And you have come to deliver me. Yes, we will go out from here. But not yet, for I am sick and bruised. Let me rest awhile."

"Yes, we will rest awhile," he said; and he looked about him for some place of greater security. For they were not safe as they sat directly in front of the statue. They might be seen by any stranger who chanced to enter. And if any one passed and saw that the lamps were extinguished, search might be made for the author of the profanation; and whoever was found in the building might be accused of it, and it would not be well to be dragged before some priestly tribunal for such a thing as that.

There was an opening in the rear wall. Cleotos remembered having seen it but a week ago, though then he knew not whither it led. Now, placing Ænone gently down, and bidding her be of good courage until his return, he groped along the sides and rear of the building until he found the place. It was an aperture of small size, being only about three feet wide and four feet high, and Cleotos feared lest it might lead only to some inner recess of no great utility as a place of concealment. But to his delight, he discovered, upon passing through the opening, that there was a turning to the right, and here his foot struck upon a stone step. It was the commencement of a flight leading upward—how far he could not tell. But it was sufficient for his purpose that he had found a place of temporary concealment, for, by ascending a very few steps, he would not only be out of sight but also out of hearing. Returning, therefore, to where he had left Ænone, he lifted her gently in his arms and bore her within the recess. There, ascending several of the steps, he sat down upon one of them and placed her beside him with her head upon his shoulder.

"Now for a few minutes we can talk together," he said. "The gods be thanked that I did not at once take the route to Ostia. For this, at least, I owe them gratitude, since, by putting it into my heart to linger around, they have for once given happiness to a poor and lowly man. See, dear Ænone! Here is your ring which you gave me, and here is the gold. I have not used either. Your commands were that I should at once fly to Ostia; but something told me that you would need me yet, and so I tarried."

"Did you then see me at the garden gate?" she said. "And why not, therefore, have come to me before?"

"I did not tarry at the gate, for what should you be doing there? But I stole around to the front of the palace, and there I waited. Yet nothing happened. I saw the guests go away and the lights one by one extinguished; and gradually all became silent. Then, feeling happy that I had at least watched over you for an hour, I came away."

"And why not, after that, have commenced your journey?" she said. "Do you not know that it was intended to have thrown you to the lions? That you are even yet in danger, dear Cleotos? Oh, go now. Stay not for me."

"Nay, I will not now go alone," he said. "But I will confess that having watched over you for that little while, I believed that no harm had come to you, and, with this cheering assurance, began my journey. But then it seemed to me as though all Rome were awake. Wherever I went, I met crowds of men, and in one place a concourse of heated revellers forced me to turn back with them and join their ranks. Then they surrounded the cage of a wild beast just entering the city, and still drew me along in their train. And as they passed this temple, the cage upset, and among the flying crowd I saw a figure in white upon the portico steps. What possessed me at that sight to think of you,—what made me see in that torn and dishevelled form you whom I believed to be resting in your own home,—how can I tell? A turn of the head, perhaps,—or a gesture of the body as you flew up the steps. I know not what it was; but something spoke the truth to my heart, and it beat quickly, and I stole back from where I had fled away, and coming in, I found you. And you, Ænone?"

"He has driven me away," she said in a low voice. "But it was all a mistake. Something or somebody has made him hate me for the moment. He will forget it all to-morrow, when he sees me again."

"He shall not see you again," exclaimed Cleotos. "Henceforth you are mine alone, and we will share each other's lot forever."

He spoke calmly and deliberately—not as one who makes a mighty resolve and anticipates opposition to be overcome, but as one who mentions a fact about which there can be no controversy, and regarding which no doubt can arise. Never for a moment since he had entered the temple and found Ænone stretched senseless upon the pavement, had he doubted that thenceforth their destinies were linked together. Nor was it unnatural that he should so believe. He knew from the first that she must have been driven from her lord's house, though the time and manner of the act were still a mystery to him. But by the act itself, however done, he felt that Ænone had become free again. It was as though Sergius, by withdrawing his protection, had restored liberty of will and action to her—giving her, as it were, a sort of informal divorce. In this light he believed that even the law would regard the matter, and that no fault would be found with whatever might be her subsequent conduct. Since, therefore, she was thus rendered free, upon whom should she more naturally lean for protection than upon that earliest and best friend, her childhood's lover? She had loved him once; and now that every bar seemed removed, she could certainly do so again. Had not the Fates led them together again after two partings, as though it was foreordained that they should never more be separated?

But the first word that Ænone spoke in response dissipated that pleasant dream. She had hitherto paid but faint and listless attention to what he said—listening to his words simply for their tone of kind and brotherly interest, and without reflecting comprehensively upon their true meaning. But now that he expressed himself so much more openly, the light began to dawn upon her, and she felt that she must at once correct the mistake into which his hopes had betrayed him.

"Speak not thus, Cleotos," she cried. "That can never be. I must go home."

"And your home is with me alone," he faltered forth, turning pale with apprehension. "Where else can it be, indeed?"

"Where else but with my lord?" she said. "Oh, Cleotos, cherish no longer these vain hopes, or I shall begin to regret that our last parting was not the final one, and that your fate has brought you hither, were it even to my own rescue. Speak no further, therefore, of what you have in your heart. Let your thoughts rest there unuttered; and only strive, as a friend and brother, to have me restored to my own home."

"From which you have been cast out!" he responded,

with bitterness. "And you would return thither, to be again ejected, perhaps! Where is your pride that you should suffer this?"

"I have no pride," she answered. "It may be that I ought to feel it, and that most others in my place would do so, but I cannot. There is but one thought in my heart—to make my peace again, though I may be obliged to win it through deep abasement and by imploring pardon for doing what I have not done, trusting to the calmer reflections of the future for my justification. Nor, if I had the pride which you desire to see in me, would it profit you. Would you wish that I should come to you simply because my affection had been outraged, and that I must therefore contract new ties in order to show my resentment and my indifference to the former ones? Would my presence in such a state of heart be pleasing to you? Would such a motive prove a sufficient substitute for that calm, trusting love which alone should have power to bring me to you?"

"But surely you would love me, Ænone. You loved me once."

"Yes, once I felt for you the love of a young and inexperienced girl. Whether or not that was the real love which the heart craves, I cannot now say. It is sufficient that it is gone, and gone forever, Cleotos. Were I really free,—were I to know that I could never look upon my lord again, even then that former love for you could not return. Be content, therefore, to be my brother alone."

He knew now how hopeless he must remain. But still he could not refrain from speaking further.

"Yes, I see it all now, Ænone. You never had for me

more than a young girl's fancy. You gave your real love to this man who has treated you like a plaything and now has cast you out. And worse than all that, you still love him."

"I still love him, indeed," she said. "Whether it be right or wrong, I cannot tell, but my heart whispers to me that I must yet cling to him. It is woman's lot, I suppose, ever to sacrifice herself for some one person or thing; and though she may mistake the object and find her devotion unrewarded or received with dull appreciation, she cannot easily disunite herself from the old enchantment. Better for her happiness that she should remain self-deceived, than that she should fall away and try to stand alone. I know all that you would say to me ;—that I have been cast out, ill-treated, and suspected of wrongs which I would not admit even into my thoughts,—that my lord has perhaps taken his love from me never to restore it,—and that I may never henceforth receive from him any thing but scorn and neglect. All this I can sometimes feel. Nay, when I consult my judgment and coolly dare to weigh the merits of the case as a strong-minded man might do, I may still more freely admit the truth of all you tell me. But when I let my judgment pass aside, and, instead thereof, consult my heart alone, it speaks softly and pleasantly to me in other strains. It tells me that if my lord has acted harshly towards me, he has done so in hasty passion and not in cool reflection,—and that, it may be, he has even now repented of it. It tells me that he has been angry with me because I have unwittingly aroused his jealousy. It tells me that all which he has seen amiss in my conduct can be explained, and that, perhaps, the evil influences which now surround him may some day lose their charm, and he be led back again to love me as before. You wish that I may be happy, dear Cleotos? What, then, do you advise me to do? Shall I henceforth trust to my judgment or to my heart?"

"To your heart—to your heart alone!" he responded. "It may be less true than your judgment, but why seek for truth when it brings unhappiness with it? Better be deceived, if thereby any of the pain of life may be stifled. And this gift of self-deception which women have in so much greater degree than men—what is it, after all, but a gift from the gods, and one which should not be despised, since it enables them to gild with delusive fancy so many ills which they have not the natural strength to vanquish? Dear Ænone, I will accept my fate and speak to you no more about love."

"Thanks, dear Cleotos, my brother. And now, let us prepare to leave this place, for I am somewhat rested, and by leaning on your shoulder can easily walk. Once more I bid you farewell. See! I touch you with my lips, for there is no one here to misinterpret the act, and you cannot now misjudge me. So—it is over now—and we will descend. Let us hasten, ere the night is past. You will go with me no further than the corner near our garden front. From thence I can find my way alone. And from there, do you hasten to Ostia. Stay not a moment, for you know your fate if you are taken."

"There is no fate for myself that I dread. Let me only know that you are safe and I will ask nothing further.

Now let us hasten, for I fear that already we have talked too long and that daybreak is upon us."

Ænone looked up in affright. It was even so. Already it seemed as if the dark winding stairway was lighter than when they had entered it, and that a reflection from below had imparted a dull gray to the rough walls. Above, all was black and obscure as before; but below, in that faint gleam, they could now count the steps which led down to the next turning. Startled with apprehension, Cleotos clambered down the stairway to make a further observation, half hoping that the faint light he had seen might come from some artificial cause, rather than from the actual break of day. But the further he descended the brighter grew the passage, and, at the lower turn of the stairs, he saw that the full radiance of morning was pouring in at the opening. Then, more cautiously, he passed the last step, and peering out at the low door, looked through the temple into the street, bright with the full blaze of sunshine and astir with groups of men in gay festive dresses and noisy with joyful shouts and laughter.

"It is, indeed, daylight," he said, again ascending to Ænone. "But what of that? Is it too late for you to return?"

Too late, indeed; and they both felt that it was so. She was too well known in Rome not to be recognized whenever she appeared in the open streets; and for her now to be seen, with torn garments and dishevelled locks and leaning upon the arm of a slave, would be to give currency to insinuations which would never thenceforth lose their malign effects. Nor was it likely that her lord would be as well disposed towards a reconciliation; if the world at large made evil accusation against her; for there are few men with sufficient singleness of heart to preserve their love for an object contemned by others, and thereby endure the ridicule of being considered the victims of weak and transparent deception. It was, therefore, all-important that she should contrive some method of return without attracting observation; and if she could succeed in that, and it had thus far chanced that her lord's ejection of her had remained unknown, all might yet be well. And there was the certainty, moreover, that Cleotos could not venture abroad in open daylight without bringing sure destruction upon himself.

"We must stay here till night again comes," she said, after a moment's thought. "Will you grow weary of me, Cleotos, for a few more hours?"

"Grow weary of you!" he exclaimed; and again the impulse came upon him to point out how the Fates had brought them together and would not let them part, and how it was a certain sign that all was meant for the best, and that she should yield to the omen and fly with him. And once more he repressed the thought, for he knew that its expression would not only be useless but ungenerous.

"We will stay here, then," she said, and it may turn out for good, after all. It may be that my lord will inquire for me when he awakes, and finding me not returned, will become troubled about me. And who can tell but that his anxious thoughts may bring back his love? And then, when night again comes and I return to him, perhaps our reconciliation will be easier and more complete."

"Yes, we will stay," said Cleotos, "but a safer place than this must be found. At any moment some straggler in the temple, drawn hither by curiosity, may ascend these steps and discover us. Let us go up further."

Slowly rising, she leaned upon his shoulder and they began the ascent. Deeper grew the shade as they followed the winding of the passage in the thick wall, until they could no longer see the steps before them, but were obliged to feel their way. And still the stone stairway wound up, and they continued the ascent, knowing that at some time it must come to an end.

At last, when they thought they must nearly have reached the roof, a glimmer of light appeared before them, and in a moment more they could see the rough wall at the side and could look upon each other's faces. Then, after making a few more steps, they stopped. The stairway still wound up, but it was useless to go any further, for now they were safe. They were upon a landing,—a space large enough to sit down upon and rest. The cobwebs which they brushed aside gave proof that the place had not been visited for months, and it was no less likely that as long a period might elapse in the future without interruption. It was here that the light came in, pouring through a narrow horizontal aperture running along the top of the entablature and hidden from below by the projection of the mouldings. Feeling safe at last, Cleotos and Ænone here sat down upon the stone landing, and through this opening in the wall, gazed out upon the city spread at their feet, and with enforced patience awaited the return of night.

CHAPTER XX.

To those faint and heart-sick watchers, it was a long and weary day. As they sat constrained in the narrow wall, oppressed with anxious thought, the minutes seemed to drag like hours, and the sun to climb his upward course so slowly, that at times the shadows upon the cornice of the temple scarcely moved. It was hard to realize that, in the city below, there were so many thousands basking in a general joy and festivity which made the whole day pass as though Apollo's steeds were doubly winged.

And yet, had Cleotos and Ænone been free from care and uneasiness, there was much in their position to have given enjoyment. From the opening along the entablature there lay spread out before them the finest view that Rome could offer. It would almost seem as though the temple had been located where it was with especial reference to splendid scenic effect. Raised upon the Capitoline Hill, its grand chaste mass looked down upon all about it—and gave to the watchers above unequalled limits of fair landscape. The Capitol itself was beneath them; and further down lay the Forum, with its intertwining courts and colonnades. At the right was the palace of the Cæsars—at the left, the Appian Way began its course, at such an angle as was best calculated to give a view of its palaces for a long distance away —and in front stood the Colosseum itself. In all that medley of magnificent architecture there spread out, but few buildings of mean appearance could be seen ; and these were blended by the distance into pleasant combinations of shapes and tints concealing their defects, and giving, by contrast, superior magnificence to the edifices gathered closely about. And thus at one view was to be witnessed more that was beautiful and grand in architecture than at that time could be presented to the gaze in any other portion of the empire—temples and courts and baths and amphitheatres in a confusing yet not irregular array, stretching away for miles, until gradually their grandeur gave place to the quiet beauty of suburban villas, and these, in turn, to the open country rolling out, with its wealth of vineyards and olive-groves, until met by the blue sea.

And this scene, so imposing, had now a new attraction in the life which flowed in and about it, for there had collected half the population of Rome. Senators and plebeians, soldiers and slaves, all classes and degrees were there met together ; each, whether rich or poor, powerful or abased, now smiling and joyous with festive animation. Jewelled imperial uniforms, and less rich but more picturesque costumes from all the tributary nations of the barbarians, mingling together—new arches raised upon the cross-ways—new statues of the gods, for the first time unveiled in the open squares—fountains and altars and loud music, and all that has ever been contrived to give life to a city made wild with a delirium of long-anticipated festivity were now presented to the sight and hearing in that most magnificent quarter of the great city of the age. Even the gladiators, who, at an early period of the day, walked two by two across the Forum to the amphitheatre, from which it was certain that half of them would not return alive, forgot their dangers and shook their weapons aloft with a wild cry of triumphant exultation.

But to Cleotos and Ænone, there could be no such sense of joyousness. The outside sunshine and gaiety could only serve to remind them of their own isolation and unhappiness. Those hours of festivity which had been so eagerly anticipated by thousands, were to themselves only a sad abyss separating them from safety. Would that the night were come, so that they could depart! What might not happen before then? Perhaps, at that very moment, the imperator was engaged in the double search after his wife and his slave; and if so, what assurance could there be that some one might not have seen her as she lay upon the outer steps, and thus be able to point the way to her retreat? Or a mere chance might reveal them. Some priest of the temple might, for the first time in many days, climb up the stairway for the purpose of gazing out upon this view now so fraught with unaccustomed animation—or a workman might come to complete some forgotten task, for slaves did not always have their holidays insured to them; and if the two fugitives were discovered in this hiding-place, all would be indeed lost to them. No eloquence of language could then give cogency to their explanations, or lead the world to believe that such concealment for a night and a day together had not been planned deliberately and with forethought. It was with trembling, almost, that they looked forth upon the panorama below them; nor could they always give due credence to that reasoning which told them how impossible it was that a gazer from below could see those two pale faces pressed against the inner side of that deep-grated aperture. Once, when a soldier pointed upwards with his spear, it seemed as though he motioned at them; and they shrank away from the opening, and, for awhile, anxiously listened, as though at each moment they might hear the tramp of guards coming to drag them down. Far away, past the amphitheatre and the suburban villas, Cleotos could see the track of the paved road leading to Ostia. Not many miles could he follow it before it was lost in the distance, but in imagination he could still trace its line until it reached the sea. There, now, lay the vessel freighted for the Grecian isles. Perhaps it might yet linger until he came—perhaps, on the contrary, the sails were ready to be spread, and the commander, with one parting glance along the shore in search of him who was to come and present a ring for a token, was turning to give the order to unmoor. But if too late, there must surely be other vessels soon ready to sail, thought Cleotos. He would conceal himself and await his chance for one of them; and if ever he had the good fortune to find himself far out at sea, then he would be safe. The arm of the government was long and powerful, indeed, and reached to every corner of the empire. There was no obscurity, however dark, into which it could not penetrate. But it was not likely that its whole machinery of detection would be employed for the apprehension of a lowly fugitive. He would, therefore, be at rest; and when once at home again, might trust for protection to his own insignificance. And whether at Samos or elsewhere, he could surely find some quiet nook in which to pass away the remainder of his life in peace and tranquillity.

Can it be wondered that he should long for the hour of escape to approach, even though at his side now rested the only being whom he had ever loved with a calm and enduring affection? She had told him that their paths must ever be separate; what hope, therefore, could there be for him, and why should he wish to linger? Their parting must come in a few hours, at the latest; why then wish to needlessly delay it? And before him, as a dread warning not to pause, towered the amphitheatre, already fast filling with an impatient crowd, eagerly waiting to glut their eyes upon the misery of some who, like himself, had committed no other fault than that of offending their masters in perhaps yet more trivial particulars. Accident only—the momentary compassion of one who had hitherto treated him unpityingly—had hindered him from being one of those unfortunates. And he had not yet fully made good his escape. The victims for that day were now groaning in their underground cells, listening, perhaps, to the howlings of the beasts that were to devour them; but the spectacles were destined to last for many days to come, and each repetition would require its separate quota of living food for the lions. He must, therefore, hasten. He could not, at any risk of life or limb, desert her who had been thrown upon his protection; but that task once accomplished, there must be no long delay before placing the waves of the sea between himself and the imperial city.

To Ænone there was no such journey in anticipation. She needed not to fill out the narrow limits of her bodily vision with fancied pictures of distant seas and shores. The end of her path lay directly before her. She could see the marble front of her lord's palace—the fountain in the inner court—the twin statues at the entrance. All these were but a few steps off, and had she been endowed with invisibility, not many minutes could have elapsed before she would be at her home again. But there, far different from the lot of Cleotos, her other troubles would begin. To him, home would be the restoration of peace and safety; to her, it might be only the entry into new trials. Could she feel sure that her lord would not again eject her, and perhaps this time with open and public ignominy? Or, if he received her again, would it be with repentant love? Would it not rather be because he would dread the comments and strictures of the world? Might not her life, from that moment, be still more embittered with suspicion, reproaches, and insults, until she would look upon her refuge in the temple of Ceres as a place from which she should never have departed?

"Tell me, Cleotos," she said, "will he take me again to his love as before?"

She knew that Cleotos could not answer that question as well as she could herself; and yet she would fain have heard some words of comfort and assurance from him, even if they only whispered of deceitful hope. And what could he say? He understood her thoughts, and how, by a few forced expressions of confidence, he might bring present peace to her heart; and yet he dared not speak them. He knew too well all that was to be dreaded from the anger and suspicion of the imperator, and he could not bear to raise within her breast a false security. Better that she should be miserable now and yet prepared, than to be lulled into deceitful forgetfulness and again rudely awakened.

"We cannot read his heart," Cleotos answered. "Let us only hope that he will not be unrelenting."

She bowed her head.

"If I thought otherwise, I would pray the gods that I might not live to meet him," she said. "Do you not think, dear friend, that it would have been better if I had died upon the cold pavement below? Or, since I did not, that I should yet die here, rather than return?"

"Why talk of dying, Ænone? You are too young for that; and there should be many years of happiness before you."

"Yes, I am young, Cleotos, but the young as well as the old can die. And as to happiness, does it often last through a long life? Age should not count by years alone. Whenever happiness has fled, then all that is precious about life is gone forever; and the soul is old, however few may have been the years of the body. Do you know, Cleotos, there was one moment, not many hours ago, when it seemed to me as though I should never leave this place?"

"What idle fancy is this?" he said, striving to smile encouragingly.

"Nay, let me tell you what I dreamed while I slept below. It was not as I lay upon the pavement; but after that, when you had left me for a moment by myself. Then, for the instant, I sank into a troubled sleep; and I dreamed that I saw this winding stairway. So natural did it all seem, that when you afterwards supported me up from step to step, I felt as though I knew the place and had been here before. And I dreamed that I went up higher and higher;—and then a great fear seemed to fall upon me, and something told me that death stood near, but in what way I could not tell. And I awoke."

"And found that it was all a dream;—what then?" Cleotos said, still trying to smile. But it was a troubled smile, for those were days when it was thought that dreams were sent by the gods for a purpose, and were not to be lightly disregarded. "You were tired and bruised. Is it strange that your mind should have indulged in some distempered fancies? Think no more of it."

"True,—I should not think of it again," she said. "And I remember now that my dream was not in all things like the reality. I seem to know these steps as though I had seen them before; and yet it was not as though we stopped here at this narrow opening, for we stood in the open air, beneath the sky. In this, at least, it was unlike."

"And that very falsity, therefore, proves that the whole was false—does it not, Ænone?"

"It must, indeed, Cleotos. And even if it were all true, why should I feel fear? For I remember that the evil dream did not seem to last, but that I awakened, not, as you might think, cast down by the overshadowing of the great dread which for the moment had drifted over me, but rather buoyed up with a strange and unlooked-for feeling of comfort nestling in my heart and whispering of relief. What make you of it all, Cleotos? Had succor really come at the end, and the threatened doom been driven away? Or was it that I did not any longer fear to die, but rather wished to court death! Would he—would my lord come to look upon me if I died, Cleotos? Would he weep for me then, do you think? I would not wish that he should be unhappy, either; but if my death would cause him to think upon me with tenderness again, then would I rather die than live on and be still under his displeasure."

"These are but uncomfortable words, Ænone, and you should not speak them. Rather, if you cannot encourage cheerful hopes, strive to give up all thought whatsoever, and, like any other idle spectator, look upon the scene before us. See! there comes the Emperor Titus; and now, at last, the games will commence."

Cleotos pointed towards the palace where a crowd of expectant thousands, which had long loitered about the principal portal, began to break away and leave a clear passage for the emperor, who, mounted upon a decorated steed and heralded by loud music, now made his appearance. Surrounded by his chief officers and an escort of the Prætorian guard, he slowly rode through the ever-thickening crowd, until, saluted with uninterrupted acclamations, he gained the amphitheatre and disappeared beneath one of the ornamented arches. The next moment, fresh bands of music struck up their strains of triumph within, telling the world that the emperor had taken his seat, and was ready to open the games.

Slowly the shadows moved along the moulding of the entablature; and gradually, as the sun rose higher in the heavens and the noonday heat increased, the more intense fermentation of the city population subsided. Those who were outside the amphitheatre, and who for the most part had hitherto moved to and fro, as, one after another, new objects excited their attention, now, little by little, withdrew into shady and cool by-ways and passages;—all, except a few thousands who still stood outside, listening to the shouts of men and the growls of wild beasts within, and joining with greedy sympathy in each burst of applause.

But inside the great building there was as yet no lack or decay of interest. As the heat increased, a hundred slaves had swarmed up the tall posts planted along the upper edge, and thence had spread from side to side the great silken velarium. Thus protected from the fervid sun, the sixty thousand spectators still sat with undiminished patience, and watched the many real tragedies which each hour unrolled before them. Where Cleotos and Ænone sat, the interior of the amphitheatre could not be seen; for high as were the walls of the temple, the walls of the former building were higher. But the distance was not too great for sound to be conveyed; and ever and anon would be borne along across the Forum the sullen fierce snarl of beasts or a single sharp cry of a human victim, closely followed by the united sounds of thousands of hands clapped together like the distant pattering of hail.

Still the shadows crept along the entablature, slowly but surely; and, at last, the sun began to approach its western goal. Then, upon a sudden, there arose from the amphitheatre a mingled tumult and din, eclipsing all that had gone before. There were the roarings of infuriated beasts, snarling and fighting over their prey,—the shrieks of victims,—the loud bursts of music,—the clapping of hands and the shouts of thousands of voices, all swelling forth in one chaos of wild confusion. Was it merely the combat of some favorite gladiator with a beast of inordinate power? Was it no combat at all, but the simple destruction of an unresisting slave or Christian captive? Or was it one grand closing piece for the day,—a cunningly prepared chaotic struggle of scores of famished beasts for hundreds of contributed human victims,—a spectacle designed to surpass all that had gone before, and, at the same time, to whet the public appetite for the more brilliant spectacles that were to come upon the morrow?

Whatever it might be, it was soon over. Gradually the shrieks ceased and the roar of savage beasts died away; and then, in a few moments, as the sun touched the western plains, the whole multitude began to pour out from the different arched entrances. The sports for that day were at an end; and the enchanted, but not yet satiated, audience streamed off in different directions, across the Forum and down the Appian and Sacred Ways. First, the emperor with his escort, as he had arrived,—then, the nobles and richer citizens,—and, lastly, the slaves and the plebeians from the upper benches;—all criticising the performance of the day in the several lights in which their position or education led them to look upon it, but no one appearing to have a thought of pity for those who had suffered for the common amusement. Laughing and shouting, as they wended their way homeward, or, as still unsated with magnificent show, they followed the imperial procession to the palace, there was, perhaps, no one among them all who looked upon the record of the day with any thing else than careless levity.

Only Ænone, who, bowed down with her own troubles, still felt for the woes of those who had that day suffered in the arena. Long after their voices had been hushed, their shrieks continued to ring in her ears, and her soul rebelled at the injustice and heartlessness which could extract amusement out of a fellow-mortal's agony.

"Are there gods in heaven at all?" she cried. "Tell me, Cleotos, can there be gods and yet this thing be suffered to exist? Oh, for some other world, where the errors of this one cannot prevail; or, while we are here, for some quiet nook in this world, apart from such mocking strife and cruelty! In your own Samos, is there no such spot, Cleotos?"

Cleotos felt his eyes sparkle with joy and anticipation of hope. Could it be that now, in her indignation and abhorrence of that imperial fountain of corruption and inhumanity, she was at last about to consent to leave all and follow him?

"Ænone," he said, bending over her, "in my native island there is no such cruelty as is here found; and though there is no place in all the world where man's injustice cannot reach, yet we may shun all open communication with it. Will you go thither?"

"Would that I could!" she said. "But, alas! what is there that could turn my lord's heart so that he would consent to give up this hollow world of imperial vanity, and with me seek for such an innocent shelter as you describe? No, there is no hope of that!"

And Cleotos sank back despairingly. Why had he trusted himself to misconstrue her few words and once again nourish such vain dreams? Must she be obliged each minute to forewarn him that he could have no part in her future life, but that, through every ill and indignity, her nature would attach itself yet more firmly to the hope to which it had learned to cling? And he spoke no more; but, as they sat side by side, watching the sun go down and the deeper shadows steal over the earth, and the streets empty of their moving masses and the dim lights here and there flicker out, and thus waited until the time might come for them to descend and take their homeward way, he thought how terrible would be her awakening if her lord should still overwhelm her with his disdain; and how much better it might have been for her, after all, if she had died upon the cold pavement at the foot of the marble goddess!

CHAPTER XXI.

And at last the hour came for the attempt. It was not safe to descend to the street in the early portion of the night, by reason of the many bands of revellers still roving about, any of whom, through wanton sportiveness, might interfere to stop the fugitives, and thus perhaps lead to their recognition and detention. But one by one these parties hurried past into the darker and more obscure recesses of the city or else dispersed, and single wayfarers became less frequent, and here and there the lights in different houses were extinguished; and at length comparative repose fell upon all around. Then Cleotos arose.

"It is time," he said. "I will first venture down and see that the way is clear."

Then, leaving her, he began to descend the steps; slowly groping his way with his outstretched hands touching the wall on either side, and with a strange feeling of dread lurking in his heart. Why was it that now, when all the city seemed asleep, he felt more strongly than during the day a something warning him of interruption? Was it a mysterious prescience impressed upon him by some guardian spirit? Or was it a mere nervous fear, resulting from an overtaxed and wearied system now aroused to unwonted action? Whatever it was, he felt that morbid foreboding circling about his heart closer and closer as each instant he descended nearer to the pavement which his reason told him he would find unwatched and vacant; and when, at the last step of all, something clasped him by the leg and a powerful form rose up dimly before him, he stopped—not in surprise, but in despair.

"Whither away so fast, my master?" came in gruff tones to his ears. "Let me first know who it is that would slip by so slily."

"Is it you, Drumo?" murmured Cleotos, recognizing the voice of the armor-bearer. "Alas! then all is indeed lost! How and why have you tracked me? Could you not have waited one day until I was beyond your reach?"

"And is it you, valiant cup-bearer?" exclaimed the armor-bearer with a loud laugh. "Nay, fear me not. I have not come out, seeking to carry you back to your prison-house. Am I not myself a fugitive? And how do I know but what you have been sent out to capture me?"

At the idea, the giant threw back his head and laughed yet more heartily. It was evident that, if a fugitive, he did not take his position much to heart, but would be merry and careless whatever fate awaited him.

"But sit you down, Cleotos, and tell me how it is that you are here. Yet, bah! What is there to tell me? Do I not know it all,—how that you were set free by that black-eyed Leta, and thence have, somehow, found out this hiding place, which I thought was known only to myself? Tell me, though! You do not know, perhaps, that afterwards your mistress was left out in the street, passing through the same gate at which you escaped. Have you seen or heard aught about her, in your wanderings to and fro?"

"I have not," answered Cleotos, instinctively foreboding mischief.

"It matters not," mused the armor-bearer. "I shall yet find her. Certainly she has not returned to the palace. Nor would she think of doing so, believing that she would be again cast out. But if I could only meet her—"

"And for what purpose?" faintly asked Cleotos. "Surely she could not now assist you?"

"Assist me?" roared the armor-bearer. "As though I would ever ask assistance from any one,—much less from a woman! Nay, I would extend aid to her. She has been cast off from her own place, and she must believe that all such ties are broken. Thenceforth she should go with me, and be mine alone."

"Yours?" murmured the amazed Cleotos.

"Ay, is there any thing so wonderful in that? Because you have given yourself up in love to her, is it a good reason that no one else should do the same? What there is about that puny weakly form and that meek little face of hers to enchant me, who can tell? I only know that, for months, I have thought about her and dreamed about her, and wondered whether time might not, at last, bring some hope to me. It is dark, Cleotos, and I cannot see your face, but I know that you must be laughing. I would laugh, myself, if in your place, at the thought of such a great burly fellow as I am, becoming enamored of an innocent little lamb like that! And the merriest thing about it is, that I cannot understand it myself, but merely know that it is so. And thus, for months, I concealed my love, and wore a brave, indifferent face, and smiled upon my master;

and struggled hard to resist the temptation I sometimes felt to put a knife into him for very hatred of his happiness. But now that I am at last a free man—"

"A free man?" ejaculated Cleotos.

"Yes, a free man," responded the armor-bearer. "It does not look much like it, these stone walls—this hiding-place —does it? But sit you down upon that step above me, and I will tell you all about it."

Cleotos sat down. He must yield to the necessity, for he could not venture to leave the armor-bearer without the danger of awakening suspicion, or what would equally lead to discovery—being followed. No matter how anxiously Ænone might be waiting, he must leave her alone until an opportunity occurred to steal away. And a great aching pain spread over his temples with his dread, lest, after long waiting for him, she might begin to reproach him in her heart with trying to make his escape alone, or might herself descend to find out what detained him.

"And first, refresh yourself while you listen," said the armor-bearer. "Here is some black bread and a flask of wine that I purchased at a shop as I fled to this place. It will serve to keep up your strength and courage for what you may yet have to go through. No? You are wrong, there, but be it as you will. To me no drink ever came amiss, and more especially not now, that I must pass half this night in this damp cell and upon these cold stones."

With that he lifted the flask, and throwing back his head, indulged, by way of illustration, in a prolonged drink —not by any means the first one of the evening, for already in his thickened utterance and disorderly gestures, he gave evidence of having exceeded the bounds of a reasonable discretion. Then, replacing the flask at his side, in readiness for further applications to it, he leaned against the wall and continued :

"All the rest of that night I followed my master about ; never, when I could help it, losing him from my sight, for his action was strange, and at times I feared lest he might do himself some mischief. Once, towards morning, he started up, took the keys and passed down through the garden ; and I crept along softly at his heels, for I suspected where he was going. Entering the slave-prison, he unlocked the outer door leading into the alley behind—the same door at which our mistress had been bolted out—and then, passing through, he gazed about him. I knew that he was looking for her, thinking that perhaps she might yet be crouching near. But she was gone. It was still dark, though not so dark but that he might have seen her white dress if she had been at hand. Yes, he not only looked for her, but once called her by her name ; and I heard a sort of sob come from his throat as he waited in vain for an answer."

"He would have taken her back again, if she had been there," cried Cleotos.

"Not so, I think ; though I believe he was sorry he had not been less rough with her. Well, he called her by name ; and then, turning suddenly around, saw me, in spite of my efforts to keep out of his way. And he grasped me by the neck and pressed me against the side of the wall.

"'What do you here, dogging my steps ?' he cried.

"'I do not dog your steps, master,' I said. 'But I have come to tell you about my mistress. Knowing full well that you would soon be anxious about her, I dispatched a slave to inquire, and he returned but a little while ago. He tells me that she has found her way to the house of her father, the centurion Porthenus, where she now rests in safety.' In saying this, of course I lied, Cleotos; but you will see that it was necessary, for I did not want him to search too long after her."

"And he—what did he do then?" demanded Cleotos.

"He released my neck from his fingers and paused for a moment in thought. Then he told me that I had done well; said something about never meaning to see her again—that he should not have treated her so roughly, but would have done better himself to have sent her carefully and safely back to her father's house—but that it was all the same, since she had, at last, got there—and so, walked back to his own room. There I still hovered near, keeping my eye upon him; for though in the one matter of her safety he was relieved, he did not yet in all respects seem to be in his right mind. Every little while he would drink more wine—a bad practice, Cleotos, for he had had enough; and would sing songs and break into all kinds of forced and extravagant merriment. Then he would sink back into a state of stupor, and sometimes it would seem as though he slept, except that I heard him muttering to himself. I could not catch all that he said, but from a word or two, he appeared to be talking about our mistress; and sometimes I began to think that he really cared for the poor little creature, after all, and regretted her. Or, was it the disgrace of the matter that overcame him? I could not make it out; but I know this, Cleotos, that it is well for you that you escaped, for never yet has man had such vengeance wreaked upon him as you would have endured if you had remained in his power until morning."

"But I was innocent," said Cleotos. "You surely must know that."

"Bah! I know it well enough, but what would that have mattered as long as he believed you guilty? Have innocent men never suffered before now? Well, there for awhile he lay, until, as morning dawned, a message came to him. The comedian Bassus had sent for Leta, whom, it seems, he had won at play, and she had asked to see our master. Perhaps she fancied that she might yet work upon his feelings so that he would retain her. But he would not see her even for a moment, and she went away to her new home, with all the gold and jewels and rich attire that had ever been given to her, but without a single kind word of farewell. So that was the end of her. And then, the imperator rose up from the couch, poured water over his face and hands, and began to dress himself with more than ordinary care. I had thought that he would not go out, but I was mistaken. There came a new mood upon him, and he set his lips together with the air of one who had become inspired with a great resolution.

"'Reach me my purple tunic and let my hair-dresser come to me with his perfumes,' he said. 'She shall not have it to say that I have shed a tear or altered a day of my life on account of her. I will tear her from my heart! By the gods! I will forget that she has ever lived.'

"He mentioned no name when he spoke, but I knew well

that he was not thinking of the Greek girl, but only of our mistress.

"'And can I therefore—' I commenced; and I stopped pretty much as I had begun; for something seemed to warn me that it was not yet time to speak out what I had in my heart. There was an ugly look in his face, and, like a slave as I was, I was afraid to go on.

"'Can you what?' he said, turning upon me sharply; and for the moment I dreaded lest he had fathomed my meaning. But he had not.

"'Go to the amphitheatre,' he continued, after a minute or two, 'and see that my place is made ready. Upon this day, of all others, I shall not let them see that I am absent. Have my whole escort at hand to accompany me.'

"And so, Cleotos, you see what a man this was, who called us his slaves. Hating him as I do, I must still wonder at and admire him. For, instead of remaining at home, tossing upon his couch and moaning forth his complaints as I had expected, and feared indeed,—for it would not have been becoming to have shown such passion for only a woman,—he acted the brave part, dressed himself in his gayest apparel, perfumed his beard, and, with his whole retinue, took his place at the amphitheatre, and there sat laughing and nodding to his friends as though his heart was light as a feather. I do not know whether the story of his disgrace had yet gone the rounds. If so, no one dared to hint the knowledge of it to him; for, though he smiled and jested with all, there was a certain dangerous look in the corner of his eye, that showed how ill he would brook any mention of what had happened. Ha! it makes me thirsty to think of it, only. Let me wait a moment and take one more pull at the flask."

"But your freedom; what has all this to do with it?" asked Cleotos, more for the sake of saying something than because he felt in any way interested in the subject. For there was still upon him the same continued dread lest Ænone, alarmed at his protracted absence, might descend to look for him; and he hoped that in such a case the sound of his voice in conversation might reach her ear and warn her to stay back. Once, indeed, it seemed to him as though he heard the rustle of her dress against the wall and even her suppressed breathing at his ear; but it was merely the wind sighing through the vaulted passage.

"I am coming to that," responded the armor-bearer. "Will you not give me time? And what use or benefit is there in being a free man if one cannot tell his story in his own way? Well, you must have heard that our master has had a long-standing wager with the proconsul Sardesus as to which of the two could produce the best gladiator. How many thousand sestertia were staked, I know not. That mattered little to me. I only know that, as the weeks had run on, our master had failed to find the right kind of man to put into the arena, and had about made up his mind to give up the contest and pay the necessary forfeit with a good grace. But now there was a devil of obstinacy and recklessness raised in him; and he began, even at that last moment, to cast about him for even the slightest chance to win. And so the time for the single combats arrived, and the proconsul was ready with his man,—a great stout Rhodian slave, taller than I am by an inch, and I am of no small height,—with the neck and forehead of a bull and the muscles of Hercules. At the first sight I remembered the caitiff; for he had been among our prisoners from the East, and had thence somehow passed into the proconsul's possession. There the man stood waiting for his opponent; in default of whose appearance the proconsul would claim the stakes. · A hard thing for the imperator to lose so much, just for want of a little hired brawn and bone, was it not, Cleotos?"

"And did he lose?" said Cleotos, still without interest, but yielding to the necessity which forbade silence.

"You shall hear. Our master looked at the Rhodian for a moment despairingly and then touched me on the breast.

"'Twenty sestertia, if you slay that man for me,' he said.

"'Will twenty sestertia mend my broken bones?' I answered, shrugging my shoulders. 'Large and strong as I am, that knave in the arena will, with one hug, crack my joints apart, like an egg-shell. Nay, nay, master, I have oftentimes proved myself no coward, but now, some other man must undertake that work for you.'

"'Thirty—fifty sestertia,—your freedom if you succeed in killing him,' said he.

"'No, no,' I still said,—but while I spoke I began to reflect. It would be, after all, a great thing to be free,—to polish my own armor instead of that of another person; or, better yet, to have a slave of my own to polish it for me. And then I thought that, as a free man, I might stand nearer my mistress, who, having been cast out, would, perhaps, if I ever met her again, learn to forget that I had ever been any thing other than a free citizen of

Rome. And with that the impulse seized me, and I snatched up a weapon and leaped down into the arena."

"And slew the Rhodian?"

"Yes, or I should not have been here now. But it was a hard struggle; and had it not been that I had the most activity to set off against his greater strength, it might easily have gone the other way. But he slipped in his own blood, and I plunged my weapon into his throat, and he fell back with a dying groan, and the people shouted their applause, and I clambered back into my seat; and the imperator, in his joy, not only proclaimed my freedom, but flung me a purse of gold pieces besides."

"And then you left him?"

"Not yet. I was entitled to do so, of course; but I had given him my escort from the palace, and, as a matter of grace and courtesy, would attend him back again. So I returned at his side; and, as the Fates would have it, when alone with him in his private chamber, he said something more about my mistress. What it was, I remember not; but the mention of her name put it into my heart to say what I had before vainly attempted to say. Then, I had been a slave and had not dared to utter the words. Now, I was a free man; and what was there that I might not have the courage for?

"'Nay, master,' I said. 'You have cast her away from you. You have therefore no further care about her. Leave her to me.'

"By the gods! Cleotos, I had better not have said it, even then; for he turned upon me like a tiger, and there was a savage glare in his eye which I would not care to meet again, big and burly as I am. Then it flashed upon me,—all that I had before but dimly suspected,—that he had loved the woman, even though he had cast her off; and that though, for awhile, that fiery Samoen girl had ruled his soul by some devilish charm, yet that now the spell was gone and his thoughts were turned once more back to his meek little blue-eyed wife. I read all that in an instant, even as his clenched hand was raised over me; and I knew that, in the demand I had made, I had done him an insult which he could never pardon. But it was too late for me to draw back;—I could only go on and make the best of it.

"'Dog!' he said, standing for a moment as if stunned by my words, and as yet doubtful of my meaning. 'What insolence is this? Shall I strike you dead upon the spot, vile slave that you are?'

"'Not now a slave,' I said. 'Do you so soon forget that you have given me my freedom,—ay, and proclaimed it, too? I am a Roman citizen, and, so far, am the equal of yourself. You have cast off your wife, and cannot now oppose me if I take her to myself.'

"That, at least, is what I began to say. Whether I said it all, I know not; for there came a blow across my face that sent me reeling against the wall and covered me with blood. Could you have borne that, Cleotos? Answer me, could you have borne that? Think of it! I was a free man, and he had struck me like a hound! He had often struck me before, but then I had been a slave and had scarcely minded it. But now that I was a citizen, the blow seemed to make a scar upon my very soul. How I did it, I can hardly tell; but in a minute I had crushed him down with the weight of my naked fist, and he lay quivering at my feet."

"Dead? Surely not dead?" exclaimed Cleotos.

"No, not dead, or even insensible, though I had given him a fearful blow. But I might as well have slain him, for what safety could there be for me now? First, there had been this insult to him and then this blow; and how, after all that, could I hope to escape his vengeance, except by instant flight? What happens to a slave who strikes his master? And though I was a slave no longer, and the law might not give me over to his power, how could I expect him to make close distinctions between the slavery of the one hour and the freedom of the next, and thereby forbear his private vengeance? No, I knew that I must fly; but before setting out, I did this. I leaned over him, placed him half upright in the corner of his couch, pinned his arms closely at his side and clasped his mouth so that he could not struggle or cry for help; and then,—then, by the eternal Jove! I told him all that he would have liked to have been told but one day before! I told him how that his wife was innocent,—how that you were to her only an old friend of her youth, whom she was trying to deliver from slavery and restore to his own country. This I knew; for, in my jealousy of you, Cleotos, I had watched you both, and overheard your conversation. And I told him, furthermore, that it was not she who had released you from prison, but that it was the black-eyed Leta. For here, too, I had watched and seen for myself."

"Thanks to you for telling him that!" cried Cleotos with animation and seizing the hand of the armor-bearer with a convulsive pressure of gratitude. "This was noble and generous-hearted,—to spend those last moments in removing from the eyes of the man who had smitten you, the veil of error which had blinded him!"

The armor-bearer burst into a roar of savage laughter, which echoed through the whole building, and, if any one had been passing at that moment, would have certainly drawn attention to his place of concealment. But no one was abroad or near at hand to be attracted by it.

"Poor innocent little soul!" he cried, after another draught from the flask of wine, and still shaking with inward merriment. "Have I not always said, Cleotos, that you should have been born a priest or a woman or a scholar,—any thing rather than a man intended to cope with this troublesome world of ours? Why think you that I should care to benefit the man who had so used me? Truly, forgiveness and magnanimity may hold fair places in your catalogue of virtues, or may be used by those high in power who can afford the luxuries of such qualities, now and then, as a new sensation; but they can have no position in the mind of a slave. Had I the least expectation that this man could ever again meet his wife so as to be reconciled with her, then it would have been a forgiveness and a benefit, indeed, for me to have told him what I did. But knowing that he can never see her again,—this is where my revenge shall strike home to his heart."

Cleotos sat stupefied and wondering. What devilish device could this man have contrived that he could so turn apparent benefits into instruments of vengeance? And in the momentary silence, once again he listened for the sounds of a light descending footstep, and again seemed to hear the rustle of a flowing garment against the wall. Was the sound real, this time? Or was it, as before, the sighing of the evening wind?

"Now listen to me!" continued the armor-bearer. "He will never see her any more, for this night I will carry her off with me. I know not where she now is, but I will find out, and that easily. I have discovered for a certainty that she has not returned to her father, and it is probable that she must be lurking from sight in some lowly and not far-off quarter of the city. Some persons who were abroad last night must have seen her, and there are few of these but must know me. Gladiators and slaves and keepers of wine-shops, and all who would be apt to range the streets after nightfall, know Drumo the armor-bearer; and when I come and ask here and there whether any among them has seen a pale white woman dragging herself about the streets and crouching out of sight, some one, at last, will be sure to lead me to her hiding-place. I will find her before the morning. I will drag her out. I have now the double incentive of love for her and revenge towards the imperator to help me. That light frame of hers,—I can carry it in my arms as another person can carry a child. Before the sun is high, we will be miles away. I know old ruins and quarries where we can be concealed by day; and ere a week is over, I shall have her in safety in some mountain nook where no pursuit can reach me. And then—"

"And then—oh, and then?" cried Cleotos in a transport of agony, as the dread malice of the plot began to become apparent to him.

"Then, Cleotos, I will write to the imperator telling him that she is with me, and that we are where he can never lay hands upon us again. Will not the tidings sting him and bow his head with shame and agony? If he believed that she had been guilty, he would not regard the matter so much. He would feel rage, to be sure, and would curse me from the bottom of his heart, and would wish that he could lay his hand upon me once again ; but the paroxysm would not last long, and soon he would forget her, as one unworthy of him. But knowing that she is innocent,—that she has never wavered from him in thought or deed,—that in driving her away from him he has done an injustice which he can never repair,—and that now she is in the power of the buffeted slave,—will not his newly awakened love for her burn and burn until it eats into his soul and makes him frantic with despair and hopeless regret? Will not this be a revenge worth seeking?"

" A revenge, indeed !" murmured Cleotos.

"Ay, trust to me for contriving schemes to repair my wrongs. But why so silent? Is it from fear lest you, too, may not escape? Nay, I meant not to leave you here alone. You shall go with us, my tender cup-bearer—I pledge you my word for that. It will be good, indeed, that we should join our wits together, for we can be vastly useful to each other on our journey. You can, at proper moments, steal out and buy bread and wine for us, while we are in hiding here and there ; and I—I will give you the protection of my strength and valor. Shall it not be so ?"

" As you wish," muttered Cleotos.

"Nay, it is a good arrangement," responded the armor-bearer, " as fair for you as for me, though you seem to treat it but lightly. But no matter for that. The end will tell which one has been of the most use to the other. And now that we have nothing further to speak about, let me sleep for an hour or two. I, at least, need rest, for I have worked hard to-day, and it was, in itself, no easy task to cut the comb of that Rhodian gladiator."

With that the armor-bearer threw himself lengthwise across one of the steps, placed his hands under his shaggy head, and, in an instant, fell into an uneasy slumber.

CHAPTER XXII.

For a moment Cleotos sat uneasily crouched in the angle of the wall, and confusedly striving to arrange and reconcile the conflicting emotions which overwhelmed his soul. Mingled with his deep and fervent joy at the knowledge that Ænone could now be restored to her home and to her shelter in the breast of her erring lord, came dark forebodings regarding the difficulty of departure from the narrow prison-house into which her fate had led her. For how could she hope to pass, without detection, that bulky form, stretched like an unwieldy log across the only avenue of escape;— insensible now, to be sure, as he lay awaking the echoes with his heavy and uneasy breathing, but yet sleeping with all the instinctive alertness of a hunted man, and ready, at the slightest incautious touch of an intruder, to spring up into instant and savage action? And yet, something must soon be done, for the night was rapidly wearing away.

Softly Cleotos at length raised himself, crept away from the prostrate giant and began to ascend the stairway, still pondering as he went. But no satisfactory scheme of relief crossed his bewildered brain. And now he remembered Ænone's dream, foreboding misfortune, and he shuddered as he wondered whether that dream might not, indeed, be a warning voice. Was it mere chance that had led the armor-bearer to the same place of refuge? Or was it not rather a predestined fate working out some settled and premeditated purpose? If so, was it a kind and beneficent fate, acting simply with the generous wish that Ænone should hear of her dear lord's just repentance? Or was it a revengeful Nemesis, which, with hateful eagerness to punish some forgotten fault of her past life, had craftily decoyed her into the power of a monster? It must at least be a fate—Cleotos thought—for such things do not come by chance.

Carefully and noiselessly climbing the steep ascent, he returned to Ænone. The moon, which had been hitherto concealed by drifting clouds, now shed a slender, flickering ray of light through the grated aperture of the wall and dimly revealed the interior ;—and he beheld Ænone, not resting upon the stone step where he had left her, but leaning over upon her bended knees and with her head bowed in her hands.

"Hush!" she softly whispered. "I am giving thanks to the gods for the glad tidings which I have heard. I know it all, now."

And as she turned towards him, he could see, even in that faint light, that her face was transfigured with radiant new-born joy.

"Have heard all?" he murmured.

"Not all, perhaps," she said, "but enough to assure me that my lord's kind favor is once more turned towards me. Shall I tell you how I learned it? I was awaiting your return hither and I heard from below a sudden loud laugh. It came not from yourself, I knew, and I stealthily glided down to where I could listen. I am not dreaming, am I,

Cleotos? Tell me that I am awake, and that the good news is true. That man was my lord's armor-bearer, was he not? And he told you that my lord once more loved me, had always loved me, and would take me to his heart again,—is it not so?"

"It is true, indeed, Ænone. But did you hear further what that man uttered?"

"I heard him make threats of what he would do, if he could succeed in finding me, though I know not wherein I have offended him. But what of all that? I fear him not. Are not the gods now with me? Surely they cannot have suffered me to hear these happy tidings, with the intent that I should be miserable at the last? They are too merciful for that. All we must do is to avoid that man. He cannot find us, unless he comes up hither; and if he does, you will protect me,—will you not, Cleotos?"

"With my life, if it is needful," he answered. "That man is stronger than I am, but it seems as though, for your safety, I should have twofold the strength needful to prevail against him."

It seemed strange how little, in the overflowing joy of her heart, she regarded the savage utterances of the armor-bearer; while, with Cleotos, the dangers springing therefrom nearly banished from his startled and less elastic mind, every other feeling than despair. Why did they look so differently upon the same thing,—the one with a thrilling tumultuous transport of delight, which refused to admit the perception of any sense of accompanying ill; the other, with a dread apprehension which weighed down his soul and forbade his climbing to catch even a ray of that light of hope which shone so brilliantly upon her? Was it the premonition of a coming fate, leading them apart into the separate paths of safety and destruction?

"Yes, Cleotos, now are our sorrows over. Now do I know that my lord loves me and will receive me again. In what he has done, he was surely not himself. We can pardon much more than that, to those coming to us with penitence in their hearts, can we not? I know what he will say, when I first again greet him. He will wish to ask my forgiveness, but I will not suffer him to do so. I will stop the words upon his lips with my tender love, ere he has time to utter them, for why should I let him degrade himself with unaccustomed avowals of repentance? It is so hard, indeed, for a man to say that he has done wrong. And you, too, Cleotos—you shall be pardoned and made free, and you will remain ever after this our open trusted friend and brother,—will you not?"

In his single-minded solicitude for her safety, he had not yet thought about himself, but now that the subject was forced upon him, he sadly shook his head. Forgiven he might be, and freed from the perils of the amphitheatre, since, with the innocence of the wife, his own innocence was, of course, made manifest; but here the bright picture must end. Though inexperienced in the ways of the world, he knew too much of human nature to believe it possible that Sergius Vanno could long endure the presence or sight of one, whose name had once, even through mistake, been connected in disparagement with his own. There might, indeed, be some show of gentle forbearance at the first, and even a wish to make up with kindness for past harsh treatment; but, in the end, other feelings would too surely prevail. There would come dislike and hatred, and then, perhaps, new oppressions. No; there was but one way left for himself to act. He must guide Ænone safely back to the shadow of her home, and then, bidding her a last farewell, must stealthily follow out the interrupted project of a flight to his native land. But he forbore to tell her what he now thought. It were not worth the while to deprive her of the present happiness she felt in spreading out her bright plans for the future.

"It will all be well, at the last, Ænone," he said. "I feel that it will. Only let us first escape from this place."

Slowly he again descended the stairway, carefully feeling his path before him, and sustaining his mind by the faint hope that, while they had been talking, the armor-bearer might have awakened and have departed to commence his promised search. But the hope was vain. The giant still lay stretched clumsily across the narrow passage at the bottom of the steps, in such a posture that it would be impossible for any one to pass without awakening him. Nor was there any apparent prospect that he would soon depart. The wine that he had so bountifully drank seemed to have made his slumber heavy, if not deep, and there appeared to be but little chance that he would become fairly aroused again to his situation before the return of light. Then, unable to depart without the danger of detection, he would be obliged to conceal himself more effectually in the deeper recesses of the wall; and what could hinder him from there stumbling upon his prey?

Once more, with sinking heart, Cleotos returned to Ænone.

It was best, he thought, to tell her the truth at once; and taking her hand, he said:

"There is, as yet, no escape. All departure from this place is closed."

She did not, even now, give way to despair, as he had expected. Her new-born happiness still seemed to make her reckless of all possible misfortunes, and to endow her with unwonted strength. Certainly, she was now the most firm and hopeful of the two.

"Is there no other way, Cleotos? Let us think."

He shook his head. There was no other way.

"This stairway winds still higher, Cleotos. We have not traced it to the end. It may be that it will turn and descend again, with another outlet."

"Where can it further go than to the roof itself, upon which we should be yet further removed from help?"

"Let us, at least, try, Cleotos."

And hand in hand they followed the winding of the steps. It was but a short distance; and then, as he had suggested, they found themselves standing upon the flat temple roof, and gazing up at the arched sky, once more overcast with clouds which here and there would spread out for a moment into broken rifts, letting a chance ray of the full moon steal through, and again would close up into thicker and more lowering folds than before. Beneath lay the great city, its blocks of houses clustered together in dark undistinguishable masses, except where here and there a few dim lights indicated some well-kept and wealthier locality. There was but one place where more lavished brightness prevailed—the Cæsars' palace—whose windows glowed with light, and whose central court was alive with men bearing great torches. For there, as elsewhere, it was a festive night, and Titus was giving welcome to the rulers and governors of his provinces. There were also a few scattered lights glimmering far off in the usually dark streets—singly or in groups, as here and there a belated artisan, lamp in hand, would plod his weary way through labyrinthian passages, or a quick-moving and noisy band would brighten the walls upon either side with the flaming of their collected torches. One such group, for the moment, Cleotos mechanically watched—tracing its course from a distance, and noting how, as it came nearer, the torches would now separate and wind through diverging narrow lanes, and again would come together into one compact body when the several lanes here and there united in some broader esplanade. Were these the torches of revellers, who had sallied forth to provoke midnight quarrels with loitering strangers—or of slaves taking advantage of the festival license, in order to perambulate the city in quest of booty—or of some wealthy noble of the court, passing, with all the dignity of a large retinue, to the imperial banquet? Alas! what could it matter to Cleotos? And he strove to withdraw his mind from this useless and listless contemplation and to fix it more suitably upon the emergencies of the moment.

The cool breeze from the sea, gambolling over the plains, fanned the two fugitives' cheeks, giving a grateful relief from the heat of the close wall in which they had been so long confined. But apart from this, there seemed no change in the hopelessness of their situation. And as Cleotos gazed at his companion, perhaps with the weak purpose of gaining resolution from her strength, he saw that the period of her fortitude had passed away, and that her face was pallid with some new apprehension.

"Did I not tell you?" she said, convulsively grasping his hand. "Is not this my dream, speaking to me of death? See! The open sky overhead as I then saw it!"

He, too, shuddered as he recalled her description of her vision. But it was no time to falter; and, by a desperate effort of will, he seemed at once to assume the strength which she had lost.

"Have I not said that dreams are but the chance fancies of a disordered brain?" he responded. "Or, if it were otherwise, do you not remember, that in your dream, hope came to you at the last?—And see!" he cried, moved as by a sudden inspiration. "Here is your hope, for here, indeed, are the means of escape!"

He pointed below. It happened that the ground made a gradual ascent from the front to the rear of the temple, so that, where they now stood, the height of the wall was not as great as elsewhere, and, in that dim light, seemed yet further foreshortened. The distance was still too far to jump or fall, and the most expert athlete could scarcely hope to swing himself to the bottom and live; but enough had been taken from it to diminish much of that acute perception of danger which, at a greater height, would naturally overcome even a strong brain with giddiness, and thus inordinately magnify the perils of a descent. At a space of about four feet down the temple wall and parallel with the roof ran a horizontal moulding, some eighteen inches wide, and thus ample enough to serve for a temporary foothold; more especially as a person standing upon it could, for further security, grasp the edge of the roof itself. Below this moulding, the wall continued smooth and perpendicular to the ground, and hence, unless further assistance could be obtained, the safety of one standing upon that narrow edge would scarcely be as well assured as if he were upon the roof itself. But as the moulding was carried around towards the corner of the building, it met an angle beneath which jutted a piece of sculptured stone, the top of a pilaster or other projection, a foot across,—and beneath this again was another and a sloping roof, the covering of some smaller building adjunct to the temple, and after that more mouldings,—and so, in like manner, there ensued a continuous ladder, as it were, of pilaster-capitals, roofing, mouldings, and sculpture, reaching to the ground itself. Fearful as the experiment might at first appear, it really needed but little close observation to show the ease with which a person of well-balanced brain and cool deliberate caution could climb from the ground to the temple roof and back again; the only hazardous portion of the way being the passage along the highest moulding, a task occupying, at the longest, but a few seconds.

"See, Ænone!" cried Cleotos. "We have but to descend upon that, and we shall be safe! Fear not to attempt it. It is broad and firm; and though the way may seem long, yet it is not so very far, and I will go before to sustain you."

Carefully he grasped the edge of the roof and lowered himself down until he stood firmly upon the projecting moulding. As he did so, he glanced below and saw that the party of men with torches had come nearer, and perhaps in a moment more might pass the temple. But what were they to him? Should he delay on that account? They might yet turn down some other avenue; and even if they passed, it was not likely that their flaming lights would send a glare so far up the temple wall as to reveal the fugitives. No,—time was too precious to be wasted in awaiting the coming and going of a few wandering revellers. Therefore, looking up to Ænone, he gradually soothed her fears and prevailed upon her with new assurance of security, until she, too, gradually lowered herself over the edge, and then, supported by his arm, prepared to pass with him along the moulding.

"Oh, Cleotos, I fear to try! The way below me looks dark and far—"

"Courage, dear Ænone! The way is shorter than you think, and, in a minute more, we will be at the end. Let me lead you now."

"One moment, dear Cleotos; let me strive to regain my courage. But when I look upon this black abyss below me,—oh! let me first say one prayer to the gods!"

"Not to the gods, dear Ænone, but to the only God, the God of the Christians. He alone will help us, for, unlike the others, he is not the God of the rich alone, but also of the poor and suffering."

She moved her lips. Was it to the gods of Rome or to the Christian God that she appealed for help? Cleotos could not tell; but he could see that a strange, earnest light glowed in her upturned face, as though her soul had kindled with the sudden perception of some truth now for the first time comprehended by her. And when her lips had ceased to move, he could see the same hopeful brightness lingering like a twilight of thought upon her expression as she looked tenderly down upon him.

"Now let us descend, dear Cleotos, for again I feel brave."

"Not yet! not yet!" a harsh voice above her at that moment cried out with startling vehemence. "Stop there, and let me first see who you are!"

Was it chance again,—or a fate? For there stood the armor-bearer, who had too soon awakened, and, in restless mood, had groped his way up the stone stairway. In that dim light, as he now looked over the edge, he could at first only distinguish the outline of a female figure; but that was enough for him, and he grasped her by one hand.

"Let me descend," she murmured in affright.

"Not till I have looked at you, my pretty one!" he cried; and leaning still further over, he grasped her head in both his hands and turned her face up full to his view. She could not relax her hold upon the roof, and therefore had no alternative to enduring his scrutiny until he might please to let her go. The examination did not last long, for in an instant he recognized her and proclaimed the discovery with a loud oath.

"My mistress,—you here?—And with that poor cup-bearing slave, who has lied to me about you, pretending that he knew not where you were hidden, and who surely cannot deserve you as I do? Did I not know that I was destined to see you again? By Hercules! but the Fates themselves must have contrived this lucky meeting!"

"Drumo—is it you who thus insult me?" she cried. "How dare you so speak and act! Release me at once, I say!"

"Release you?" he answered, grasping her only the more firmly. "Nay, but that would be a sorry joke after the gods had so kindly sent me to you! Nor need you feel that my love is an insult to you. Am I not now a free man? And have not you been cast out from your own house? So then, you could do far worse than remain with me. Surely you would not fly away with that poor weak wretch beside you, when here stands the conqueror of the strongest gladiator of the arena, offering his love. Stay, therefore, and we will go off together to some other land and lead a gay life indeed!"

As he spoke, he grasped her by the waist and prepared to lift her back upon the roof. A moment's delay in that, however; for now the men with the torches came still nearer and were about to pass the temple, and faint murmurs of voices came up from among them. Strange, perhaps, that, at the first, there came no motion or cry from all that desperate party above; but so it was. With the armor-bearer, indeed, there could be but the one resource of silence, until the torchlit strangers should have passed by and be no longer able to hear and interrupt;—with Ænone there was the complete paralyzation of fear, rendering utterance impossible;—while Cleotos, knowing the savage nature of the armor-bearer, and the straits into which he might be driven if interfered with, and how little could be done from below in prevention or anticipation of any sudden impulse of wild and excited desperation, felt that the only hope of safety lay in maintaining his own composure, and trying what could be gained by gentle and soothing entreaty. Thus, therefore, they remained in breathless silence,—the armor-bearer half kneeling on the roof, with his arm thrown around Ænone, who, supported by Cleotos, stood upon the narrow moulding; when, of a sudden, louder voices swelled up from the torchlit party now directly beneath them and at once changed the current of affairs.

"Freedom and a hundred sestertia to the one who finds her!" cried a well-known voice.

"It was near here that they say she was last seen," added another. "Jupiter! to think that a daughter of the house of Porthenus should be wandering alone about the streets at night!"

"My lord! My father! Oh, my lord!" cried Ænone, at once finding utterance as the familiar sounds fell upon her ear.

The cry was heard, and the passing party at once arrested its steps. Then the torches, raised high in the air, disclosed the fugitives; and with an oath, the armor-bearer lifted himself upon his feet, dragging Ænone again upon the roof. What now should he do? Detected and baffled, —driven to bay like a tiger in his lair,—with every evidence of his violence thronging about him,—the past and the present both combining for his destruction—should he deliver himself meekly up and be thankful for whatever mercy might be dealt out to him by the outraged lord below? Or should he resist to the last, and then unite all in one common destruction with him, and thereby make his death more memorable? Perhaps, if he had been able to reflect with cool deliberation, he would, after all, have chosen the former course; but the fumes of the wine which he had drunk yet seethed in his brain, and produced in him an unwonted recklessness of all consequences. Why, indeed, should he, a free man, submit to humiliation or ask mercy of any one?—he thought—playing with that newly purchased bauble of liberty, without considering that its jealous and ill-timed maintenance was luring him to his destruction. And while he thus, for a moment, balanced himself between two courses, a harsh command from below turned the scale.

"Freedom and wealth to whoever will slay that caitiff for me and rescue her!" cried Sergius Vanno. With that, the torches flamed yet higher to cast a light upon the scene, and twenty slaves leaped upon the first low range of roofs and cornices, and began to climb like cats towards the top.

"Say you so?" cried the desperate armor-bearer. "Then look up and learn how little my death will profit you!"

With that he lifted Ænone like a feather in his brawny arms, and held her poised high in the air over the edge of the roof.

"Say you so, indeed?" he repeated. "Is it your wife that you want, proud imperator? What hinders me now from flinging her down to greet you? I dare not, do you think? By Pluto! if you do not call back your slaves from climbing up towards me—yes! if you do not yourself go down upon your knees and beg and whimper for her life like a very slave yourself, I will loose my grasp and dash her down in fragments at your feet!"

A murmur of horror arose from below. Sergius, who had himself sprung towards the ascent, stood as though palsied—the slaves who, climbing upward, were now clinging in various stages of advance to the different roofs and cornices, discontinued their progress—none could tell but that any instant would be rendered hideous with the threatened tragedy—when a new and sudden diversion was given to the scene. For, with one bound, Cleotos, dragging himself up, sprang upon the armor-bearer, crowded him back by the mere force of the onset, compelled him in like manner to drop his light burden upon the roof, bore him off his feet, and now lay writhing with him in deadly struggle. One loud shout below told that the threatened danger to Ænone was, for the moment, past; and then, as the frenzied contest went on above, the slaves once more began to swing themselves from one ascent to another in order to gain the temple top.

For an instant the armor-bearer fought but sluggishly, deeming it a careless and easy matter to overcome the slight force brought against him. But, with the desperation of the occasion, the vigor of Cleotos had increased twofold; and soon the armor-bearer, not yet entirely recovered from the enervating stupor of his wine, found himself obliged to put forth all his strength if he would hope to release himself. The light activity of the one, animated by loyal love, was a potent match for the brute power of the other; and, with almost equal success, they rolled over and over upon the sloping roof, locked tightly in each other's grasp. And so, each unable to conquer and refusing to be conquered, they strove together with blinding fury and continually slid nearer to the fatal edge.

"Release your hold!" hissed the armor-bearer, during a momentary pause in the conflict. "Or do you wish that I should fling you over into the street below, like a dead dog?"

"We will go together, then!" gasped Cleotos, feeling that at last his strength was failing him, and that another moment might place Ænone once more in the giant's power. "I have sworn to protect her, and I will do so to the end. I have sworn to give up my life for her, if needful; and what better time to sacrifice it than now?"

There was a parting struggle. Then, with a half-stifled cry, the closely-knit and writhing mass slid from the roof, and striking upon the projecting moulding, bounded off and fell with a crash into the street below.

A moment more—and the moon, which, until now, had remained hidden behind a veil of clouds, as though reluctant to look abroad until the tragedy should be complete, glided serenely forth and poured a flood of light upon all things around;—upon palace and hovel—upon grove and river—upon the narrow street where a group of slaves stood with gathered torches and gazed affrighted upon a silent broken mass which lay motionless upon the pavement in their midst—and upon the temple roof, where other awe-stricken slaves surrounded Sergius Vanno as he knelt beside Ænone, with her head pillowed upon his knee, and called upon her to look up and forgive him!

THE END.

www.ingramcontent.com/pod-product-compliance
Lightning Source LLC
Chambersburg PA
CBHW022100230426
43672CB00008B/1231